ISBN: 978-1-963565-61-4 (Paperback)
ISBN: 978-1-963565-62-1 (eBook)

Library of Congress Control Number: 2025901667

Printed in the United States of America

Published by:

info@thequippyquill.com
(302) 295-2278

Dedicated to the memory of the lives and work of

Martha Morton
Madeleine Lucette Ryley
Evelyn Greenleaf Sutherland
Beulah Marie Dix
Rida Johnson Young

CONTENTS

ACKNOWLEDGMENTS

THIS PROJECT WOULD NOT HAVE BEEN POSSIBLE without the generous help and support of many colleagues, friends, and institutions. Since this book began as a dissertation, I must first acknowledge the guidance of members of my committee at the University of Texas at Austin, especially my advisor, Dr. Oscar Brockett. Later, I received funding for research and travel through a PSC-CUNY Grant from the City University of New York and Faculty Research grant from Borough of Manhattan Community College while teaching there.

David and Helen Day Meyer not only brought to my attention Madeleine Lucette Ryley's entire play collection at the University of Manchester, but copied several of her plays and sent them to me when I was in Austin writing my dissertation. When I was able to visit Ryley's archive at the John Rylands Library, David and Helen graciously hosted me in their lovely home, providing meals and stimulating discussions. Many heartfelt thanks! I owe a huge debt of gratitude, as well, to my friend and colleague, Susan Croft, who assisted me with various British archives and traversed the extra mile by arranging flat-setting situations for my stays in London.

Librarians and experts have helped to facilitate my work and have provided valuable information over the years. With its vast resources and helpful librarians, the New York Public Library is indeed a blessing for any scholar. I am grateful for the assistance of Linda Long and Lesli Larson at the University of Oregon McKnight Library, Peggy Haile McPhillips at the Norfolk Public Library, and Marc Warren at the Maryland Historical Society. I appreciate the friendly helpfulness of Mary Anne Chach, Sylvia Wang, and Mark Swartz each time I visited the Shubert Archives in

New York. And to the librarians at BMCC who helped with loan requests for obscure plays, thanks so much. Thanks as well must go to librarians at the Harvard Theatre archives, as well as the British Library, John Rylands Library, Boston Public Library Special Collections, the Harry Ransom Center and the University of Texas libraries.

Warm gratitude to friends and colleagues who have encouraged this project. Thanks to my department chair, Susana Powell, who provided collegial support in so many ways. Noelia Hernando-Real helped with typing the appendix and reading chapters, as did Barbara Ozieblo; Maria Beach generously shared information from her dissertation research on Dix and others; and David Gunderson not only drove me to Connecticut to find Young's will at the Stamford Courthouse and trek with me through an up-state cemetery to locate Martha Morton's grave, he provided editorial suggestions on the Introduction. More recently I owe many thanks to Kathleen Pharis and Pat Farkas for lending an ear and encouragement.

My children, Drew Johnson and Brooke Gonzales, and grandchildren always keep me grounded and looking forward. Lastly, I must thank my literary agent, Catalea Collins, and the production folks at Quippy Quill for their care, suggestions, patience and diligence in updating this project. Many, many thanks!

Progressive Era Women Dramatists

> Miss Morton is the latest recruit to the ranks of our native playwrights. The fact that she is a woman imparts an added interest to the event.
>
> —Ali Baba, *Dramatic Mirror, 1891*[1]

> If you look at the new writers, you must note that the woman dramatist is coming into greater prominence than she has ever reached before.
>
> —Rida Johnson Young, 1917[2]

WITH THE BEGINNING OF THE PROGRESSIVE ERA, 1890 to 1920—a time of reform and change "in all policies at all levels of society, economy and government"—American women began to advance in most careers.[3] Thus, it naturally followed that this period would foster the rise of America's professional woman dramatist. Entering a field that had always been "a man's job," the women dramatists in this study served as pioneers in American theatre. Learning about their work and their experiences gives insight into the process of Progressive Era theatre, as it also affirms that succeeding as a professional playwright inevitably involves hard work, know-how, buckets of determination, and more than a little luck.

This study looks at Martha Morton, Madeleine Lucette Ryley, Evelyn Greenleaf Sutherland, Beulah Marie Dix, and Rida Johnson Young, each of whom rose in prominence as professional dramatists at the turn of the century. Essentially, they have been overlooked by theatre scholars, their legacy to American theatre often overshadowed by "canonized" male writers of the period.[4] These dramatists collectively serve well to represent the large number of women who wrote plays and musicals for the stage during the Progressive Era.[5] Archival documents, including census records, birth and death certificates, and correspondence, along with interviews and articles from a variety of journals and newspapers, offer a glimpse into their lives, their opinions, and their writings. Each chapter explores their early years and evolution as dramatists, discussing significant plays, along with their public and critical reception.

Although prominent plays and musicals are highlighted, lesser-known works or even commercial failures are also examined when they represent a particular challenge or thematic departure for the dramatist.[6] A comprehensive listing of each dramatist's work is included with each chapter, demonstrating the sheer volume of their creative work.

It is fitting to begin this study with a discussion of Martha Morton (1864–1925), the first American woman to establish a lengthy career as a professional playwright and who gained national fame and significant earnings for her stage successes.[7] As noted in Chapter One, Morton's professional career took off in the spring of 1888 with a staging of her full-length melodrama, *Hélène*, and concluded in 1915 with a New York production of a detective-genre play, *The Three of Hearts*. Of Morton's thirty-seven known titles, fourteen received New York productions, including three plays for comedian William H. Crane—*Brother John* (1893), *His Wife's Father* (1895), and *A Fool of Fortune* (1896); Sol Smith Russell staged *A Bachelor's Romance* (1896) in New York and toured throughout the country.[8] Morton, known in her day as the "Dean of the Women Dramatists," is now remembered primarily for spearheading the formation of the Society of Dramatic Authors in 1907.[9] When women were not allowed membership into the American Dramatists Club, they formed a society admitting both men and women. Morton's eloquent and ironic speech to members of the American Dramatists Club is included at the end of Chapter One.

Madeleine Lucette Ryley (1858–1934), discussed in Chapter Two, began her theatrical career performing in comic opera for a number of years before writing for the stage.[10] She and her husband, J. H. Ryley, both English, lived and performed in New York for about twenty years. By the time she began writing plays, Ryley was known as an American; possibly her dual citizenship contributed to being overlooked by both English and American scholars. Between 1894 and 1907, she achieved eleven New York productions and an equal number in London. Critics praised the wit and dialogue in Ryley's comedies and farces, which included in New York, *Christopher, Jr.* (1889) for Maude Adams and John Drew and in London, *Mice and Men* (1901) for J. Forbes-Robertson and Gertrude Elliott. Ryley's transatlantic career was typical of turn-of-the-century theatre professionals who sailed from New York to London and back on a regular basis. Although her playwriting career seems relatively short, after returning to London in 1901, Ryley remained active within the theatre community and continued to write and occasionally perform. Compared with the other women in this study, Ryley appears to be the most visibly active in campaigning for women's suffrage, serving as Vice President of the Actresses' Franchise League in London.[11]

Chapter Three focuses on the collaborative relationship of Evelyn Greenleaf Sutherland (1855–1908) and Beulah Marie Dix (1876–1970). Individually, each was accomplished in her own right and served as an example of the "literary" New Woman. Sutherland worked as a columnist and drama critic in Boston for about twelve years before she began writing plays. She had at least eighteen one-act plays produced, at times earning praise for her depiction of class and racial differences. Before teaming up with Sutherland, Beulah Marie Dix began writing short stories when young, then historical novels and plays while a student at Radcliffe." Following a successful playwriting career, she moved to Hollywood and wrote scenarios for the early movie industry.

Sutherland and Dix began collaborating around 1901 and went on to create at least sixteen plays within seven years, the majority receiving professional stagings in London and New York.

Their dramatic works consisted primarily of "costume" plays such as the swashbuckling *The Breed of the Treshams* (1903) and *Boy O'Carroll* (1906), made popular throughout Britain by actor Martin Harvey (later Sir John Martin Harvey). Their most enduring American success, however, proved to be *The Road to Yesterday*, the hit of the 1906 Broadway season;[12] this comedy-fantasy toured in road companies for several seasons and in 1924 was made into a musical, *The Dream Girl*. Dix and Sutherland formed a strong friendship, regularly attending theatre together and traveling to Great Britain to see productions of their plays. Their collaboration ended with Sutherland's death in 1908. Today, Dix and Sutherland's plays serve as examples of the historical plays so popular in turn-of-the-century theatre and demonstrate what women could achieve through collaboration.

Although Rida Johnson Young's (1875–1926) lyrics, musical books, and over sixty song titles ensure her place in American music history, she has yet to be fully explored as a dramatist.[13] Chapter Four traces Young's beginnings in theatre as an actress and looks at her most significant plays, such as her first major success, *Brown of Harvard* (1906), and the notable *The Lottery Man* (1909), which at one point had four companies simultaneously touring the country. It also discusses her musicals, including *Naughty Marietta* (1910) and *Maytime* (1917), the former now a frequently revived classic, while the latter was so popular with audiences in its day that the Shuberts had two productions running simultaneously in New York. However, Young's other musicals, such as *Her Solder Boy* (1916) and *Sometime* (1918), not only entertained World War I audiences but also reflected the era. In addition, Young's correspondence with the Shuberts shows that she closely monitored contracts and royalties, providing a look into the business side of playwriting and the relationship between playwright and producer.[14] Compared to the other women in this study, Young was very likely not only the wealthiest but the most prolific; she adhered to a daily writing schedule throughout her working life, generating more than thirty-five plays and musicals, of which at least twenty-nine were professionally produced.

REPRESENTING THE "NEW WOMAN"[15]

Collectively, these five subjects were refined and, for the most, educated women who came of age between 1875 and 1895. Each came from a middle-class family, and none seems to have inherited particular wealth or status.[16] Ryley, who began on stage as a teenager, is the only one of the five who did not advance beyond public school, whereas, Dix, the youngest, attained both her undergraduate and graduate degrees from Radcliffe. All five dramatists began submitting short stories or poetry to magazines and newspapers early in their writing careers, and each ultimately earned substantial royalties writing for the stage. Morton helped to support her family throughout her working life, continuing her support for two sisters in her will. Although Ryley's husband was a working actor, her royalties very likely served as a major source of income. Early on, Dix strove for financial independence through publishing novels and writing plays, ultimately establishing a career in the early film industry. Sutherland, whose husband served as dean of a medical school, may not have been as dependent on royalties as the other women, but she nevertheless earned her own money first from journalism and then playwriting. Young's considerable income from royalties not only enabled her to support her mother, but also provided a luxurious lifestyle.

Each of the five women married, although Young's marriage lasted only a few years. Dix had a daughter and Sutherland adopted a son, but the others apparently remained childless. A New Yorker of English parents, Morton spent her married life in a well-to-do home on Riverside Drive. Ryley and her husband resided in New York City and New Rochelle, New York, before eventually settling in London. Dix and Sutherland were from the Boston-Cambridge area, where they lived during their collaborative years. And Young, originally from Baltimore, owned homes in Greenwich and Stamford, Connecticut and another in Long Island, New York, residing part of the year in various New York City hotels. Other than Dix and Sutherland, who worked together, it is not known whether the women were friendly, critical, competitive, or supportive of one another, but they had to have been acquainted socially and professionally. As contemporaries, they were discussed in various articles on women dramatists of the era. Morton and Ryley, for instance, were often featured together in articles on earlier women playwrights between 1895 and 1900, while in 1908, Lucy France Pierce included all five women in "Women Who Write Plays" in *World Today*.[17]

Women's clubs served as social arenas for women in all professions, but attending a club meeting or event might very well have provided these dramatists opportunities for networking. In *The Torchbearers*, Karen J. Blair discusses the profusion of women's clubs throughout the United States beginning in the 1890s and the importance of clubs in helping women "rebuild their intellectual powers" and "feel entitled to self-expression."[18] Theatrical clubs for men such as the Lambs (1874), the Players (1888), and the American Dramatist Club (1891) had existed for some time. One of the earliest organizations for theatre women was the Twelfth Night Club, which was formed by actresses but included Martha Morton as a prominent member. By 1913, a number of active organizations in New York City were connected with theatre—the American Playgoers, Professional Woman's League, Century Theatre Club, and the Shakespeare Club of New York City.[19]

In the early 1900s, prominent women playwrights, as celebrities, were often invited to club meetings or events as guests or speakers. Martha Morton, for example, spoke before a large audience at the Brooklyn Section Council of Jewish Women on comparing the movie industry with the stage.[20] At "Women Dramatists' Night" at the Hungry Club in 1910, Rida Johnson Young and Rita Olcott were among a handful of invited women dramatists. The published report of this event told: "Each dramatist present made a happy little speech" and that "Mrs. Chauncy Olcott was introduced as the 'baby dramatist'" because *Ragged Robin*, co-written with Young, was her first play. Today, we might interpret this sort of report as condescending. Even so, with 150 club members present to greet the guests of honor, this event provided valuable advertising for *Ragged Robin*, which had opened the week before; conceivably, members went home after the meeting and urged their husbands to take them to see *Ragged Robin*. Indeed, various clubs provided opportunities for women dramatists to meet with other women, to advertise their productions, and even to enhance their celebrity.

WOMEN AND THE OCCUPATION OF PLAYWRITING

If the women in this study had not supported themselves through playwriting, what other options were open to them that would have proved as lucrative? Very few, if any. According to the 1900 census, only one in five of the female population older than age ten were in "gainful occupations"; but by 1920, the number had increased to one in four females over ten, with most positions as domestics, waitresses, counter help, or factory workers.[21]   Teaching increasingly became a respectable occupation for women, but they were paid much lower salaries than men.[22] Indeed, playwriting, from all accounts, appears to be one of the few occupations for women that remained on an equal basis with men. Frances Elizabeth Willard, in *Occupations for Women*, described in 1897 a vast range of work suitable for women, from various types of domestic work to such jobs as architects, photographers, artists, musicians, bankers, and doctors. Willard also included playwriting as a viable and respectable occupation for women, citing ten women as successful examples, including Morton, Sutherland, and Ryley.[23]

In 1911, producer/director/playwright David Belasco in *Good Housekeeping* called playwriting "the great opportunity" for women, declaring: "There is no profession in the world which offers such splendid emolument to a woman, when she has made a success of it." Indeed, an average Broadway play, according to Belasco, yielded for a playwright an income of $300 to $500 a week, which a fortunate writer could average from thirty to forty weeks of the year; and if a play caught on with the public, it would then be performed by stock companies throughout the country.[24] *Every Week* claimed in 1917: "A good comedy takes in about $9,000 a week, of which the author gets from five to ten per cent."[25]

Concurring with Belasco, Rida Johnson Young disclosed in a 1920 interview: "Very few plays pay the playwright less than $300 a week for every company that is producing them. In the larger cities, they may pay double that amount." And "production on the stage is not the end of a successful play," told Young. Movie rights "vary from $25,000 to over $100,000 for a play," and there are "stock-company royalties, which may go on for years." Indeed, one "successful play may net a playwright anywhere from fifty thousand to several hundred thousand dollars."[26] Income from royalties earned by women created news in early journals and newspapers. In *Theatre*, November 1913, "Big Earnings of Big Plays" put women dramatists alongside men as moneymakers. Within just two years, claimed the article, Martha Morton netted $50,000 from her first play, *Hélène*, sold her second play, *The Merchant*, for $15,000, and made "an additional $250,000" from her biggest success, *A Bachelor's Romance*.[27] Accounts such as this—exaggerated or not— must have prompted women readers to rush to their desks to have a go at writing for the stage.[28]

Rida Johnson Young unabashedly admitted in interviews that she wrote for the money; she, in fact, excelled at finding ways to extend the life of a creative work.[29] For instance, in 1911 when Young wrote *Barry of Ballymore* for singer/actor Chauncey Olcott, she also included the lyrics to "Mother Machree," a song the Irish tenor instantly made popular with the public. Once the song caught on, Young capitalized on it by writing a novel, *The Story of Mother Machree*, published in 1924, and that same year her short story version appeared in *Munsey's Magazine* in February. A film based on the short story, directed by John Ford, was released in 1928.[30] Altogether, at least nineteen films were made from Young's plays and stories.

Today, $300 to $500 per week may not sound like significant income. However, U.S. income tax did not take effect until 1913 and the cost of living during the Progressive Era was considerably lower than it is now. Garff B. Wilson relates that in 1902 prices at New York's first-class theatres varied from 25 cents to $2 and many good shows could be seen for 50 cents.[31] Advertisements in a

Boston newspaper from 1908 list gingham fabric at 7 cents per yard, men's dress shirts for 75 cents, a three-piece mahogany parlor suite for $80, and a complete brass bed for $25.[32] Perhaps even more telling is the *New York Times* article, "Living on $100 a Month," which informs 1912 readers that "a young couple living in New York or any other large city" could easily live on $100 a month by budgeting their income; indeed, states the article, "Little apartments of four or five rooms may be found in a good neighborhood in Upper Manhattan, the Bronx, or Brooklyn for $25 a month within the five-cent car fare limit."[33] It is no wonder that popular playwrights in earlier times could afford sprawling estates in upstate New York, Long Island, or Connecticut.

What constituted a successful run during the Progressive Era? When Clara Morris produced Martha Morton's *Helene* in 1889, the two-week run was enough to establish it as a "Broadway play" and ensure a good road tour.[34] By the latter 1890s, a month's run in New York was considered a good showing for a production. Occasionally, a production might become a "runaway hit" and last through a theatrical season— from the end of June through the middle of the following June. Some managers, however, kept productions running even if not doing well at the box office in order to go out nationally as a "New York success." Strongly objecting to this practice, a Chicago drama critic complained in 1898 that "plays are kept in New York right through the season, whether they pay or not, in order to come before the country as New York successes. After that they go to London, and Chicago is fortunate to see them eighteen months after their first appearance."[35] In general, the trend was for productions to run longer. During the 1899–1900 New York season, only thirty-four productions of approximately eighty-five achieved more than fifty performances, or about one and a half months. Twenty years later, during the 1919–20 season, of 141 plays, musicals, and spectacles produced in New York, at least forty-five achieved more than 100 performances or approximately three months, with sixteen chalking up between 200 and 452 performances.[36]

WRITING FOR PROGRESSIVE ERA THEATRE

Almost ninety years ago, renown theatre historian Arthur Hobson Quinn prefaced a discussion of Rachel Crothers by stating that other women who wrote plays in the latter part of the nineteenth century "need not detain us" because their writings were "usually romantic or farcical comedies and merely followed a mode of the time."[37] Quinn was not alone in both his disparagement of Progressive Era plays and his shunning of all women playwrights other than Crothers. American theatre at the end of the nineteenth century was indeed dominated by popular melodrama, musicals, light comedies, farce, burlesque, and vaudeville. Theatrical conditions contributed to playwriting that now seems contrived, formulaic, sentimental, and melodramatic. Consequently, a large portion of popular turn-of-the-century comedy and drama, including those written by most women dramatists, is viewed today as dramatically inferior. As historian Oscar Brockett posits: "In theatre history there is a tendency to judge an era by the excellence of its drama. In most instances the best plays come to be treated as typical, while all lesser works and entertainments are swept aside as unimportant."[38] Not only has "lesser" work been "swept aside," but by and large most dramatists of Progressive Era theatre have become marginalized, if not forgotten. Of the scores of men and women writing plays between 1890 and 1920, only a few are acknowledged today in theatre history texts—David Belasco, Henry C. DeMille, Clyde Fitch, William Gillette, Bronson Howard, Percy MacKaye, William Vaughn Moody, Edward B. Sheldon, Augustus Thomas, and Rachel Crothers.

In addition, anyone taking a random look through reviews of the Progressive Era would undoubtedly agree with Howard Taubman, who depicted this theatrical period as being ruled by "the personality of the players rather than their plays."[39] Most of the considerable number of women and men who grew rich from writing for Progressive Era theatre did so by playing a subservient role within the production process, tailoring dramatic work to fit star performers or making changes to appease theatre managers, who in turn sought to satisfy the paying public. Although the star system promoted rushed and poorly written plays, it also created a demand for new work and, concurrently, generated opportunities for women playwrights. As Morton described: "There is an almost frenzied demand for plays, especially for the conventional 'star' plays, which can be sold like potatoes. If the author is enough of a juggler to combine all the characters into one grand central light, surrounding it with shadowy, transparent forms, which act the part of echoes, or of an old Greek chorus, he will never be without work."[40]

Once a dramatist's work caught on with the public, he or she was inevitably approached by managers or performers with requests for "star" vehicles. The mode of writing might depend on the personality of a particular actor. For instance, before writing *American Citizen* for Nat C. Goodwin, Madeleine Lucette Ryley questioned the actor about his preferences, but he was "characteristically laconic" and did not even request to see a synopsis of the play. As Ryley told: "'Go home and write me a comedy,' said he [Nat Goodwin], 'and don't let me see it till it is finished.' 'Good clothes?' I queried. 'No,' he answered. 'Wig or no wig?' 'No wig.' 'Nat Goodwin or somebody else?' 'Nat Goodwin.' I did not see him again until the piece was completed."[41] Ryley sums up the difficulty of writing a play to order as being in "the number of personages one must satisfy":

First, of course, comes the star who is to be fitted. He, or she, must feel in perfect sympathy with the part provided, or failure is inevitable. Then, hardly less important, is the manager . . . to be appeased in every detail of construction, more particularly in the matters of expense and what will attract the masses. Thirdly, the public itself is to be considered. . . The matinee girl, too, is a factor that, in these days, comes more and more to be considered every hour.[42]

As Ryley mentions, a major factor contributing to the increased numbers of women writing for the stage during the Progressive Era was that the paying public consisted predominately of women and girls. The term, "matinee girl," came into popular usage in the 1890s to designate women of all ages who regularly attended theatre, flocking to afternoon matinees in groups and often displaying zealous devotion toward star actors who thus became "matinee idols." Theatre critic Walter Prichard Eaton stated in 1910 that theatrical managers estimated almost 75 percent of theatre audiences in this country were women.[43] The prevalence of the matinee girl became a major influence on the drama, and in order to succeed, playwrights were forced to accommodate the tastes and preferences of women and girls. Young certainly knew the importance of catering to women in the audience: "I am supposed to write musical comedies which will please the 'tired businessman.' But if I do not please the lady whom the tired businessman brings with him, the show will not last long."[44]

To a great extent, star performers served as early "play doctors," trying out plays on touring circuits, cutting and embellishing as needed. Popular comedians like Nat C. Goodwin, William C. Crane, Sol Smith Russell, and Max Figman were superb at comic timing and attuned to audience reaction, often freely reworking scenes and bits. In most cases, they would not bring a comedy before New York audiences until they honed it on the road, a process that took from two weeks to two years. Although playwrights generally trusted their work to the experience and instincts of star performers, occasionally disagreements occurred. Dix and Sutherland, authors of the period play, *The Lilac Room*, were so unhappy with Amelia Bingham's alterations to their work by the time it opened in New York in 1906 that they withdrew the play after only a few days. Around the same time, Mary Roberts Rinehart (writing as Rinehart Roberts), exercised her right to close *The Double Life* when Henri De Vries, the lead actor, not only made unauthorized alterations to the play, but blatantly contacted Rinehart's agent, Beatrice DeMille, to ask for "a percentage of the royalties for rewriting the piece."[45]

Emerging dramatists also gained valuable lessons from seasoned directors or performers as seen in Rida Johnson Young's experience: "When I think of *Brown of Harvard* I think mainly of my quarrels with Mr. [Henry] Miller. When I was forced to rewrite and rewrite, to cut and elaborate, I felt that Mr. Miller was murdering my child. One day, after a vehement quarrel, he ordered me off the stage. But I can never thank him enough for having had the patience to put up with me at all."[46] Novice playwrights who observed the "doctoring" of stars and endured the playmaking criteria Ryley described advanced in the craft of playmaking. After serving their "apprenticeship" and becoming established in the profession, a dramatist could, if so inclined, heed her personal artistic vision and take risks with more challenging or experimental themes. Morton, reflecting the Progressive Era's theme, described it as being "pioneers to a better art, torchbearers that shall shed the light of progress."[47]

Looking at the lives and work of these five women dramatists provides more than a "feminine" take on theatre history; it also gives insight into what Progressive Era audiences enjoyed and preferred for their dramatic fare. Each of these women exercised a certain tenacity and grit in pursuing playwriting, and as they gained financial independence, respect, and celebrity, they influenced and encouraged other aspiring women writers. Women and girls throughout the country attended touring plays written by women dramatists. They read in the women's section of the local newspaper: "Women Playwrights, they are supplying the stage with splendid material," as shown in the *Fort Wayne News* in 1900. Or those in Mansfield, Ohio, read in their local newspaper: "Famous Women Playwrights as the Camera Catches Them," which displayed sketches of seven women who wrote successes for the stage and announced that Lottie Blair Parker had "made $150,000 in a year."[48]

Indeed, in both subtle and direct ways, each of the dramatists discussed in this work must have had a positive influence on girls, women, and society. The aim of this work is to inform readers about the lives and works of Martha Morton, Madeleine Lucette Ryley, Evelyn Greenleaf Sutherland, Beulah Marie Dix, and Rida Johnson Young. In so doing, it is hoped that it will lift them from obscurity and acknowledge their contributions to American theatre.

Martha Morton, 1901.

CHAPTER I

DEAN OF THE WOMEN PLAYWRIGHTS: MARTHA MORTON (1865-1925)

> A woman, by her sex, is debarred from being "in the swim," as the vulgar parlance has it. This is a very serious difficulty a woman has to overcome, and there is no doubt that this explains why so few women have succeeded in writing for the stage.
>
> —Martha Morton, 1891[1]

> It is very hard to tear one's self from a task that is so pleasant as the work of playmaking.
>
> —Martha Morton, 1896[2]

IN AUGUST 1892, THE AMERICAN DRAMATIST CLUB gathered in Atlantic Highlands, New Jersey, for their monthly meeting. Martha Morton, an up-and-coming playwright, was the invited guest, but while the men met at the Grand View Hotel, Morton lunched with their wives in a nearby cottage.[3] Fifteen years later in March 1907, the American Dramatist Club finally broke their long-standing men-only tradition by inviting established women dramatists to join them for their yearly dinner at Delmonico's. It was at this auspicious event that Morton, now known as the "Dean of the Women Playwrights," announced the formation of the Society of Dramatic Authors, consisting of thirty women and one man. In her address to Club members Morton concluded: "Gentlemen, we are not going to blame you for something of which you are entirely innocent—about which you were never even consulted—*your sex*—we are not going to ostracize *you* because you are *merely* men—we invite you all!…All dramatists are one in their work; therefore, as moderns we make no restrictions of nationality or sex."[4] Shortly thereafter, the two groups merged into the Society of American Dramatists and Composers, forerunner to today's Dramatists Guild.

Well respected by her peers, Martha Morton was described in various articles and interviews between 1891 and 1915 as articulate, educated, and confidant—a woman of culture and taste. Photographs from the 1890s depict a stylish, corseted young Victorian, while later photos show her in more loose-fitting dresses and gowns. One article from the era describes twenty-six-year-old Morton as "a profound student," "ardently ambitious," a playwright who works "for pure love of the profession" and is "keenly critical of her own work." Outwardly, she possesses "charmingly unaffected manners" as a "delightful conversationalist," with fine powers of reasoning "intuitive perceptions, and close observation, combining to render her unusually attractive and entertaining."[5]

By 1907, Morton had become a leader among the growing number of women playwrights. In fact, Lucy France Pierce cites Morton as one of the veteran women dramatists who "tore down the wall of opposition" in a field where the odds of women succeeding were strikingly low.[6] Shirley Burns's detailed description of Martha Morton in 1910 reinforces the impression given by other journalists: "Mrs. Conheim is a charming woman to meet. Her personality is delightful. She has the gracious ease of manner of the well-accustomed woman of society and the world, and her mind is so well poised and abundantly stored that everything she says is worth listening to. She stands very straight, is always beautifully gowned, and the grasp of her hand is firm and sincere. She is wonderfully alert— nothing escapes her—and she is a gifted conversationalist."[7]

Born in New York City on October 10, 1865, Martha Morton was one of eight children of Amelia and Joseph Morton, a china importer.[8] Morton credited her mother, "an ardent student of Shakespeare," for transmitting to her a taste for reading plays.[9] But dramatic writing was apparently in her genes, since ancestors included Thomas Morton (c. 1764–1838), a well-known English dramatist of the early 1800s, and his son, John Maddison Morton (1811–91), who wrote comedies, melodramas, and farces; John Maddison's best-known work, *Box and Cox*, is considered by some to be the best farce of the nineteenth century.[10] Edward Arthur Morton, an English critic and author of books for the musicals *The Merry Widow*, *San Toy*, and *The Geisha*, was her cousin.[11] A major influence on her educational development occurred when the family returned to London for seven years; Martha was between ten and seventeen years of age. The family resided in London's Regent's Park, where the Morton children were exposed to literary and theatrical figures, including Mrs. Charles Dickens and the critic Dutton Cook.[12] It was Cook who advised Martha to make a study of the drama by systematically reading "all the English dramatists and afterwards the dramatists of Germany, France, and Spain."[13] Morton maintained in interviews that she had always written, her earliest writing as a child consisting of poems and short stories. When her mother suggested she send a story to a magazine, it was accepted, earning the budding writer $25.[14] Thus, when considering the literary figures in Martha Morton's family, her formative years abroad, and the encouragement given by her mother and other adults, it is no wonder that she developed not only a propensity for writing but a love for the stage; stated Morton, "It seemed a natural drift."[15]

EARLY SUCCESSES

After the family returned to New York in the early 1880s, Martha attended the Normal College (Hunter College), although health problems apparently kept her from graduating.[16] Her brother, Michael, wanting to learn more about the theatre in order to write plays, became an actor under producer Daniel Frohman at the Madison Square Theatre, where he was directed by David Belasco.[17] Her brother's connection with Frohman very likely helped Martha secure her premiere showing. Having seen Belasco's first New York musical success, *May Blossom* in 1884, she wrote a parody of it for the amusement of friends. When he heard of the skit, Daniel Frohman used it in a benefit for one of the Hebrew charities in New York. The "travesty" of *May Blossom* presented at the Academy of Music in May 1885, "enlisted, for the Montefiore Home, no fewer . . . than a hundred well-known amateurs."[18]

While connections through her brother contributed to her initial successful showing, it was a combination of youthful daring and sheer desperation which prompted Martha Morton to rent the 5th Avenue Theatre on a Monday night for a preview showing of her first full-length play, *Hélène*. This melodrama, set in France, reflects dramatic work that was typical of the day, revolving around a misunderstood heroine and the two men who love her. After attempts to interest theatre managers failed, the novice playwright "offered her play to a charity, relinquishing all her interest in the receipts."[19] Of the event, a *New York Times* reviewer mentioned that both the dramatist and Minnie Seligman, playing the title role, had "a host of friends" because the house filled to capacity, forcing the band to play under the stage.[20] The *Tribune* also covered this one-night event and labeled it a "creditable first attempt," reporting that *Hélène* had "many strong situations" but noted that "in the hands of an experienced playwright," the play would have been exciting.[21]

The melodrama attracted the attention of well-known actress, Clara Morris, known for a highly emotive acting style in playing tragic heroines such as Camille. Indeed, most reviewers later agreed that *Hélène* served very well as "a medium for the exhibition of the extraordinary personality and curious theatrical method" of the actress.[22] Clara Morris presented *Hélène* on October 29, 1889, at the Union Square Theatre and ran for a week; subsequently, *Hélène* became the chief feature of her touring season, and, according to *Theatre*, netted the playwright $50,000.[23] Riding on the play's commercial success, Morton wrote a novelized version of it, published as *Hélène Buderoff; or, A Strange Duel* in 1889, and dedicated it to Clara Morris.[24] The play, under the title, *The Refugee's Daughter*, served as a viable vehicle for actress Cora Tanner in the early 1890s.[25] Eight years after *Hélène*'s initial showing, Morton told an interviewer "some kind players out on the Pacific Coast" were doing yet another production of the play. "I almost could wish," confessed the playwright, "that they would consent to shelve it, for it does not now seem to me so great an achievement as once it appeared."[26] Most significant, however, is that *Hélène* launched the professional career of the twenty-four-year-old playwright.

Morton's next play, *The Merchant*, also had a rather fortuitous route to production, made legendary by various published accounts. When she completed *The Merchant*, Morton submitted it to New York theatre managers who declined it, one after another. Discouraged, she put the manuscript away. About six months after *Hélène* was produced, the *New York World* offered a prize for the best American drama. At the coaxing of her family, Morton submitted *The Merchant*. One account has her carrying the manuscript downtown and "absent-mindedly" leaving it on a counter in a shop, forgetting all about it until just before the deadline.[27] Another account claims that Morton rolled it up "in a hard roll," addressed it "to *The World* and placed it on the outside of a street letterbox" hoping that "someone would steal it for stamps" since it had given her so many disappointments that she was sick of it.[28] To ensure impartiality by the judges, contest entrants were instructed to submit plays under assumed names. Morton explained that she signed the manuscript Henry Halliton, fearing if a woman's name was attached, it would "place an obstacle" in the way of its success.[29]

After being "kept on the anxious seat for about three weeks," Morton received a call from three gentlemen of the committee who were surprised to learn that Henry Halliton was a woman; they informed her that *The Merchant* "had won the prize, and that the *World* would give it an early production."[30] *Critic* stated that the newspaper also awarded several thousand dollars for winning the competition. The *Dramatic Mirror* mentioned no cash prize, but stated that *The Merchant*'s special matinee performance at the Union Square Theatre "cost *The World* about $1,500" and that the "advertisement alone was worth $10,000."[31] Indeed, the special matinee on June 26, 1890, introduced *The Merchant* to New York audiences. According to Odell, "Two weeks before the play was produced, it was bought for $5,000, by Thomas B. Macdonough and H. C. Kennedy."[32] Leading roles in the production went to Nelson Wheatcroft, E. J. Henley, Selena Fetter, and Blanche Walsh in her New York debut. "One day," Odell predicts retrospectively, "we shall reckon on the ability of Martha Morton."[33]

The American setting of *The Merchant* illustrates that Morton must have heeded cousin Edward Arthur Morton's advice to "Throw away that French trash. Look at the life about you and write of that." Having grown up with a father in businesss, Martha knew the "ups and downs," of the merchant life and put those "ups and downs into a play."[34] *The Merchant* also foreshadows Morton's later use of themes of the businessman who lives beyond his means, the evils of extravagant living, and the folly of keeping up appearances. The comedy-drama centers on Mr. and Mrs. Vanderstyle in their luxurious villa on the Hudson. It is learned that the husband has deceived his wife, Myrtle, about their financial precariousness. Now, as he teeters on the brink of financial ruin, he considers shooting himself, but upon hearing his wife's voice singing in the next room, decides to live. A compelling moment comes when he confesses to Myrtle that the diamonds he has given her are only paste. Fred Dupre, a supposed friend to Vanderstyle, makes advances toward Myrtle and, when repulsed, plots to get even. He maintains the upper hand by lending her husband money to save him from ruin. Dupre, however, has a change of heart and pleads for Myrtle's forgiveness in a speech overheard by her husband. Although there is no bloodshed at this crucial juncture, the villain's check is returned, and he is driven away while the curtain falls on husband and wife in each other's arms. Several minor characters provide comic aspects, along with a subplot concerning Lord Northwick and his attempts to run off with Jess Morgan, a pretty young girl.

Almost a year after its special matinee showing, *The Merchant* reopened at the Madison Square Theatre in May 1891 with a new cast that included Henry Miller, Edward J. Henley, and Viola Allen.[35] Generally, reviewers' comments on the play remained conflicted. The *New York Times*, called it "a clean, simple play," in which the "comedy element is better than the tragedy," concluding pointedly: "*The Merchant* is not dull or stupid, nor does it drag. Some of the dialogue is very good and bright. When the actors have committed their lines to memory, it will be well acted."[36] Yet five days later, possibly a different *New York Times* critic shook his head over the success of *The Merchant*, calling it "false and shallow and obviously artificial."[37] However, the *Tribune* stated that while the play is "absolutely conventional . . . it tells an interesting story and tells it well." Evidently holding a bias against women playwrights, he credited the play's weaknesses to "the usual feminine faults of over-statement," "glib verbosity," and moralizing, and suggested a "blue pencil judiciously and vigorously used . . . would leave *The Merchant* an effective play." Commenting on the strength of the acting, the *Tribune* reviewer also noted that Edward Henley, "excelled in the character of the evil-doer who reads all women like an open book," and pointed out that this "is an innocent and inexperienced woman's invariable idea of a bad man." Even so, he commended Morton on her theme and "a depth of conviction that inspires absolute respect."[38] *The Merchant* ran just over seven weeks, a strong cast and excellent staging by Eugene Presbrey contributing to a well-received production.[39]

Morton attended performances of *The Merchant* every night, closely monitoring audiences and showing "all the enthusiasm of a regular first-nighter."[40] Clearly, the dramatist did not rest on her laurels when it came to learning her craft. In spite of the odds against her—youth, inexperience, and gender—the successful run of *The Merchant* established her as a credible playwright, prompting the first of many articles on Morton. *The Illustrated American, for instance*, described the dramatist as "the brilliant young person whose latest success has instantly ranked her among the foremost playwrights of this country."[41] The *Dramatic Mirror* followed with:

"And in her debut as a writer for the stage Miss Morton has achieved that which per se must command respect. She has been very successful... from the pecuniary standpoint; fairly successful from the artistic standpoint."[42]

In October 1891, Morton made a trip to Minneapolis for the first performance of her next play, *Geoffrey Middleton, Gentleman*, performed by the Pitou Stock Company. Praising the production upon her return, she indicated that the play adhered "to the theories of the so-called new school."[43] Morton referred to the trend toward realism in theatre and the move away from the broad, artificial acting style of melodrama. The "new-school" trend was used in Morton's third play through contemporary scenes that were "quiet and natural." Set in New York City, the play tells a straightforward story about aristocratic Geoffrey Middleton who marries Margaret Merrit for money, not for himself, but for his father. He believes that Margaret is aware of the arrangement all along and that she has basically sold herself, and thus, he proceeds to make her life miserable. But Margaret, who loves Middleton, does not learn about his real motives until well into the marriage; it is Middleton's father who contributes to further complications before their eventual reconciliation.

Concerning *Geoffrey Middleton*'s March 31 opening at the Union Square Theatre with a strong cast—Nelson Wheatcroft, Minnie Seligman, William Faversham, and Vida Croly—the *New York Times* commented on Morton's improved skills, finding her third play "truer to the facts of life than her first and vastly more logical and interesting than her second." Even with Morton's use of "old stage types" for some characters, noted the critic, her study of the stage is beginning to show. Her "quiet and natural scenes" must have improved her playwriting; the critic stated: "she makes use of her technical knowledge with so much facility that we sometimes forget the stage in looking at the play. 'Geoffrey Middleton' will, indeed, compare favorably with recent American plays more pretentiously put forward. It is quite as true to life and quite as well written, for instance, as the dramas of [David] Belasco and [Henry] De Mille." Despite the production's "well-worn scenery and auction room furniture," the audience responded not only to the "simple story, told in a direct and effective way" but also to its incidental humor.[44] *Geoffrey Middleton, Gentleman* ended Pitou's run at the Union Square Theatre on a prosperous note.

Within three years of her first New York production, Morton, like many emerging playwrights, attracted the attention of stars and managers. A June 1891 article reported that Morton had "a new drama ready to place on the boards," and "work laid out for several years to come."[45] An October report stated that she had been "commissioned by Mr. Pitou to write a one-act comedy for his company."[46] By November another publication stated that "Miss Morton's pen is in great request by managers and stars. She has more orders to fill than she can possibly find time for."[47] It was around this time that Morton wrote *Miss Prue* and *The Little Blacksmith*, produced outside of Manhattan, for Lizzie Evans.[48] But the star who would boost Morton's career into greater prominence was actor-comedian William H. Crane.

HITTING HER STRIDE WITH FOUR PLAYS FOR WILLIAM H. CRANE

William H. Crane, at forty-seven, had been acting for close to thirty years, initially with "low comedian roles." Early in his career as a star actor, Crane announced his intention to encourage American playwrights, and Morton's was his fifth American play at the Star Theatre.[49] Crane's appearances were always anticipated events in New York, his fans finding his humor "broad, unctuous, and perfectly understandable."[50] His company changed relatively little from year to year, constituting more of a "traveling stock company."[51] Crane put considerable care and expense into *Brother John*, the first play Morton wrote for him; the comedian planned more elaborate staging than usual and added four new actors to the company for his March 1893 opening at the Star Theatre.[52] This production served as Martha Morton's first major New York opening, without benefit of an out-of-town tryout or trial matinee.

Central to *Brother John* is John Hackett (Crane), a prosperous hatter with a factory in rural Connecticut, who provides for and dominates the lives of his younger siblings, Beck, Sophie, and Bobby. Hetty, Hackett's forewoman, comes to their house most evenings to teach him chess, although he is generally too preoccupied with business to fully appreciate the handsome Hetty or that his sisters are bored to death with their knitting. Sophie and Ed, her beau, along with Beck and Bobby, manage to secure brother John's permission and a hundred dollars for a trip to the seaside. In Act Two, the group arrives at Long Branch, where they hire a lavish cottage, buy expensive clothes, and entertain the Van Spragues, a socially elite family who ultimately turn out to be swindlers. Hackett follows his siblings when they do not return home, and ends up staying at Long Branch. He extricates them from various difficulties and exposes the greedy nature of the "society" friends. By Act Four they all return home, more appreciative of the simple life, and everyone, including Brother John, winds up happily paired with the person of his or her choice. *Brother John*'s subplot concerns Hetty and the elder Van Sprague, who cheated Hetty's father out of his life's savings and prompted his suicide. Similar to *The Merchant*, the play exposes the false values and shallowness of those who pursue social status—"asserting the superiority of bucolic goodness over civic evil."[53] Both the *Tribune* and the *New York Times* felt Morton's characters were too extreme but commented favorably on her dialogue and humor. The amiable hatter, for instance, when showing off his newest creation to his sister's beau, pitches: "What is the cause of so many bald heads in this community? Hats Sir! Close heavy hats. Now this is lighter than cork! with a free circulating ventilator, and when the air blows on the head sir—the hair grows on the head sir—it will suit you sir— becomes the very plainest face—Try it on sir—try it on."[54] At the resort, when the usually demure Beck makes an impressive entrance dressed in an outrageously low-cut gown, Brother John declares: "You've been bottled up so long—you exploded all at once—didn't you?"[55]

Credit for the vociferous, rapturous reception of the opening night audience went to the star, rather than the play, with critics predicting a long life for *Brother John*. After a healthy run at the Star Theatre, Crane toured with the play and brought it back to New York the following February with the same cast, playing again to full houses. During the interim, the playwright and the star must have heeded the *New York Times'* initial dramaturgical advice, because upon its return, *Brother John* had been "greatly improved since last season, simply by the omission of irrelevant and consequently ineffective episodes."[56]

His Wife's Father, Morton's second play for Crane, is a translation of *Der Compagnon*, a four-act German farce by Adolf l'Arronge, which she condensed and adapted into American characters and setting. The action of *His Wife's Father* focuses on Buchanan Billings, a wealthy grocer and doting father of Nell. Act One opens on Nell's wedding day at the Billings's home in New York City; Billings tells Frank, his new son-in- law, that not only is he signing over his entire grocery business to him, but he (Billings) also expects Frank to move in with them. In addition, the father of the bride announces that he has a wedding trip all planned out in four or five weeks so he can tag along. The lovers, however, find an opportunity to slip away and take the wedding trip they have already planned. Upon learning the bridal couple has left, Billings, at the end of Act I, mournfully declares: "They're gone . . . I'm an orphaned father."[57]

Later, the situation grows intolerable for the newlyweds with a retired Billings constantly coming between them and creating havoc in the household. This leads to a confrontation between Billings and his son-in-law, who secures a place of their own and moves all the furniture out of Nell's apartment. At the end of Act Two, the distraught father alone in Nell's empty room, sits on the only piece of furniture left in the room, a mineral water box. Yet even on their own, the couple receives her father's unwanted help in the form of his faithful servant, Matt, who is sent to serve them. The young marrieds quarrel, Frank leaves on a business trip to Europe, and a grief-stricken Nell ends up bitterly reproaching her father; this third-act confrontation causes Billings to realize that his excessive devotion to his daughter is ruining her happiness. In Act Four, Billings turns his attention to Mrs. Canary, the neighborly widow who has served as Nell's surrogate mother. Frank returns from Europe, determined to break the contract with his supposed "silent" partner, but Billings will not hear of it; eventually, things iron out and the play ends as Billings and Mrs. Canary depart on *their* wedding trip. Lending diversity to this otherwise simple plot is a secondary romance between a mismatched pair, Mrs. Canary's daughter, Kitty, and Billing's nephew, Ferdinand. As do most romantic comedies of the period, the play culminates in the union of several happy couples.

Following successful tryouts in Philadelphia and Washington, DC, *His Wife's Father*, opened in February of 1895 at the 5th Avenue Theatre, running 104 performances. The enthusiastic reception on opening night caused the *New York Times* critic to complain that because of audience members' "warm personal liking" for the comedian, "they are disposed to count every merit of the play at least twice and to pay no attention to its faults."[58] Nevertheless, Buchanan Billings, the meddlesome father in *His Wife's Father* suited William H. Crane extremely well. A second article in March called it "a rich and memorable portrayal," stating that it "fits his personal manner, and exhibits the best side of his talent."[59] Although the supporting cast was strong, the only other actor singled out by reviewers was Anne O'Neill, who played Billings' daughter, Nell. Crane returned in November of the following year with *His Wife's Father* at the 5th Avenue Theatre, playing eight performances with a new supporting cast. The *New York Times* reviewer commented favorably on Morton's skill in transferring the play from a German to a Harlem setting with "extremely probable New Yorkers," and translating its humor into familiar forms for speech, yet he complained about a "general sense of triviality" and the "commonplace."[60] The following week, apparently a different reviewer in the same newspaper, instead, found the reality of the play its "best quality"—"thoroughly human, and delightfully droll, with a few touches of appreciable pathos"; the reviewer felt the characters to be "natural human beings" and their "love-making and squabbling . . . like bits of actual life."[61] During the summer of 1897, the play chalked up forty-two performances at the Criterion Theatre in London as *The Sleeping Partner* with an English cast playing renamed roles.

In spite of the monetary rewards of tailoring plays for Crane, after *His Wife's Father* Morton suggested to the comedian that the public needed to see him in "something not by Martha Morton," that after a break, she "would write for him again if he wished it."[62] Had Morton, as the "sub-servient" playwright, begun to feel overshadowed by the star performer?

The lack of discernment on the part of Crane's fans certainly reflects the difficulty for a playwright who wished to be taken seriously by critics and audiences. Possibly Morton felt a need to develop more complex characters and themes, or perhaps she simply decided it would be a wise "marketing" strategy to temporarily break away from Crane, as she put it, "for the benefit of the public, Mr. Crane, and myself."[63] Although the comedian agreed, he nevertheless came to see her several months later: "'Martha,' he said, 'there's no use talking. You've got to write me a play. I've read dozens and dozens of them in the last few weeks, and I'm so sick of the work that I won't read another one. I haven't found anything to suit me. Now, don't you see, you'll have to write me one?'"[64] A few days later Morton proposed an idea for a storyline of a play, using the Wall Street theme he had suggested. With Crane's approval, she began creating "a part entirely different from anything he had done before," and a year later she read the first draft of the play to the actor.[65]

The role was that of Elisha Cuningham, a successful investor at the point of retiring in luxury who returns from Europe only to discover his partner has "involved him in a speculation which, through the treachery of a financial associate, reduces him to penury."[66] In brief, Cuningham takes to drink and becomes a wreck, but through the help of his daughter's suitor, he effectively turns the tables on the man who ruined him. The victory, however, takes a physical toll on Cuningham, and at the end of the play he dies. Morton describes Crane's horrified reaction: "When we came to the death scene, he exclaimed in a startled way: 'Why, Martha! I can't die. Dear me, no! You'll have to fix it some other way.' But I persuaded him that was the only logical and legitimate ending which the story could have; that without it the play would be absolutely unconvincing."[67] Persuading the star comedian that his character must die to maintain the integrity of the play, is, in itself, a feat that indicates Morton's position as a playwright by this time. Although in May she referred to the new play for Crane as *The Fortune Hunter*, by the time pre-production notices appeared in late November the title had become *A Fool of Fortune*.

Opening on December 1, 1896, *A Fool of Fortune* with only forty performances, had a shorter run at the 5th Avenue Theatre than did *His Wife's Father*, yet critical reception remained more favorable. The *New York Times* compared *A Fool of Fortune*'s "stock ticker" theme to *The Henrietta*, calling it "the best of its kind since that comedy by Bronson Howard, which is the best American play ever written."[68] Critics agreed on the weakness of the second act, although the strength of the other two acts counteracted this fault, agreeing with the *New York Times*: "The first act is sprightly and entertaining, and the third is stirring and pathetic, with an infusion of rich humor."[69]

The work is essentially a comedy with a touchingly sad ending, leaving the viewer with "a genuine thrill of sympathetic emotion."[70] By the third act, Elisha Cuningham, now a broken man, has attempted for a year to regain his fortune by selling off household furnishings and his wife's jewelry; but speculations have netted little gain. The action occurs in the Wall Street office of Karl Woresdorf, the German banker who loves Marjorie, Cuningham's daughter. Count de Cluny, in love with Jennie, Cuningham's youngest daughter, and Cornelius Green, an old family friend from the country, have also lost money in the "Sunset" scheme of the unscrupulous Ezekiel Powers. Foreshadowing the end, Green, puts an arm around Elisha Cuningham and pleads with him to "quit this feverish life—it will kill you in the end—I can almost hear your heart galloping like an overdriven thing. Come back with me to Nature—the blue Heavens—and God."[71]

But, rushing in, Woresdorf announces: "I have secretly bought up Sunset at a nominal price and with Mr. Green I control the whole stick— for you... BUY IT MAN, BUY IT and force Powers to come to you for it." In response to Cuningham's request for financial backing, Woresdorf assures him that "he'll carry him to any amount." The pace of the scene turns high-pitched, as Powers gets tricked into selling the Sunset shares and—just as the price begins to climb—Cuningham buys them all and ruins Powers. Enjoying their moment of victory, Cuningham and his partner, Lloyd, shake hands across the table. "Our last deal, Lloyd," says Cuningham. "We couldn't stand another like this—Bessie's ring did it." Cuningham drops his head on the table. Marjorie calls out to her father while Mrs. Cuningham (Bessie) goes to him, touching his head; "He's tired—He's fallen to sleep," she tells the others. "Don't wake him—he's worn out—he hasn't slept for weeks." But Woresdorf, who has been watching Cuningham, puts his fingers to the man's pulse and quietly tells Green to "Take the women away." Unaware her father has died, Marjorie crosses lovingly to Woresdorf who takes her in his arms and guides her off with a backward look at Cuningham. Now alone with his partner, "Lloyd staggers to Cuningham's side and sinks down beside him."[72]

Critics commended the dramatist's skillful delineation of a complex central character who was "particularly sympathetic and touching in the last act," and welcomed a play that gave an actor "so good an opportunity for consistent and powerful acting."[73] Arthur Hoeber's review in The Illustrated American featured production photos, including two which show Crane's make-up "metamorphosis" as Cuningham—dapper and prosperous in Act One, while broken and aged in Act Three.[74] A Fool of Fortune represents one of Morton's most enduring works; when Crane and his company revived the play fifteen years later in a special matinee performance, the New York Times declared the story to be "quite as fresh today as it was [in 1896]."[75]

Morton did not work with Crane again until fifteen years later. The Senator Keeps House's opening in November 1911 marked not only their reunion, but also William H. Crane's fiftieth season on the American stage.[76] The eighty performances at the Garrick Theatre must have provided a boost for Morton, as it had been about nine years since she enjoyed a healthy run. In the comedy, Senator Larkin, from the Northwest, is a wealthy widower living in Washington, DC, with his nephew, Patrick. Their domestic life is constantly disrupted by frequent changes of housekeepers—it seems they always end up trying to marry the Senator, who harbors "a prejudice against second marriages."[77] A fellow congressman, Judson, introduces Larkin to "the best of all housekeepers," Ida Flower, accompanied by her daughter, Eva. Ida commences to set the Senator's house in order, as Eva and Patrick commence to fall in love. But just as the Senator begins to soften toward Mrs. Flower, he learns that Judson planted her in his home so she might influence him to support a claim she is bringing against the government. Larkin physically confronts Judson, punches him in the nose, and kicks him out of his house. Later, after Ida Flower has gone, Patrick asks his uncle: "What will become of us?" "Become of us?" replies the Senator, "Why, we're going back to honest burnt toast and bad coffee!"[78]

It takes the senator another act to learn that Ida did not know of the "injustice of her claim and has not been guilty of dishonesty and treachery."[79] He continues to be surly towards her until Eva and Patrick announce they are married; he helps them break the news to Ida and, in the process, restores harmony in his home. A reviewer in *Bookman* called *The Senator Keeps House* "an innocent and amiable play," which was "sufficiently humorous, sufficiently sentimental." He remarked that "The author does not ask us to take life very seriously, but bids us don a tender-hearted smile. There is a gentleness about this comedy that must be called old-fashioned; but old fashions, like old shoes, are comfortable; and it is sometimes rather restful to be relieved from novelty."[80] Overall, critics concurred that Morton's play, together with Crane's acting, made an enjoyable evening of wholesome entertainment.

SO PLEASANT A TASK AS THE WORK OF PLAYMAKING

The Best Plays of 1894–1899 mentions *A Fool of Fortune*, stating that "It is commented on here only because, up to now, very few women had attempted playwriting either here or abroad."[81] Indeed, Morton had made an impression upon the critics and the public: "Very nearly at the head of the list of modern women playwrights stands the name of Martha Morton," states a clipping from the *Dramatic Mirror*, May 1896—the only other women contemporaries as widely known as she being Frances Hodgson Burnett and Madeleine Lucette Ryley. Since 1889, with *Hélène*, the dramatist had achieved six New York productions and was yet to experience failure. In addition, the Pacific Coast stock company obtained the use of *His Wife's Father, Brother John*, and *The Californian*— a westernized version of *Geoffrey Middleton*. *His Wife's Father* was to be produced in Swedish in Stockholm and *Brother John* in London the next season. William Crane continued performing in his repertoire the plays she had written for him.[82] And in the process, Morton became one of the most widely interviewed and publicized American woman dramatist of her time.

That Morton took her work seriously is demonstrated in a description of her daily schedule: rising early, she walked in nearby Central Park before commencing work in her "workshop."[83] After a noon rest and second stroll, she returned for "another spell of work" and at times, "if deeply interested in the task," she wrote "on far into the night." Explained Morton: "Of late, it has been necessary that I should push my pen nowadays a bit harder than usual, and so the late hours frequently find me at the study desk toiling away as if life depended upon it, for it is very hard to tear one's self from a task that is so pleasant as the work of playmaking."[84] By this time, she had hired an assistant to help with correspondence and business details. "For gentle art," explained Morton, "in these rushing days, goes hand in hand with roughshod commercial interest, and one may barely live without the other."[85] Morton could certainly afford an assistant by then, since *Theatre* revealed that the playwright earned a total of $250,000 from the first three plays for William H. Crane, a small fortune in the days before income taxes. Indeed, Morton ended 1896 with her star on the rise and her reputation as a professional playwright firmly established.

When Morton was asked why more women were not successful as dramatists, she expressed the opinion that it was because "most of them who attempt the work are appalled . . . by the difficulties which it presents."

> You understand, merely writing the manuscript of a play is not sufficient. No dramatist can succeed who does not understand all the technical points of stage setting, costuming, the most effective entrances and exits, and a thousand and one details which seem trifling, but which are vitally important. It is not so easy for a woman to acquire this practical knowledge as it is for a man, and I suppose many women have become discouraged at their failure to get hold of what is technically known as "theatrical business." Nevertheless, it is entirely possible for them to do so, if they will go about it patiently, persistently and with the right sort of spirit. [86]

Morton became indoctrinated early into the politics of casting when Grace Sherwood, an actress, sued William H. Crane for breach of contract. Apparently, Sherwood had been "conditionally" hired by the company manager for the role of Martha in *Brother John*, but both Crane and Morton found her acting poor. The *New York Times* reported: "Miss Morton testified that Miss Sherwood was an utter failure as Martha." And Crane was quoted as saying after seeing Sherwood in rehearsals he felt she "would not do at all as Martha" and did not want her in his company. Even so, a jury returned a verdict for Clara Sherwood, which Crane said he would appeal. [87]

One technique Morton utilized in the process of creating a play, was using a chessboard to visualize the ground plan of scenes, and moving characters through the scenes to keep track of entrances and exits. In fact, Esther Singleton told in "American Women Playwrights" in 1898 that Morton wanted to include a theatre in a house that she was building where she might "try the effects of her combinations, exits, and entrances," although it is not known whether her plan came to fruition. During rehearsals Morton often took control of the staging of her own plays, which enabled her to "devise business that [was] fresher and more lifelike than the conventional arrangements of professional stage managers."[88] In 1910 she reflected: "When I first started in . . . the idea of a woman directing a rehearsal was unheard of. But now they think nothing of it."[89] In addition, the playwright paid close attention to reactions of opening night audiences by sitting in an "obscure corner of a stage box" to watch the faces of theatregoers. If a scene does not "produce sufficient effect," she stated, "there is something wrong with it. The only way, after all, is to learn from one's own mistakes. There is no other training school for dramatists except that. It is a long and often a trying one, but the lessons are worth mastering in the end."[90]

Morton's first few years of playwriting must have been exhilarating as her career picked up momentum, but happiness was interrupted by her father's sudden death in August 1895 in Providence, Rhode Island. Joseph Morton had retired from his business as "one of the oldest and best-known china and glass importers in the United States" but recently had returned to work in connection with a well-known importing firm. After his death, it fell to Martha to provide primary support for her mother and five of her siblings, or at least her unmarried sisters—as expressed in her 1908 will, she felt "my brothers as men, are naturally able to support themselves."[91] Even later in life, Morton continued supporting younger sisters, Phoebe and Victoria, and provided income for them in her will.[92]

Morton, however, did enjoy some luxuries with her earnings, purchasing a cabin in upstate New York.[93] Her cabin was at Merriwold, located at the foot of the Catskill Mountains, where a cluster of New York playwrights and other writers regularly spent their summers. This literary "colony" formed the focus of Baily Millard's article "Merriwold Dramatists" in *Bookman*, August 1909. At Merriwold, dramatists William C. De Mille, Charles Klein, J.I.C. Clarke, Margaret Turnbull, and Martha Morton, among others, worked on their plays, swam in the nearby lake, walked in the woods, socialized, and shared works-in-progress with one another. Millard described Morton's "cozy little cabin" as "the Mansion"— so named because of its "ornate appointments"—containing "a sunlit study, daintily decorated and furnished."[94] According to various news clippings, Morton spent quite a lot of time writing at Merriwold, even after her marriage.[95]

At the age of thirty-two, on August 25, 1897, Martha Morton married Hermann Conheim, a New York businessman. The wedding was performed in an intimate ceremony at the home of her mother, who by then had moved to Saratoga, New York, after which they took a "bridal tour" in the Adirondack Mountains.[96] Hermann Conheim, born in Koenigsberg, Germany, immigrated to the United States at eighteen. In Germany, he received training for a banking career, but after settling in New York, he established a firm that imported bristles, one of three such firms in New York City at the time.[97] A photo, circa 1902, shows Morton lunching at home with her husband at an elegant round dining table with a manservant attending. Dressed in a suit, with a mustache and dark receding hair, Conheim portrays "a wealthy importer and cultured gentleman of New York."[98]

After marriage, Morton continued using her own name professionally, with most publications referring to her as "Miss Morton" or "Martha Morton Conheim." The Conheims lived at 265 West 90th Street off Riverside Drive in New York City, their home described as handsome and even "rarely beautiful." Shirley Burns mentions every room being "one of unusual originality and charm," declaring the library as "one of the most beautiful" and containing "more than three thousand volumes, hundreds of which are *editions de luxe*."[99] The October 1909 *Theatre* includes a large photograph of Morton's richly appointed study and another with the playwright posed in a "morning negligee" and seated in a high-backed chair at an ornately carved black oak table with a fireplace beyond.[100] Although they never had children, their twenty-eight-year marriage remained mutually supportive. A month after Morton's death, her husband "established a scholarship fund in her memory at the Hebrew University in Palestine."[101] When Conheim's death followed two years after Morton's, his obituary included the sentiment: "The death of Mr. Conheim is believed by his friends to have been partly due to grief over the death of his wife."[102]

MORTON'S BIGGEST HIT, *A BACHELOR'S ROMANCE*

At the end of August 1897, while the newlyweds enjoyed their honeymoon trip, a short announcement in the *Tribune* stated that "the bride will return to this city in time to be present at the first night's performance of her new play, entitled 'A Bachelor's Romance.'"[103] When Morton began writing this "distinctively American" play for Sol Smith Russell, he was already a well-known actor-comedian. A specialist in awkward, eccentric roles, Russell reflected "a quaint, simple and lovable strain" that contributed to his appeal with audiences. The comedian was especially popular with playgoers of the South and West, so tended to perform infrequently in New York, despite a loyal following there.[104]

David Holmes, the central role in *A Bachelor's Romance*, proved tailor-made for the forty-eight-year-old Russell. The script describes David Holmes as "a man of about forty" who looks older, his hair "streaked with gray," and when he first appears, carrying "books, papers, and umbrella," his attire is "careless," epitomizing "a type of hard-working journalist."[105] Literary critic for the *Review*, Holmes lives in the top floor of a comfortable, old-fashioned studio building in Washington Square. The beginning of the play reflects a literary and decidedly masculine atmosphere, with Holmes seen as a "modest, diffident man of books and manuscript, whose calling puts him forward as a student of humanity, interpreting man to men, but who really knows men very little and women not at all."[106] Other male characters include Martin, his secretary, Savage, a modern literary man, and Mr. Mulberry, an older impoverished classics scholar reduced to periodically selling off cherished volumes.

Two aspects in the story soon become apparent, the first being that Holmes must select the winner of a $10,000 prize offered by the *Review* for the best serial story. Not only have Martin, Savage, and Mr. Mulberry entered the contest, but also Harold Reynolds, a young *Review* staffer. But most central to the plot is Holmes' ward, Sylvia, the daughter of a deceased friend. Having placed her with an older woman in the country, Miss Clemantina, Holmes has conveniently forgotten his ward, periodically telling his secretary to remind him to go see the "child" on Sunday, but Martin *has* reminded him "every Sunday for the last ten years."[107] When Sylvia, now seventeen years of age, makes an unexpected appearance into David Holmes's apartment, she is shown to be a "very quaint, little figure of a country girl, dressed in an old-fashioned but picturesque way." Initially, she tells him she is another hopeful entrant in the essay contest: "My story's called 'The Charity Child' because I live on the bounty of people. My father died and left me in the care of a gentleman whom I have never seen. I'm living with a maiden lady. *He* pays my board. She's very good to me, but she's kinder soured on things, and I get so tired of listening to how wicked the world is. She's opposed to everything—are you?"[108]

Holmes, unaware she is his ward, remains preoccupied with writing and absent-mindedly agrees that, yes, she ought to go to a glee club concert with a nice young man she has just met. When his widowed sister, Helen, and pleasure-loving brother, Gerald, pay a call, differences between the bookwormish Holmes and his social-minded siblings become immediately apparent. Miss Clemantina, "a maiden lady with a sharp tongue," then shows up to suggest that Holmes take her "unruly, disobedient, disrespectful" young charge off her hands. Sylvia returns with her date, Harold Reynolds, causing Miss Clemantina to storm off in a huff. David Holmes must now contend with Sylvia's presence in his staid, comfortable world, and asks his sister to take charge of the young woman. Sylvia's youth, vitality, and disarming naturalness charms everyone, especially her guardian who begins to rediscover his own lost youth.

Eventually Holmes must wrestle with an ethical dilemma concerning the final decision for the literary contest—should he award the $10,000 prize to his "rival" for Sylvia, Harold Reynolds, who has actually submitted the best entry, but who would then be in an advantageous position to marry? Or should the prize go to Savage, whose story is only second-best, but who has no interest in Sylvia? At the end of the third act, when Holmes' brother accuses him of being jealous of every man who approaches Sylvia, Holmes confronts his own feelings: "In love!—In love—Yes—but I have never called it by that name—even to myself. . . . Gerald—is it too late?" His brother is not encouraging: "I—I hate to say it—but if you ask me—it would be the worst of folly for you to marry a young girl—and I'm—I'm afraid you wouldn't have very much chance with Sylvia—." Unaware of Sylvia's affection for him, a resigned Holmes tells Sylvia she ought to marry Harold, and as the curtain descends, he discloses to Martin, his secretary, that "Harold Reynolds—has won the prize."[109]

Act Four opens on a rustic setting in the front yard of Clemantina's country house and reveals changes in several characters. Harold, whose prize winnings have altered him from a carefree Bohemian to a foppish snob, argues with Sylvia to whom he is now engaged. But city-sophisticates, Gerald, Helen, and their friend, Harriet, have become charmed by country life, discovering the simple pleasures of fishing, milking cows, and collecting eggs. After Holmes arrives with Savage, Mulberry, and Martin, various misunderstandings resolve themselves, especially when Harold and Sylvia call off the engagement and he departs for the city. David is then free to admit his feelings for Sylvia. Romantic pairings at the end of the play are abundant, including David Holmes and Sylvia, Helen and Savage, Gerald and Harriet, and even a reunion between Miss Clemantina and her old friend, Martin.

After a copyright matinee performance in New York on September 16, 1896, at the Gaiety Theatre, Russell began touring throughout the country with *A Bachelor's Romance*, faring well with audiences and most critics.[110] A December notice of the Chicago opening declared the show a hit: "The author has studied the player's personality and methods closely, and produced a play of genuine interest with few exaggerations of plot or character." It was decided "to present nothing else in the three week's engagement."[111] Two weeks later, the *Chicago Tribune* deemed the play "the comedy success of the present season."[112]

Common sentiments resonate throughout reviews of the New York production, opening with Annie Russell (no relation to Sol) at the Garden Theatre on September 20, 1897. Reviewers displayed a kindly respect toward the talents of Sol Smith Russell, possibly engendered by the actor's opening night speech. Before the second act curtain, Russell— in his "quaint, pleasing manner . . . expressed the hope that since his last professional visit, public appreciation in this neighborhood had broadened sufficiently to take him in."[113] The *New York Times* critic felt a need to interpret an opening night audience that was less exuberant than most: "A lack of noisy demonstrations on a theatrical 'first night' in this town generally indicates that the proportion of intelligence in the audience is unusually large. No actor in the world deserves a warmer and kindlier greeting than that given to Mr. Russell; but it is true also that variety 'comedians' and 'farce-comedy' tenors are often received more noisily."[114] Metcalfe, at variance with Charles Frohman in the past, now tossed laurels to the producer for *A Bachelor's Romance*: "Mr. Charles Frohman deserves a nice, fat halo for his generosity in supplying so excellent a cast to an artist like Mr. Russell, and also to a clean meritorious play. Perhaps even he foresees a better era for the New York stage."[115]

Dramatically considered, however, the play did not fare as well as did the cast in its critical reception. The story of an older man falling in love with his young ward was a well-used one and critics quickly pointed out *A Bachelor's Romance*'s similarity to plays with similar themes, specifically, Garrick's *The Guardian*, Henry Arthur Jones's *The Physician*, and J. M. Barrie's *The Professor's Love Story*. But the most hurtful charge against Morton was that of plagiarizing a novel published in 1891, *A Little Rebel*, by "The Duchess" (Mrs. Hungerford). In November 1897, toward the end of the New York run, newspaper stories appeared, reporting: "It is alleged by many persons who have read the novel and have seen the play that 'The Duchess' story has merely been put into dramatic form by the playwright, that almost every character has been lifted from the book to the play, and few changes made." In addition, continued the *New York Times*, "critics who accuse Miss Morton of plagiarism further maintain that scene after scene in her play is taken in sequence just as first presented in the book." The "critics" claimed that Morton had lifted passages from the novel with "scarcely the changing of a word," which Morton "emphatically denied" in the *New York Times*:

> "This is the old story," she said, "and a part of the price one pays for success. A year ago, when the play was running in Chicago, *The Times Herald* came out with a bitter and personal story charging me with using this story by 'The Duchess' in the preparation of my play. I took no notice of it. Now some enemy of mine has been following the same thing up and brought it to New York. I never even saw the book referred to until the Chicago papers attacked me. Then I read the book. To be sure, the motive is much the same. We are all of us obliged to use an old motive in the construction of our plays. The whole thing lies in the fact that the play has been unusually successful, and someone is trying to cause trouble."[116]

A reading of the novel, *A Little Rebel*, does reveal marked similarities between the novel and *A Bachelor's Romance*.[117] The novel concerns Thaddeus Curzon, a solitary professor who teaches and engages in scientific research and who lives in a small dingy flat on the Strand in London. Curzon is unexpectedly appointed guardian to the daughter of a friend who has died in Australia. Relieved to learn she will be living with an aunt in London, he promptly forgets about her until several months later when she appears in his flat, not at all the child he imagined, but a lovely seventeen-year-old named Perpetua. Unhappy with her old-fashioned, strict aunt, Perpetua refuses to leave Curzon, and he is forced to turn to his widowed sister to take charge of the girl. Both Curzon's friend, Hardinge, "a gay young society man, with just the average amount of brains, but not an ounce beyond that," and Curzon's dissipated, titled brother show interest in the lovely Australian ward. To save her from his brother, Curzon proposes on behalf of Hardinge, despite having fallen in love with her himself, but she refuses. Fortuitously, however, Curzon's brother dies suddenly, giving Curzon both title and property, which allows him to freely propose to Perpetua for himself.

As mentioned before, May-December romances appeared to be a popular theme in the late nineteenth and early twentieth century. And while there are similarities, Morton's play reveals a richer plot and more sub-plots when compared to the straightforward story of *A Little Rebel*. A comparison of the play with the novel refutes the accusation that Morton lifted dialogue word for word from the novel, as apparently asserted by the publisher of *A Little Rebel*.[118] Morton openly denied the accusation: "I desire to say through the *Tribune* that in no way did I take any part of my play, *A Bachelor's Romance*, from a novel. I took the situation and plot from human experience, and built the play around it without in any way using another's language or ideas."[119] Rather, it appears that she took a clichéd idea that resembled *A Little Rebel*, setting her story in a literary atmosphere with decidedly American characters—stated Metcalfe, "it is American in every particular; in atmosphere, authorship, and acting."[120] Despite Morton's conventional theme and falling back on the old-fashioned notion "that a month or so in the country will transform urban character and purge away all its faults," critics and audiences found the story easy to digest.[121] After six weeks at the Garden Theatre, the production returned the following April for another week at the Grand Opera House.

At the same time it was being introduced to New York audiences, *A Bachelor's Romance*, put into an English setting, toured England and Scotland under John Hare's management, reaching

London and the Globe Theatre in January 1898. English audiences must have agreed with the *Daily Mail*, which declared the play as being "full of Dickens tenderness and full of Dickens laughter" and "never for an instant dull" since it played ninety-five performances, surpassing the New York run. "It is undeniable that the play was a great success," stated J. T. Grein, owing something to John Hare's "personal popularity," the other actors, "and a good deal to the authoress."[122] George Bernard Shaw, in *Saturday Review*, remarked, tongue-in-cheek: "Miss Morton's success as a playwright is, of course, founded on a clear gift of telling stories and conjuring up imaginary people. But her easy conquest of managerial favour is due to the aptitude with which she sketches congenial and easily acted parts for good actors to fill up, and to that sympathy-catching disposition to be good-natured at all costs, which is so agreeable to the public just at present."[123] Although *A Bachelor's Romance* may not hold up on today's stage, it nevertheless, remained one of Morton's strongest works and became her most widely produced play. It continued to be produced throughout the country by various stock companies well into the 1920s. Published by Samuel French in 1912, *A Bachelor's Romance* was later released as a film by Adolph Zukor and Daniel Frohman's Company, Famous Players in 1915.[124] *The Dramatist*, however, expressed that the "shoddy photo-drama" and the performance of John Emerson could not compare to the stage version and the "exquisite artistry" of Sol Smith Russell.[125]

Russell did not even come close to his success with *A Bachelor's Romance* in his second Morton play, *Uncle Dick*, tried out briefly in the fall of 1898. The only available review comes from the *Boston Transcript*, which routinely condemned Morton's work, making it difficult to know the merits of the play, if any. Generally, however, it appears nothing much came of Russell's portrayal of the avuncular Dick, who served as an instrument by which other younger fun-loving characters learn lessons about life's true values. His supporting cast included several of the same actors from *A Bachelor's Romance*, with the addition of a twenty-year-old Lionel Barrymore.[126]

For the first time in fifteen years, during a two-year period, 1899 through 1901, Morton had nothing new staged on Broadway. Having written about twenty-two plays, with twelve professionally produced— including seven New York productions and two in London—she had certainly earned a break. Morton continued writing during the dawn of the new century, however. *Veronica*, a five-act drama, copyrighted in 1902, was apparently never staged, and a reading of the manuscript (entitled *La Veronica*) indicates a heavy, cumbersome plot resembling a romance novel and filled with numerous diverse characters. Even so, the storyline with a woman at the center suggests that Morton wanted to write something other than comic vehicles for male stars. Indeed, giving forth her ideas on marriage and lifestyle, Morton wrote two plays at the beginning of the century, *Her Lord and Master* and *The Movers*, both which comment upon the behavior of American women.

INDICTING AMERICAN WOMEN

In April 1901, Morton postponed a trip to Europe to "retire to her cottage in the Adirondack Mountains and there devote the entire summer to the composition" of a new play for Ada Rehan. Evidently, she had been contracted by managers of the well-known actress to create a "society play for Rehan's season which began in August."[127] But in early August, it was announced that Effie Shannon and Herbert Kelcey would be starring in Morton's new play, *Her Lord and Master*, with Ada Rehan's sister, Hattie Russell, playing a supporting role, along with Douglas Fairbanks in his New York debut.

When *Her Lord and Master* opened at the Manhattan Theatre the following February, it enjoyed a respectable run of sixty performances, but the play's theme caused indignation among the critics and very likely some discussion among theatre-goers. Morton's "up-to-date version of the Taming of the Shrew" pits American versus British manners in a culture clash, which leaves Americans in a poor light. Indiana Stillwater (Effie Shannon) becomes acquainted with Englishman, Viscount Thurston Canning

(Herbert Kelcey), who, with his uncle, is a guest at her millionaire father's Colorado ranch. As an only child, Indiana has been lovingly pampered by her family. When Lord Canning reveals his love for her, Indiana, despite an admission that she does not return his feeling, senses that this man is different from other suitors and agrees to marry, telling him "I want to be something more than what I am—something better," and "I wouldn't marry you if I did not think I could love you—someday." But she warns him of her spoiled nature and secures his promise that when she becomes "inconsistent" and willful in a way that is not good for her, he must not give in.[128]

Lord Canning's promise to his young wife forms the flimsy premise upon which the plot hinges. In the second act she is a changed person, repressing her usual robust personality to impress her new mother-in-law. The script describes her as: "the personification of English maidenhood, in plain English gown. She wears a bonnet with strings and carries a prayer book, uses a decided English accent."[129] Her overly demure manner prompts even her husband to question why she does not act natural, but she insists that agreeing with his mother in everything is the only way to get along with her. The test of Indiana's new demeanor, as well as the strength of their marriage, comes when her family makes a surprise visit, bringing along Glen, her childhood beau (Fairbanks). Indiana turns rebellious when her husband considers it improper for her to socialize with her family and Glen at a London hotel late at night; to keep his promise to her—that he will not give in—he has the doors locked at midnight, forcing Indiana, with the aid of a servant—to climb in through a window. Her act of "disobedience" causes a rift between the newlyweds the next day; but Indiana begins to realize how much she now loves her husband, and rather than travel with her family, she elects to stay behind to repair her marriage. Peace and harmony are restored at the end.

Her Lord and Master is, by and large, a comedy of manners with a bite and a not-so-subtle "expose" of American attitudes and behavior. Comparisons between American and British culture begin even in the opening scene between two servants. When Flash, Lord Stafford's valet, asks Kitty, the Stillwaters' servant, how much Mr. Stillwater is worth, Kitty contemptuously replies: "A man who knows how rich he is—is not a rich man in America. He's only well off—Mr. Stillwater has reached that stage where money is never even mentioned. So in the future when they say in America a man's rich—you will understand he is not limited to figures." And when Flash becomes intimidated by Mr. Stillwater's presence, Kitty reassures him: "He's an American gentleman. He is free and easy with everyone."[130] Morton also emphasizes the youthfulness of American women; Indiana is but eighteen, her mother, Elizabeth, is described as "a very young woman," and Indiana's grandmother, Chazy Bunker, is "a woman of 50 who appears about 35." Grandma Chazy laughingly relates to the two English guests in the first act: "You'll find women like me all over the states—you see— we don't become old before our time—to make way for the girls. I had a daughter to rear and I did it as well as I knew how—then I superintended my grand-daughter's training—now she's a woman—I'm commencing all over again on my own account—." Even Lord Stafford's usual British reserve is caught unawares when Grandma spears him with: "How is it that a good catch like you has escaped the matrimonial anglers so long?"[131]

The *New York Times* reviewer took particular umbrage over the play's conjecture that American men are ruled by their wives. When Thurston expresses a serious interest in his daughter, Mr. Stillwater explains lightly that American women are "natural Imperialists. They head a despotic monarchy at home." A bit later he boasts, "every man I know is under his wife's thumb and is proud of it."[132] The *New York Times* reviewer, despite the playwright's "cleverness," questions whether the topic of an American wife or English husband

> "can be summed up in a single type in a single play. It is well known that in the cockney adage, Britannia rules the wives; but even the utmost enthusiasm of those Americans who call themselves imperialists would scarcely lead them to postulate that Uncle Sam should do the same. And is it quite true that American husbands and fathers are subject to petticoat government?"[133]

The *Tribune* found it odd that an informed playwright would write such a play "in the hope of pleasing Americans"; while recognizing Morton's sure hand at crafting plays and "deft touches," he took offense over the basic premise of the play, which makes "all the Americans" either "weak or vulgar."[134] Expressing similar dissatisfaction, a review in *Theatre* stated: "It seems unfair for an American author to place her own countrymen in an altogether unfavorable light and present as typical Americans persons whose lack of manners is seen only too plainly in contrast with the high breeding of the English characters in the play."[135] The cast received moderate praise, particularly Effie Shannon as the willful Indiana and Herbert Kelcey as the restrained and dignified Lord Channing. Shannon and Kelcey may have felt a particular affinity for these roles because she was American while he was from a well-to-do English family.

Morton also attempted more substantive themes, reflecting the national shift in playwriting toward more complex characters and realistic situations. It is the social commentary and theme of *The Movers*, Morton's drama produced at Hackett's Theatre on September 3, 1907, which make it one of her most significant works. In *The Movers*, Morton lays the blame for society's "fevered social and financial life at the door of the woman who imagines that her sole function in society is to spend her husband's money" in woeful extravagance.[136] Indeed, as the *New York Times* stated: "One recognizes it at the outset as a purposeful play."[137] Act One of *The Movers* introduces Chudleigh and Marion Manners, an up-and-coming couple in their late twenties, and like many in their social sphere, their lives reflect a feverish pursuit of material gain. But even before the introduction of Marion, her husband, a broker, tells his friend, Harold, that things have not gone well over the last six months and he now needs $25,000. In Marion's first scene—reminiscent of Nora with Torvald in *A Doll's House*—she displays childlike delight over a gold purse set with diamonds which her husband gives her; "Now don't lose it as you did the last one," Chudleigh tells her, "it cost four hundred dollars."[138]

Although the first two acts depict Marion as frivolous and shallow, her younger sister, Phillipina, appears even "worldlier," and it is revealed that a spendthrift life is all the sisters have known.

Their father, Archibald Leigh, "a social butterfly who makes and unmakes fortunes without changing his mode of living at any time," once again is forced to sell his house due to poor speculation.[139] But Marion reminds her family: "As long as I can remember, we were going to be put into the streets the next moment, but we were never deprived ourselves—eh, Mother? When they pressed father too hard, we just put ourselves on a steamer and sailed for Europe to economize. We had a gorgeous time in Dresden. We speak French and German, and play four-handed better than most girls."[140]

While she may be extravagant with her husband's earnings, Marion also actively participates in business dealings. When longtime friend, Dr. Sterling, comments on her nervous state, she reveals: "I'm overworked. I've always been overworked. I've never had an idle moment in my life. Father never speculated without consulting me, and when it went wrong, I managed splendidly to keep things going until he struck it again. I've made Chudleigh. I've figured out his most successful deals."[141] Sterling serves as the voice of reason in the play, often functioning as the only sane presence, giving forth sermonettes on morality and healthy living. He tells Marion, for instance, that she is "a human spider, ceaselessly spinning webs," advising her to "read an hour a day"; she must think of herself more, he suggests, "all this misdirected nervous activity is destroying you body and soul"; Sterling tells her, as well, that she is "a wild seabird who skims the surface and never dives under."[142]

After Chudleigh's potential deal falls through, the situation grows worse for the Mannerses. Fourteen months later, when Act Two opens, their furniture stands ticketed and arranged in lots for an impending auction. Although the Leighs take it all rather philosophically, Chudleigh cannot be so blasé and begins to emotionally fall apart. At the end of the act, Marion seriously considers accepting assistance from the auctioneer, Chamberlain, whose offer harbors unsavory implications for her. When Sterling, who has heard part of their conversation, tells Marion she must refuse, she lashes out at him, reaching a pitch of hysteria that ends with a gunshot offstage. Despite the doctor's attempts to stop her, she rushes into Chudleigh's room only to stagger out moments later in shock. "My husband does not need your assistance," the agonized Marion tells the auctioneer, who has entered the room, "He has moved away—moved away—moved away."[143]

Eighteen months after her husband's suicide, Marion has moved on and, with Dr. Sterling's encouragement, pursues a two-year nurse's training program. The Leighs and the Rays (Phillipina and her husband, Harold), now own Marion's house. Marion shows up to nurse Phillipina's sick child, and Chamberlain drops by, again making advances toward Marion; he owns the mortgage on the house and threatens to dispossess the family unless she agrees to marry him. This time, however, Marion possesses enough self-respect to reject the man outright. But while Marion's values have changed, her sister's seem more entrenched. The crisis of Chamberlain's threat causes the family to examine their lifestyle. When Mr. Leigh reacts, telling Marion: "Obstinate, ungrateful child, after all the sacrifices we've made for our children," his wife finally speaks up: "We never sacrificed for them. It was our own vanity and pride. Our children must be better dressed than others, our children must be prettier, our sons-in-law must be richer. I'm tired of the sham and the lies. And you, you poor man, you've worn yourself to pieces. Nobody knows it as I do."[144] The next morning, however, Mr. Leigh finds yet another scheme and Mrs. Leigh acquiesces. Hope remains, though, for Phillipina and Harold, who decide to move to the country. At the end, Dr. Sterling and Marion remain in the nursery with the sleeping child. "Ah! The Doctor's fate has overtaken me," he says. "I have fallen in love with my trained nurse." But Marion gently stops him from coming closer and tells him, "In two years."

As may be surmised from the synopsis, *The Movers* is not without flaws, and reviewers were only too ready to point them out. While the idea of the play is not new, stated the *New York Times*, yet it seems new when characters on the stage resemble those one reads about in the daily paper. But, he qualified: "if only the people did not get into the same old snarl, and if only the prosperous auctioneer person did not insult the helpless heroine in the same old way, and if it were only less obvious that the dear, good preachy doctor would get her also in the end, you would be willing to forgive Miss Morton for dragging in every bit of local gossip she could think of, rejoicing in the fact that something of real New York had actually got upon the stage."[145] And yet, Walter P. Eaton in the *Sun* called *The Movers* the most interesting play of the season, particularly when compared with *The Ranger*, Augustus Thomas's "sad, sad melodrama."[146] But the "great dramatic weakness" of the play, stressed Eaton, lies in Morton's failure to show the audience Marion's change. For two acts, "'The Movers' is at bottom sound, truthful, effective drama. From then [following Chudleigh's suicide] to the close it is weak and ineffective." Let the change in Marion, "the most significant psychology of the drama," take place in the third act, advised Eaton, rather than during the eighteen months between acts two and three.[147]

While some critics as in the *Tribune*, for instance, promptly dismissed *The Movers* because of its faults, a few, like Eaton and a critic in *Theatre*, strongly defended the play for its ideas. Stated *Theatre*: "But a thoughtful drama like 'The Movers,' dealing with vital problems and with as strong and profoundly moving a second act as we have seen on the local stage in years, is the kind of play our stage needs if it is to be lifted up from imbecility and triviality to become once more the recreation of intelligent men and women."[148] Eaton argued for the play's continuation and discussed its "treatment of the problems of sex equality and woman's sphere" in a longer article in the *Sun* on the following Sunday. In fact, Eaton passionately defended the play:

> To sit debonairly back in the seats of the scornful and scoff it off the boards for its crudities is a critical error in judgment that amounts to a misdemeanor. The stage in this country makes few attempts . . . to voice the thoughts and problems of the age in adult speech. When such an attempt is made sincerely and with as fair a measure of success as in "The Movers" no critic . . . can honestly say that this drama with all its faults is not worth seeing, worth discussing, even at times profoundly moving and stimulating.[149]

Interestingly, the *Theatre* critic mentioned that Morton was "a student of Schopenhauer" and related her work to the philosopher's belief that drama "should lead humanity to ultimate happiness through a merciless and pessimistic analysis of the unhealthy conditions of our modern life."[150] Eaton, too, cited Schopenhauer at the beginning of his second article, quoting some of the philosopher's judgments of women.

Because of Morton's harsh indictment of a certain class of American women and her depiction of "the woman problem," as Eaton called it, *The Movers* undoubtedly engendered more critical reaction and discussion than any of her previous works—serving as a rare instance where the dramatist and her play actually received more critical attention and approval than any of the performers. Nevertheless, Dorothy Donnelly served well in her portrayal of Marion and was apparently able to achieve a believable level of restlessness in the first two acts and show Marion's sincere "regeneration" in the last two. Some reviewers felt Vincent Serrano overacted the role of Chudleigh, or, as the *New York Times* posited, "began in a mood of wild excitement and never for a moment remembered to forget it."[151] The production was "smoothed out" some after opening night, but despite its advocates, the play did not last beyond twenty-three performances. Apparently, *The Movers* received some sort of revival in 1909.[152]

A LITTLE VAUDEVILLE, SOME SUCCESS, SOME FAILURE

While *Her Lord and Master* was still playing at the Manhattan, Morton's *The Diplomat* opened with William Collier at the Madison Square Theatre on March 1902, the two productions running concurrently for approximately a month. *The Diplomat*, Morton told in an interview, was not meant to be a "regular" play in the manner of previous work but rather a vaudeville piece.[153] And, according to *Theatre*, it accomplished "well the object for which it was obviously intended: to provide a suitable vehicle for the peculiar talents of Mr. William Collier."[154] In 1903, William Collier had just played a season with the well-known vaudeville team, Weber and Fields, and, indeed, his talent for that particular venue showed in *The Diplomat*.[155] Short on plot, but abundant in character sketches, jokes, physical humor, and dancing, the comedy's central character is Nick Sportwick (Collier), "light and dissipated . . . but with the sound heart which... invariably underlies such a surface." Continued the *New York Times*: "It is a very excellent vaudeville, far and away above the wares of the roof garden. William Collier's estimable Wildoatster is quite as racy and impertinent here as in 'On the Quiet.' His lines are as packed with epigram and swift repartee, he is as invariably whimsical and humorous in his attitude toward life."[156] The reviewer voiced a "suspicion that Mr. Collier was responsible for much of the fun, both of the "business and of the lines," because of the "frequent masculine turns of humor" not evident in Morton's previous work, and because "its raciness savored at times of something undeniably not feminine or refined."[157]

Although the *New York Times* and *Theatre* showed an understanding of *The Diplomat* as a lighthearted vaudeville piece, apparently other reviewers judged it as a conventional comedy, accusing Morton of being "illogical" or not true to life. In "Martha Morton Criticises [sic] the Critics," Morton responded openly to barbs directed at *The Diplomat*:

> I wish one of them would attempt to write a vaudeville wherein one must set out to be deliberately inconsistent and illogical, to be funny, to be amusing and, above all, to amuse a certain class of cosmopolitan audience—people who are blasé, people who have seen everything under the sun. I wish one of these critics who harps about unreal characters would attempt to do all this, not forgetting that he must at the same time not be vulgar or offend in any way, and forbidding himself the luxury of horseplay, which is the bone and flesh of the farce. I should like to see him attempt to do this and remain faithful enough to certain types of life to elicit instant and cordial recognition on the part of his audience.[158]

The Diplomat fared well, in spite of (or possibly because of) such publicity, since it enjoyed seventy-five performances.

In 1903, the March issue of *Theatre* announced a "Prize Play Competition," offering a special matinee production in one of Charles Frohman's theatres "with a first-class cast" as the prize. The notice reminded readers of the "the successful career of Martha Morton," which had begun as a result of a similar competition.[159] The irony of this notice lies in the fact that after considerable publicity, nearly 300 anonymous entries, and several months' delay, the winning play announced nine months later turned out to be *The Triumph of Love* by Martha Morton. Although each of the seventeen finalists, continued the report, represented "a fine acting piece" whose authors "should have no difficulty in finding a manager," the judges felt that *The Triumph of Love* "approached nearest to the standard set for the competition."[160] There was no little chagrin on the part of the judges, William T. Seymour and F. Marion Crawford, along with the editors of *Theatre*, when, the day after the public announcement, they learned that the contest winner was not only an established playwright, but the same one cited in the opening announcement. What made things even worse was that the play did not pass muster in production. Despite the playwright's belief in her play and *Theatre* touting it as "an important work," not even a distinctive cast (Carlotta Nillson, Minna Gale Haynes, Maclyn Arbuckle, William Harcourt, Grace Filkins, and F. F. Mackay) could help *The Triumph of Love* get beyond the single, obligatory matinee. Staged at the Criterion Theatre on February 8, 1904, the play was promptly panned by the *New York Times*—qualifying as one of the harshest reviews Morton ever received from that publication.[161]

Briefly, the plot concerns a successful, poverty-stricken politician, his love for a young widow, and a scandal involving them that threatens his career. A political boss steps in to demand he give up the widow and arranges for him a respectable match with another young woman. Because of the scandal, the politician is shot, prompting the widow (now friends with her successor) to react openly over his injury, thereby publicly exposing their true feelings for each other. "It is a moment that if properly written up to, would have been thrilling." described the *New York Times*. "The situation it gives rise to in the last act is intrinsically powerful in the extreme. There is a duel of emotion between the two women, at once impassioned and magnanimous, in which the girl gives way to the natural right of the woman the man loves and has wronged. In the bare bones of her dramaturgy, Mrs. Conheim has been as Continental as in the initial situation. But how those bones rattled yesterday!"[162] Still, Morton refused to give up on *The Triumph of Love*. Five years later she told a reporter that she still believed it to be one of her best plays, expecting "to see it produced and to have a successful run in the future."[163]

The Triumph of Love's failure represented only one of several disappointments for the dramatist between 1903 and 1907. Short newspaper notices, for example, chronicle Morton's struggles with a four-act musical comedy, *A Four Leaf Clover*. In Paris during the summer of 1902, while working on the last act, Morton was taken ill and was unable to finish the manuscript until the following January; a notice in August 1903 mentions that Morton spent several weeks with the lead actress, Edna Aug, in Surrey, England.[164] Another mishap occurred when Aug had her copy of the script all but destroyed in a hotel fire. Apparently, it took more than two years to get the musical staged, a tryout production opening at the Parsons Theatre in Hartford on October 3, 1905. Aug played Clover Brown and "interpreted four characters, a mountain boy, a Dutch girl, a French *danseuse*, and a boarding school miss." A. Baldwin Sloane composed the music, while Morton wrote the book and lyrics.[165] But fate proved unlucky for *A Four Leaf Clover*.

Morton also tried her hand at a comedy along the lines of *Little Lord Fauntleroy*, which included not one child, but five. *The Truth Tellers*— the idea taken from a book by John Strange Winter—was one of her pet projects, having worked on it "spasmodically" for eight years. The plot concerns five orphaned Scottish children who are taken to London to live with a fussy, society-minded aunt and "where precepts of truth so carefully inculcated by their father cause no end of trouble."[166] Along with the piper who accompanies them, the children bring "five Shetland ponies, several sheep, an immense St. Bernard dog, a parrot, and a kitten, all of which appear on the stage."[167] The play had a modest, somewhat successful tryout production in Washington, DC, which ran for ten days in 1901. David Belasco saw the production and contracted with Morton to produce the play sometime in 1902, but after several delays, Belasco opted not to stage *The Truth Tellers* at all.[168] Fred G. Berger eventually produced it in Washington at the Columbia Theatre in September 1905, moving to the Grand Opera Theatre in New York in October.[169] As Bordman relates "The kilted youngsters rode ponies to a bagpipe accompaniment, but nothing could kindle interest."[170] Another play of Morton's during this period, which never made it to Broadway, but apparently fared well on the road, was *The Illusions of Beatrice*, written for Maude Fealey.[171]

PORTRAYING A HEROIC WOMAN

Martha Morton turned to historical drama with her adaptation from the German of Leopold Kampf's *On the Eve* which played in New York at the Hudson Theatre, beginning October 4, 1909. The drama focuses on the 1905 Russian revolution, with characters who struggle between their sense of duty and individual longings. At the center, the heroine, Anna Ricanskaya, a highborn young woman, seeks to help solve her country's social inequalities by going among the poor. When she becomes involved with a group of revolutionaries, it falls to Anna to give the signal to the person carrying a bomb that will kill the oppressor responsible for the massacre of part of their group. She does not learn until just before the assassination occurs that the one who must place the bomb and go down in the destruction is the man she loves.

Morton's version of *On the Eve* was evidently handicapped from the start by Kampf's original, "overburdened with nihilistic discussions."[172] Clayton Hamilton in *Forum* wrote that both the original and Morton's version included "too many phases of the political situation" and, therefore, had "no coherent plot." Stated Hamilton: "The piece is a chaotic jumble of episodes which exhibits no orderly progression. Many of the moments are effective and intense, and the final situation gives the pleasing thrill of melodrama, but the fabric as a whole is no more like a play than the scattered fragments of the Parthenon are like a Doric temple."[173] Critics agreed, however, that the outstanding feature of the production was the performance of Hedwig Reicher in the role of Anna. Renown for her acting in Germany, the actress also won distinction in leading German roles at the Irving Place Theatre in New York, but Morton's *On the Eve* represented Reicher's first appearance in an English-speaking role.[174] During a rehearsal for *On the Eve*, Morton said of the twenty-five-year-old performer: "If I hadn't had her I would not have known where to get anyone to play the part. I saw her two years ago in Germany... Then she was a tall, thin, awkward young girl. But she played a part so well that I recognized her power even then. I believe that Hedwig Reicher is a second Duse."[175] The *New York Times* critic went so far as to encourage readers to see the play because Reicher "deserve[d] the attention of the large general public" and went on to speak glowingly of her skillful acting.[176] It appears that Morton was, indeed, fortunate to secure Hedwig Reicher for the role of Anna, for without the German actress, the run of only twenty-four performances might have been even shorter.

"The next play I shall write," stated Morton in 1909, "will be one about suffrage for women."[177] Possibly her attempt to carry through on this promise was *The Model*, an extant unproduced three-act play which reflects issues about women's choices (marriage vs. career) and roles (doctor, wife, or mother) and merits some discussion. The central character, Margaret Matthews, is a doctor, a children's specialist, brought up by a bachelor uncle who is also a physician and has taught his niece to be independent and career minded. When she expresses an urge to marry and have children, he tells her: "Give up your profession or give up marriage. You cannot make a success of both." Margaret replies: "If I could, wouldn't it be a feather in my cap? The greatest example for other women to follow! If I prove *she* can *run* business and marriage together as a man does—"[178] Margaret marries Paul Gordon, an artist, and for over two years they live contentedly, pursuing their individual careers, even after the arrival of a baby daughter. But when, in Act Two, Paul's secret comes out, that he has fathered a son by one of his models, the plot takes a melodramatic turn. Ursula, the mother of the boy, shows up to beg Margaret to attend her sick child, but Margaret, worried about her own daughter who has become quite ill, puts off the woman. In desperation, Ursula blurts out the truth to Margaret about Paul being the boy's father. Margaret then leaves her own child in her uncle's care and goes to Ursula's child, during which time Margaret's baby daughter dies. Act Three attempts to reconcile Margaret and Paul, but by then, the plot's credibility has been stretched beyond capacity and one ceases to care. The script shows an undefined ending—perhaps the playwright ceased to care, as well.

In her last professional New York production, Morton tried her hand at yet another new form, the detective play. Comedy "crook plays" came into vogue around 1903 with *Raffles, the Amateur Cracksman*, an early comedy-thriller, regularly revived throughout the decade.[179] Morton's *Three of Hearts*, which opened at the 39th Street Theatre, June 1915, was compared favorably with *Raffles*. A reviewer in *Theatre*, in fact, deemed Morton's play "a better and certainly more agreeable play in every way."[180] Although the complications and twists of the plot make for a difficult synopsis, the gist of it concerns millionaire Harry Hamilton who becomes drawn to a young woman in Paris and follows her back to New York. He learns that Grace Maythorne is an artist from Virginia and although she mistakenly thinks he is a baron, she, nevertheless, shows no interest; but the persistent Hamilton discovers that Grace holds a weakness for reforming "men who have gone wrong," and sets about giving her the impression that he is a thief. In the process of trying to impress Grace, he is suspected of being the thief who has been stealing jewelry off the necks of wealthy socialites. Two other characters who add texture to this play are Haggerty, a police detective, and Williams, a convict in Hamilton's employ, who gets "recruited" to steal back stolen jewels.

Evidently, George Nash as Hamilton contributed greatly to the success of the comedy, and according to the *Tribune*, enacted the role with "dash, humor, and authority."[181] The *Dramatic Mirror* stated that despite its illogical, improbable elements, "it keeps the attention of the audience from curtain to curtain, and is a very good example of a popular form for special writing in just the right proportions into a lively play of strong melodramatic tinges." The writer also mentioned that it was reported that playwright Augustus Thomas had "an anonymous hand in the piece."[182] There may be some validity to this report, since a reading of the script shows that both dialogue and plot of *Three of Hearts* possess a cleaner, more "modern" touch than Morton's other work. But the difference may also be accounted for by the genre itself and by Morton's use of the language and rhythms in MacGrath's original story. At any rate, the play provided light-hearted, summer entertainment through twenty performances.

DEAN OF THE WOMEN PLAYWRIGHTS

Martha Morton was fifty when *Three of Hearts* was produced, and it appears to be the last play she wrote. In 1924, a year before her death, her novel, *Val Sinestra*, was published by Dutton. Morton had been treated for heart disease the last five years of her life, complicated by a twenty-year history of diabetes. She died at the age of sixty on February 19, 1925, in her home and was buried with her parents in the family plot at Mt. Hope Cemetery in upstate New York. Her *New York Times* obituary cites Morton as "one of the first women to write plays successfully in America."[183]

As seen by Morton's success with *A Bachelor's Romance* for Sol Smith Russell and the four plays for William Crane, the dramatist was clearly at her best with light, romantic comedies using clear-cut, wholesome themes that affirm basic American values. She excelled at shaping characters to particular actors—no little feat in itself and often discounted by historians. Much of her dialogue was considered clever and well-written. Her plots often contained artificial situations or suffered from marked structural problems, but in production this would be balanced by the personality, charisma, or talent of a performer, thus, often forgiven by audiences and even critics. Although Morton's work may not translate effectively to modern playgoers, they do mirror the dramaturgy of her time, with characters, plots, and themes fashioned to appeal to Progressive Era, turn-of-the-century audiences. That she took playwriting seriously shows in her diligence in learning stagecraft, her persistence in placing plays with managers, her courage in trying serious themes, as in *The Movers* and *On the Eve*, and in her willingness to attempt different forms like the vaudeville piece, *The Diplomat*, the musical, *A Four-Leaf Clover*, and the "crook" play, *The Three of Hearts*. A number of Morton's plays used business themes, commenting on the folly of greed, status, and wealth, while some plays in the latter part of her career offered a critique of women and women's role in society.

Morton also directed many of her own productions. Ada Patterson, attending one of the playwright's rehearsals in 1909, observed Morton's decisiveness and ease of command. She described Morton as a slim, dark-eyed woman, "a leader in local philanthropic work, because the large humanitarianism in her is a constantly vibrant chord, a student of Nietsche [sic] and the other modern philosophers, a brilliant figure in a coterie of intellectuals."[184] Perhaps it was an inner strength that contributed to Morton's endurance as a pioneer woman playwright, serving to draw other women to her. Most interviewers mentioned Morton's supportive attitude toward other women: "the warm friend of woman, woman not merely in the abstract, as is the habit with humanitarians of the intellectual type, but the woman who is at the moment beside her."[185] Similarly, some spoke of Morton's role as mentor: "And realizing how much she can save others by giving them the benefit of her experience and advice, Miss Morton now finds her greatest pleasure in helping neophites [sic] of her profession. This rare unselfishness is a beautiful reflection of her sterling character. About her there is an anxious little coterie of satellites who look up to her as a guardian angel."[186] Said one of the "neophytes," according to Burns: "Mrs. Conheim is a great, big-hearted woman who spends her life doing things for other people."[187] An incident shared by Grace Livingston Furniss reflects the esteem with which other women held Morton: "Someone invited me to a Twelfth Night revel, and there I met Martha Morton, the playwright. 'I have read your "Box of Monkeys,"'" she said. 'Why don't you write for the stage?' I had no adequate answer, and went home and repeated to my mother as something amazing that Miss Morton had advised me to write for the stage."[188]

There have been women who have created more enduring plays than did Martha Morton and who have surpassed her commercial success. But before Morton's example as a professional woman dramatist, no American woman, and relatively few since, had achieved a lengthy career or attained the distinction that was hers during her lifetime. As a role model for aspiring women dramatists, Morton's leadership and encouragement surely serve as her greatest legacy to American theatre.

MARTHA MORTON'S ADDRESS TO THE AMERICAN DRAMATISTS' CLUB: DELMONICO'S, NEW YORK CITY, JANUARY 20, 1907

The American Dramatists' Club (founded in 1890 by Bronson Howard) invited, for the first time in its history, women playwrights to join them for their yearly dinner. Paying tributes to playwrights Charles Klein and J. I. C. Clarke, Bronson Howard then introduced Martha Morton Conheim, who represented the women dramatists. The following is her address to the group.

I take great pleasure, in the name of the woman writers for the stage, in thanking the president and members of the American Dramatists' Club for the "privilege" of breaking bread with them this evening. A diplomatic function such as this is quite unusual, where representatives of two great dominions come together—dominions so near and alas so far apart. I mean the dominions of the *sexes*. It is really beautiful, the *entente cordiale*, which prevails this evening; as we sit together round the same board, holding hands, so to speak, exchanging the most flattering of sentiments, which we mean from our souls, whilst we sip the cup that cheers and inebriates. There is another cup which has been floating in the air above my head during this entire evening—which neither cheers nor inebriates—the cup of Tantalus. The woes of that unfortunate Grecian youth, imprisoned on the borders of the lake, whose sparkling waters arose just to his thirsty lips and receded, have echoed down the centuries and found a response in the hearts of the women dramatists; for whenever they think of the American Dramatists' Club they cannot help seeing that *awful* cup of Tantalus floating gracefully toward her, and then floating away in an ultra-tantalizing manner.

I have been named the dean of the women playwrights and I am very proud to be classed among the veterans, in company with my dear friends, Mr. Bronson Howard, Mr. J. I. C. Clarke, Mrs. Charles Doremus, Mr. Charles Klein and a handful of others. It was twenty years ago! How does a man feel when he has to say that? Is there a quick, sharp pang of regret, as he looks over his shoulder, and sees Youth and sweet Inexperience scampering away like rabbits with their ears turned backwards? Men have a way of carrying off their age with laughter and jests. I have never known a woman who could do that, and my excuse for being able to look so far back is that I commenced very young. There is a fine German expression for it—"Unverschamtjung," which means neither shamefully nor shamelessly, but just "unashamed young," so *unashamed* that I wrote plays and the men shook their heads and said the drama was going to the dogs, then they crept in through the stage door and watched that "green girl" direct a rehearsal and one of them came up to me and said: "Are you going to make a business out of this?" I trembled and felt like Martin Luther before the Council of Worms. I looked him straight in the eyes and answered fervently, "God help me, I must!" Then he put out a friendly hand and crushed my fingers into splinters and gave me the comforting assurance that a woman would have to do twice the work of a man to get one-half the credit.

Since then I have been treated just as well and just as badly as a man. I have been hustled off the stage by the stage manager as the curtain was about to rise; I have been dragged on the stage after the curtain fell to bow my panic-stricken thanks to an applauding audience; I have been roasted, sizzled, frizzled to death, then resurrected and borne on the wings of praise up to a temporary heaven. I have had much success which was sweet, and a little failure which was very valuable, and tonight I have reached the zenith of my ambition—I have been present at one of those mysterious Dramatists Club dinners.

My last sensation will be experienced when The Lambs come and beg me to write a skit for their next gambol—and why not? When once the torch of reason is set to that moldy old fence of tradition it ignites very rapidly; and today is a day of tradition-burning, bonfires are being lit all over the world. We are beginning to understand many things that were riddles and that riddle of riddles—Woman—is beginning to understand herself.

Ibsen is the sign-post where the roads cross between the past and the future. Thousands of Noras have crept silently out of narrow homes into the broad walks of life, crept silently up into every vocation, every profession. As a business factor, as a creator, woman has become power in our drama.

But still she is at a great disadvantage because she has no guild, and aside from the benefits derived by a people of our profession in having a common meeting place, there is that splendid satisfaction, after the first night's production of ones play, in being able to flee from the frigidity of the managerial office into the warmth of ones own club where ones fellow author slaps one on the back, saying, "My dear boy—I mean, my dear girl—splendid work! Splendid! It was so good I might have written it myself!"

Jesting aside, the time is ripe, the material at hand, and I am happy to announce officially that an association has been formed by the women writers for the stage, which is called "The Society of Dramatic Authors."

Now, gentlemen, don't look up, this society will never be a cup of Tantalus to you, but there is something else hanging over your head, suspended by a single hair—the sword of Damocles—and when it falls, I hope it won't hurt you too much. Gentlemen, we are not going to blame you for something of which you were entirely innocent—*your sex*—we are not going to ostracize you because *you* are *merely* men—we invite you all! The president, secretary, treasurer—all who are present tonight, all who are absent, in fact, all dramatists are invited to come in and join us. The drama is universal—its unalterable laws are the same throughout the entire world—its form does not change. It is universal life crystallized into living pictures which differ in the different nations only in color and locality. All dramatists are one in their work; therefore as moderns we may make no restrictions of nationality or sex. The Society of Dramatic Authors has thirty-one charter members, thirty women and one man, a gentleman of broad views and "scientific" principles—Mr. Charles Klein. And now, returning to the cups of many vintages which life holds to our lips, the wine of which *now* we sip and *now* we drain to the dregs— this Society of Dramatic Authors, born yesterday is as yet only a cup of Promise—we extend to you the privilege of helping us make it a cup of Fulfillment.

—*Theatre Magazine*, March 1907: 84+

WORKS OF MARTHA MORTON

[Includes date and length of most significant American and English productions, source material, collaborators, leading "star" performer, publisher, and, if not published, where the typescript can be located. If no location is noted, the work is likely not extant. See legend at the end.]

1883
Daniel Deronda*, from George Eliot's novel

1884
A Capital Joke*
The Gerada Stone*
Giant's Robe,* from Astey novel
Ishmael,* from W. C. Herman novel
Vice Versa*
Treachery*

1885
May Blossom, parody of Belasco play
   Academy of Music, May 4, 1885 (1)

1886
*Berenice**
*Vixen**

1888
Hélène (Clara Morris)
   5th Avenue Theatre, April 30, 1888 (1)
   Union Square Theatre October 29–
   November 9, 1889 (2 wks.)
Hélène Buderoff; or a Strange Duel, novel
   (New York: J. W. Lovell, 1889)
A Strange Duel; or Hélène Buderoff, novel
   (New York: Lovell, Coryell & Co., 1895)

1890
The Merchant (Henry Miller / Viola Allen)
   Union Square Theatre, June 26, 1890 (1)
   Madison Square Theatre, May 4, 1891 (7 wks.)
   Produced by *The World*, winner of the best American play
   contest
The Refugee's Daughter (also *Hélène*) (Cora Tanner)
   H. C. Miner's People's Theatre, December 8, 1890

1891
Miss Prue (Lizzie Evans)
   Lee Avenue Academy, Brooklyn, November 16–21, 1891
The Little Blacksmith (Lizzie Evans)

1892
Goffrey Middleton, Gentleman (Nelson Wheatcroft)
   Union Square Theatre, March 31, 1892 (1 1/2 wks.)

1893

Brother John (William H. Crane)
  Star Theatre, March 20, 1893 (1 mo.)
  Typescript, BR

1894

Christmas, one-act (adapt. of *Je Dine chez Ma Mere*)
  Empire School of Acting, January 9, 1894 (1)

1895

His Wife's Father (adapt. of L'Arronge play) (William H. Crane)
  5th Avenue Theatre, February 25, 1895 (104)
  Criterion Theatre, London, August 17, 1897 (42)
  (as *The Sleeping Partner*)
  Typescript, BR

1896

A Fool of Fortune (William H. Crane)
  5th Avenue Theatre, 1 December 1896 (40)
  Typescript, BR
*Silver Wedding**

1897

A Bachelor's Romance (Sol Smith Russell / Annie Russell)
  Garden Theatre, September 20, 1897 (48)
  Globe Theatre, London, January 8, 1898 (95)
  (New York: Samuel French, 1912)
  Filmed, Famous Players Film Co., 1915
  Produced as *All for the Sake of Sylvia*, one-act
  The Players' Club, San Francisco, December 9, 1918

1898

Uncle Dick (Sol Smith Russell)
  Stone Theatre, Binghamton, NY, September 27, 1898 (2 wks)

1902

Her Lord and Master (Herbert Kelcey / Effie Shannon)
Manhattan Theatre, February 24, 1902 (69)
Novel by Victoria Morton (Philadelphia: D. Biddle, 1902)
(New York: Samuel French, 1902)
Typescript, BR, LC

The Diplomat (William H. Collier)
Madison Square Theatre, March 20, 1902 (76)

La Veronica, unproduced Typescript, LC, SA

1904

The Triumph of Love
Criterion Theatre, February 8, 1904 (1), *Theatre Magazine*'s
prize play

1905

A Four-Leaf Clover (Edna Aug)
Hartford, CT, October 4, 1905

The Truth Tellers
Columbia Theatre, New York, September 1905
Grand Opera Theatre, October 16, 1905 (1 wk.)

1906

The Illusion of Beatrice (Maude Fealy)
Orange, NJ, September 14, 1906

1907

The Movers (Dorothy Donnelly / Vincent Serrano)
Hackett Theatre, September 3, 1907 (23)
Typed sides, BR

1909

On the Eve (adapt. of L. Kampf)
Hudson Theatre, October 4, 1909 (24)
Typescript, BR

1910

The Model, a three-act play, unproduced
Typescript, LC

1911

The Senator Keeps House (William H. Crane)
Garrick Theatre, November 27, 1911 (80)
Typescript, BR

1914

Tango, three-act play, unproduced
Typescript, LC

1915

The Three of Hearts (based on Harold McGrath's short story,
"Hearts and Masks")
39th Street Theatre, June 3, 1915 (20)
Typescript, SA

1924

Val Sinestra, novel (New York: E. P. Dutton, 1924) Ebook, PG

*Copyrighted title listed in *Dramatic Compositions Copyrighted in
the United States, 1870 to 1916*, 2 Vols. (Washington, DC:
Government Printing Office, 1918)
    BR   Billy Rose Theatre Collection, New York Public Library
    LC   Library of Congress, Washington, DC
    PG   Project Gutenberg ebook
    SA   Shubert Archives, New York, NY

Madeleine Lucette Ryley, c. 1900.

CHAPTER 2

TRANSATLANTIC SUCCESS: MADELEINE LUCETTE RYLEY (1858 - 1934)

> I am most anxious always to stand on my own merits, and to disassociate myself, as far as may be, from my petticoats. I don't want to take refuge behind the fact that I am a woman.
>
> —Madeleine Lucette Ryley, 1902[1]

> Her sentiment is always airy and wholesome. Moreover, she can write.
>
> —Max Beerbohm, 1902[2]

MADELEINE LUCETTE RYLEY SPENT ALL OF HER working life in the theatre, performing initially as a teenager on the London stage and then touring with light opera companies throughout England and the United States. She became experienced enough to carry significant roles for a time, and when her singing career waned, she tried acting straight roles in New York productions with only marginal success. By the time she began writing light operas and comedies in the late 1880s, she was well grounded in theatre. The trajectory of Ryley's professional playwriting career was relatively short, but spectacular, from 1894 with *Christopher, Jr.*'s New York production to 1907 and *The Sugar Bowl*'s London opening. During those thirteen years, Ryley achieved a renown in both the United States and Great Britain that for a time surpassed the commercial success of most men and women dramatists of that era.

Madeleine Lucette Ryley was born Madeline Matilda Bradley to Alfred and Madeline Bradley in St. Mary, London, on December 26, 1858, the oldest of six children.[3] She first appeared on stage at age fourteen in London, playing Queen of the Fairies in one of the annual Christmas pantomimes.[4] Adopting the stage name "Madeline Lucette" early in her career, she performed roles in light opera companies, including D'Oyly Carte Opera Company's Comedy Opera Company, Ltd., in which she toured the British Isles.[5] Her American debut was in *Princess Toto* by Gilbert and Clay, her first New York performance being Susan in *Billee Taylor; or, the Reward of Virtue* at the Standard Theatre on February 19, 1881.[6] Although *Billee Taylor* had been quite successful in London, a New York reviewer called the comic opera a poor Gilbert and Sullivan imitation, yet cited "Miss Lucette" as one of the four women who "sang and acted with spirit."[7] Her portrayal of Constance in the production of *The Sorcerer* at the Bijou Opera House in October 1882 must have been one of the high points of her stage career, since even standing room was scarce. With Lillian Russell singing the lead role of Aline, the cast of the Gilbert and Sullivan operetta received commendation from most critics, the *New York Times* declaring that "a more merry and complete performance has not been given at any theatre for many a day."[8] Of Madeline Lucette in the role of Constance, critic Frederic Archer in *Music and Drama* stated: "No more judicious choice could have been made. Her conception of the part was perfect, and she used a most agreeable voice with discretion and judgment throughout. It is scarcely necessary to add that she looked the most bewitching little charity girl conceivable."[9]

Similarly, the *Spirit of the Times* noted: "She is very pretty in face and figure; she has a lovely voice, which she uses artistically, and her acting is as good as her singing."[10] During the engagement of *The Sorcerer* when Lillian Russell became ill, Madeline Lucette filled in for the star.[11]

Despite these successes, however, Madeline Lucette's performances were apparently inconsistent or the demands of performing took a toll on her voice because critics were at odds regarding the ability of the prima donna. A month after glowing reviews of *The Sorcerer*, for example, a reviewer openly condemned the singing of both Miss Lucette and her husband, J. H. Ryley:

> "Everybody who sees the lovely Madeline Lucette at the Bijou is charmed with her beauty, grace, and refinement. But all are disappointed at her singing. In the same sense everybody is pleased with the acting of her husband, Mr. J. H. Ryley, in spite of the fact that he, too, cannot sing. It seems to be a case of two clever English people being pushed by circumstances upon an indulgent public, who would like to see them in something better."[12]

Even so, Madeline Lucette continued performing roles with McCaull's Comic Opera Company. In *Virginia* in January 1883, she replaced a singer who performed so poorly that audience members actually hissed; reviewers expressed relief over the change of cast, *Music and Drama* declaring the substitution put "new life into the opera" and that one could "hear the words now, and get a clear idea of what the composer intended by the music."[13] A few months later when Madeline Lucette opened in *The Princess of Trebizonde*, the *New York Times* stated that "Miss Madeline Lucette's arch manners and petite beauty were displayed to advantage in Regina," making no comment on her singing ability.[14] The following November, however, a critic singled her out as a major flaw in *Amorita*, a new comic opera at the Casino, stating that Madeline Lucette's "unfortunate lisp is more noticeable than ever and her voice is throaty and harsh."[15] One of Madeline Lucette's last performances with McCaull's company was as the soubrette Hilaria, in Sydney Rosenfeld's *The Lady or the Tiger?* at Wallack's Theatre in May 1888. Because of considerable publicity, the production sold out opening night, but a disappointed reviewer noted that public expectation exceeded the actual performance, mentioning, however, "Madeline Lucette was very commendable in the role of Hilaria."[16] Madeline followed with roles in non-musical plays but enjoyed only marginal success.[17] She played May Hoaford in *The Power of the Press*, a melodrama by Augustus Pitou and George H. Jessop, at the Star Theatre in March 1891. Despite lukewarm reviews, however, the melodrama lasted for over fifty performances before going on tour.[18]

Madeline Lucette very likely met J. H. Ryley, when she toured with Carte's Comedy Opera Company, during which time she performed in *Congenial Souls* (1878), a curtain raiser he wrote.[19] They continued performing and touring together for several years. News clippings of *The Sorcerer*, a Gilbert and Sullivan opera in which they both performed in 1882, referred to Madeline for the first time as "Mrs. J. H. Ryley"—she was twenty-three, while he was about forty.[20] The couple became prominent within the theatre community and moved into a "pretty cottage" in New Rochelle, north of New York City. It later came as a shock to their friends and neighbors when it became known that they were not legally married until around 1890, after J. H. Ryley obtained a divorce from his first wife. Married to Marie Barnam, an English character actress, in 1864, Ryley had been "legally separated" for over fifteen years. Evidently, their twenty-one-year-old daughter, Wallace, had been living with Ryley and Madeline Lucette for nine years.[21] Marie Barnam brought undesirable publicity to the Ryleys in 1892, when she confronted her ex-husband and took him to court, in his words "under the delusion that he was a rich man," insisting on more money in their settlement. Stated the *New York Times*: "Mr. Ryley declared that all of his property is heavily mortgaged, and that it was purchased with the joint earnings of Miss Lucette."[22]

An English comedian trained in the Gilbert and Sullivan tradition, J. (John) H. Ryley specialized in comic opera roles such as Major-General Stanley in *The Pirates of Penzance*, Jack Point in *The Yeomen of the Guard*, and Wilde in the character of Bunthorne in *Patience*. Drama critic Curtis Brown referred to J. H. Ryley as being well known as "creator" in America of nearly all the comedian parts in the Gilbert and Sullivan operas.[23] By the 1890s, "Jack" Ryley had become an established New York actor, participating, for instance, with other well-known actors in the annual Lambs' Gambol and was counted as a regular member of the American Dramatists Club.[24]

EARLY WRITING ATTEMPTS AND MAJOR SUCCESSES

While still acting on stage, Madeleine Lucette Ryley wrote short stories and sketches for magazines, but she also gained uncredited writing experience while performing with the McCaull Opera Company. The attitude toward women writers at the time shows in Ryley's quote: "Colonel McCaull, finding I was quick at writing songs and fixing up scenes, employed me at what is termed 'hack work,' on the understanding that my name was never to appear. He explained that women were not supposed to have a sense of humor and that a topical song or a comedian's scene coming from a woman would not be tolerated!"[25] In another interview, Ryley mentioned that she was motivated to write comic opera librettos because of a lack of producible material and that the idea of writing plays came to her "with great force" when she headed an operatic company for a time. "Everywhere I was asked, 'Why don't you get a play?' Managers in Boston, Chicago, Philadelphia, etc., all offered me good dates and an increased percentage, provided I returned with an opera, or a musical comedy." Returning to New York to look for a play, she discovered that "plays of any merit cost money." "How absurd it is," I said, "to have a good opportunity and not be able to take it because I haven't any play! I vowed I would write one for myself, and I set to work to do it. Since that time, I have written twenty-one plays."[26] But writing plays may have been a practical decision for Ryley, as she also stated: "For five years I never saw Mr. Ryley except in the summer, and that explains why I am writing instead of acting."[27]

Ryley penned her first comedy, *Lady Jemima, in* 1890 in two weeks. Minnie Maddern (Fiske) bought the piece and eventually produced it, although Ryley admitted that it was "not much of a success."[28] Another play, *Valentine's Day*, 1891, was said to have been produced but where is not known.[29] In 1896, Ryley stated that she had written four comic opera librettos, two of which were adaptations.[30] *The Basoche*, adapted from *La Basoche* by Carre and Andre Messager, was produced at the Casino Theatre in 1893 by the Duff Opera Company and included J. H. Ryley in the cast. Apparently, this tryout production did not merit reviews, and the opera "quickly faded from public view."[31] She also wrote the book for an American production of *Lo lo l'a Dit*, produced in the fall of 1895.[32] With composer Julian Edwards, Ryley wrote two comic operas, *Honeymoon*, possibly produced at the Tremont Theatre in Boston during the summer of 1895, and very likely *The Merchant of Pongee*, an extant copy of the text located in the Shubert Archives.

Containing a fantastical, Gilbert and Sullivan–styled plot and set in a village inhabited by oddly named characters, *The Merchant of Pongee* displays Ryley's wit and proficiency with language. As the only available sample of her operatic work, it is worth a brief look.[33] The setting is the village of Pongee near Calcutta, inhabited with characters such as Trumble Hicks, an American known as "Rhumgo Chickabiddy" by the locals; Tom Dingle, Hicks's nephew and secretary; Allabedad, a sorcerer and medicine man; and Asa Lukeheart, a sergeant in the British Army. Lady Sophie Hinton heads a Blue Stocking Club and pursues intellectual research under the chaperonage of Miss Toboggan, an American missionary. The female chorus, comprising the rest of the blue stockings, consists of six school friends who accompany Lady Sophie, while her six tutors serve as a male chorus. Tom Dingle and Lady Sophie provide the central love interest, although her tendency to intellectualize marriage, along with everything else, creates obstacles for them. Initially, the fickle Sophie finds Tom too inferior, wanting only the highest combination of attributes to ensure "perfection upon the descendants."[34]

At opening, natives anticipate the return of Hicks (Chickabiddy), his Excellency, the overseer. Unfortunately, the news greeting Hicks is that a market crash has brought him sudden poverty. He decides the only way to redeem financial losses is to kill himself for the insurance money—a plan foiled by two insurance detectives, Jiggs and Jaggs, who tail him constantly.

Desperate, Hicks asks his nephew to do him the favor of killing him, an idea naturally appalling to Tom Dingle. Lady Sophie, always alert to prospects of the superior mate, meets Hicks, finds his practicality appealing, and suggests marriage. The older man, finding Sophie's wealth equally attractive, promptly agrees. When Dingle learns of the impending marriage, he becomes angry enough to kill his uncle and hires an assassin to carry out his uncle's wishes. In the midst of wedding preparations, however, Lady Sophie succumbs to feelings for Dingle. His uncle, who is now pursued by Miss Toboggan, discovers that he is not impoverished after all. In the end, the assassin is thwarted and three couples are united.

Some secondary characters prove interesting and contribute to the mayhem. The insurance investigators, Jiggs and Jaggs, for instance, talk and sing like Siamese twins, always finishing each other's thoughts. Ryley uses Miss Toboggan, the American do-gooder, to satirize Americans; in the second act, Miss Toboggan instructs a group of native women "converts," telling them that the "watchword" is "Yankee Doodleum" and awards prizes "for the highest form of reformation":

> These dainty wares I'll now dispense,/According to your merit./For Justice is a virtue which/My people all inherit./So one and all bid up for this,/An elegant confection—(Shows a hat)/For anyone who claims her vote /At the very next election . . . Just throw a sprat to catch a whale,/And don't admit that you can fail./And *that's* Yankee Doodleum!... Just keep him hard at work so he/can buy you lots of jewelree./And *that's Yankee Doodleum!*[35]

Fantastic plot notwithstanding, *The Merchant of Pongee* presents great fun, displaying the influence of comic opera on Ryley's sense of humor and the epigrammatic style that turns up in most of her later comedies.

Madeleine Lucette Ryley's career as a professional dramatist had a strong send off in 1894 with *Christopher, Jr.*'s Brooklyn showing. According to Ryley, the play took "five weeks to write and five years to place."[36] It was eventually accepted by John Drew, who was teamed with Maude Adams by their manager, Charles Frohman. The two performers had previously acted together in four plays, and although Drew maintained star billing, Adams's popularity was soaring. *Christopher, Jr.* reveals amusing and well-rounded characters, mixed with ridiculous circumstances and clever dialogue.

Chris, Jr. (John Drew) temporarily moves into shabbier lodgings and passes off Job, his valet, as a friend in order to feign poverty and impress upon his wealthy, but niggardly, father that he cannot live on his paltry allowance. When the parents arrive, Colt, Sr. remains unmoved by the humble attic flat and is still convinced of Junior's extravagance. However, he tells his son that if he marries a young woman of his (the father's) choosing a "reward" of fifty thousand pounds and all bills paid would be forthcoming on the wedding day.[37]

After his family departs, Chris confesses to his friend Tom Bellaby that he cannot take his father's offer because legally he is already married. He explains that two years earlier while he was on a voyage to Trinidad he mistakenly entered a young woman's stateroom where he fell asleep on an upper berth, remaining long enough to compromise her as she slept in the lower berth.[38] Caught leaving the young woman's room, Chris was pressed into a hasty marriage ceremony by her irate father, as the bride remained in an adjoining room "thoroughly prostrated by the situation."[39] In the confusion, Chris gave the father his friend's card and wound up being married as Tom Bellaby. The young woman selected by Colt, Sr. for Chris is, of course, Matilda, the young woman to whom he is already married and who, coincidentally, prefers being called Dora and now uses her uncle's surname. Neither Chris, Jr. nor Dora (Maude Adams) learns the truth about the situation until the end of the play. In the meantime, preposterous incidences occur, as in the second act at his sister's ball when he begins to fall in love with Dora; Chris, fearing she would not approve of the profligate Christopher Colt, Jr. hesitates when she asks his name: "(aside)

Name! By George! I haven't thought of one yet. (aloud) My name? Well, it's a blank." "A. Blank?" asks Dora. "What does the 'A' stand for? Arthur, I suppose. Arthurs are always irrational sort of people."[40]

When Colt, Sr., inadvertently learns of his son's unconventional, shipboard marriage, he ships him off to Bombay to serve as a clerk in one of his enterprises; Dora, now interested in the inexplicable "Mr. Blank," finds an excuse to visit her uncle in Bombay. The third and fourth acts take place in the Bombay quarters of Dora's uncle, during which time Chris redeems himself by uncovering the thievery of his father's manager. Six weeks after the firing of the scoundrel manager, the Colt family arrives, along with Bellaby and their friends, Mr. and Mrs. Glibb. When Dora finds out Nelly is engaged to Tom Bellaby, the man to whom she thinks she's married, she confronts Tom privately, only to discover that it is really Chris who is her legal husband. She and Tom proceed to make things difficult for Chris before he finally learns the truth.

That Ryley's "characterization is always good, and sometimes strikingly original" is illustrated in part by two older couples, the Colts and the Glibbs, as well as the servant characters, Whimper and Job.[41] Mr. and Mrs. Colt, for instance, never talk directly to each other but use Whimper as their go-between. Whimper, however, does not repeat messages verbatim but diplomatically rephrases; for example, when Mrs. Colt comments on her son's "barbarous" apartment, Mr. Colt tells Whimper to tell her, "if she doesn't like the apartment she can get *out* of it." Whimper turns to the wife, relating that Mr. Colt "suggests, madam, that it would be more comfortable for you to remain below in the carriage."[42] Mr. and Mrs. Glibb use a contrasting communication style; Mrs. Glibb does all the talking and interprets for her husband, even when she addresses him directly—Mr. Glibb has no actual lines in the play. However, Job, Chris, Jr.'s confidante and valet, enjoys his share of one-liners; for example, when Chris attempts to put up a shelf, Job is amused and Chris grumbles:

CHRIS: What are you laughing at?

JOB: At the thought of you, sir, a-wielding of a 'ammer.
CHRIS: Don't you drop your h's, Job.

JOB: And don't you drop the 'ammer, sir. It's very 'eavy.[43]

John Drew toured with *Christopher, Jr.* for nearly two years before the Broadway showing. Even the early version, in spite of being "badly shaped, ill-constructed, diffusive, and highly improbable," was still deemed as "merry and entertaining." The *New York Times* review of the first Brooklyn showing in September 1894 called *Christopher, Jr.* an actor's play, containing "a set of characters that are understandable and diverting, and plenty of dialogue that is always smart." Of the emerging dramatist, the critic stated, "Mrs. Ryley comprehends the stage, and is well-equipped, evidently, for the task of play-writing, but she lacks practice. Wherefore it is a very good thing both for her and for the public that 'Christopher, Jr.' was produced. The play is vastly better than any piece Mr. Sothern has lately had."[44]

On October 7, 1895, a revised *Christopher, Jr.* opened at the Empire Theatre in New York, and while structural weaknesses remained, most critics concurred…with the *Tribune's* statement that it was:

> admirably fitted for the abilities of Mr. Drew, Miss Adams, and the other members of the company, and it was written with so light and neat a touch, with so unfailing a presence of the frolic spirit of gayety [sic], with so much in the language, the incidents and the situations to provoke mirth, that it must be ranked among the most diverting plays in which John Drew has been seen.[45]

Similarly, Maude Adams shone in the role of Dora, "the best—in the technical sense—yet allotted to her." Particularly in the last act, continued the reviewer, does Miss Adams display her adroitness "in which she is called upon to denote sudden changes of mood, from anger, contempt, and amazement, to extravagant joy."[46] The *Critic* declared that overall, a "merrier little piece . . . has not been presented here for a long time, and the fun has the conspicuous merit of being entirely wholesome."[47] Audiences must have agreed, since *Christopher, Jr.* ran for sixty-four performances and continued in Drew's repertoire for some time.

For the London production, the setting became British and the title changed to *Jedbury Junior*, "to avoid confusion with several burlesques."[48] Of its opening at Terry's Theatre in February 1896, the *London Times* called *Jedbury Junior* "a domestic drama or comedy."[49] Another critic remarked that the audience was led through preposterous situations "into scenes of domestic tenderness," and at the moment when they prepare to snigger, "find themselves trying vainly to suppress a tear."[50] The playwright expressed bewilderment over the differences between American and English receptions of her play. Whereas the New York production "succeeded mainly by its comic element," the London version "won favor as a domestic drama." Stated Ryley: "The notices of the London press read very queerly to American eyes. One paper, for instance, reports a profuse shedding of tears at the curtain after the second act. I presume that when the play goes to South Africa, where melodrama is the popular craze, we shall hear that a black-hearted villain is the central figure of interest, and when it reaches France that the card-playing incident has been elaborated to make the greatest scene of all."[51]

Perhaps the main reason for the difference in American and English receptions of the play lies in the different casts and their interpretations of the play; the excellent English cast, headed by Frederick Kerr, displayed more pathos in *Jedbury, Junior*, whereas John Drew's jaunty interpretation of *Christopher, Jr.* emphasized the play's farcical elements.[52] Overall, audience members concurred with George Bernard Shaw, who declared that the dramatist "has a strong sense of fun, and ridicules everybody over forty, and most people under it, with much vivacity."[53] The production at Terry's Theatre ran for three and a half months, returning in December at the Globe for another fifty-one performances with a different cast, replacing the long-running *Charley's Aunt*.[54] Sometime in 1897 Ryley sold the rights of the comedy to a French manager with the stipulation that she supervise the Paris production.[55] Overall, *Christopher, Jr.* served its author far better than did most first plays.

The Mysterious Mr. Bugle, Ryley's second major New York production, provided an unexpectedly pleasing vehicle for Annie Russell as Betty Fondacre. Staged by the playwright, the comedy opened at the Lyceum in April 1897 and quickly became popular with audiences, running for fifty-six performances and playing again at the Harlem Opera House in September for another eight performances. Critics were generally in accord about both the play and Ryley's abilities. The *New York Times* called *The Mysterious Mr. Bugle* "clean, simple, rollicking fun": "The dialogue is bright, the action brisk from end to end, the situations clever, and the setting and costuming as neat and tasteful as would naturally be expected at the Lyceum. The piece went with vim, was most enthusiastically received—as was the author when she appeared to bow her thanks for a curtain call."[56]

The comedy concerns Betty Fondacre (Annie Russell), engaged to Tom Pollinger (Joseph Holland) who does not want to alienate a wealthy grandmother opposed to early marriages and who believes a man is not ready for marriage before forty. Therefore, to conceal their engagement and to provide herself with more freedom to travel about for business purposes, Betty passes herself off as Mrs. Solomon Bugle; This is all done at her fiancé's request because he possesses a jealous nature and must be absent from her for extended periods. Starting at the Lakewood hotel where Betty has taken rooms, a series of harmless events occur that become misinterpreted by the suspicious fiancé and causes Betty to seek refuge behind "the most awful whoppers." Complications begin with a burglar sneaking into her room, ultimately involving Betty's cousin, Allan, his valet, a Mr. and Mrs. Tote, and a policeman. The ridiculous aspect of the situation is that as things get out of hand, Tom begins to believe his own Mr. Bugle fabrication. Naturally, everything gets resolved in the third act.

According to the critics, there were few dull moments in this play and audiences thoroughly enjoyed the performances—Ryley's staging must have contributed to the pace so necessary in farce. Annie Russell, usually cast in more sentimental roles, surprised reviewers with her adroitness at comedy. Dithmar made one of the few negative comments about the comedy, pointing out that motive was Ryley's weak point but conceded that motive was "the weak point of most playwrights." As a dramatist, Ryley has "uncommon skill," "her ideas of 'situation' and 'climax' are excellent, and she knows the value of good 'little bits,' while her dialogue is always fresh, natural, and vivacious." Referring to her experience in comedy opera, he cited "her careful study of the printed minor drama in its tendency to punning" and concluded by declaring the farce to be "light, tripping, and brimful of honest fun."[57] In *Life*, Metcalfe simply stated: "*The Mysterious Mr. Bugle* is best criticized and described in the words of a contemporary comedian: 'It is to laugh.'"[58] Calling Ryley "one of the most successful of our modern female playwrights," *Critic* declared: "The literary quality of the piece is far superior to that generally found in farces of this description, and is not only frequently humorous, but often flashes with strokes of genuine wit."[59] Arthur Hoeber echoed other critics in his praise of the play, but he noted of the dramatist: "Mrs. Ryley's knowledge of the requirements of stagecraft is both practical and extensive and is born of no little histrionic training. Quick to grasp the possibilities of the situation, of telling speech, and of dramatic contrasts, she has evolved from a more or less simple theme a series of effective complications, uproariously absurd and thoroughly entertaining."[60]

Compared with New York's favorable reception, however, London reviews seem tepid. Opening at the end of May 1900 at the Strand, the English production with Yorke Stephens and Carrie Cronyn in the lead roles played only eighteen performances; perhaps in the three-year gap between productions, Londoners had had their fill of farce. The initial *London Times* review concluded: "Judged by its reception last night, the farce seems likely to please Strand audiences. It will certainly do them no harm."[61]

TWO PLAYS FOR EFFIE SHANNON AND HERBERT KELSEY:
A COAT OF MANY COLORS AND MY LADY DAINTY

Ryley's third New York production, *A Coat of Many Colors*, did not fare as well as her first two. Although reviewers were puzzled by the title of the comedy farce and references to the biblical story of Joseph, the title seemed appropriate for the reopening of a remodeled Wallack's Theatre on September 13, 1897. Audience members enjoyed new colors of cream, salmon, and gold, a raised parquet floor that provided a better view for the front stalls, a deeper orchestra pit, more commodious proscenium boxes, and a new showy act drop by Richard Marston—a tapestry-like painting featuring a Greek procession in honor of Daphne.[62] But, unfortunately, the same critics who praised Ryley's first two plays, now threw up their hands in despair. They lodged complaints over improbabilities similar to those contained in her earlier works, but in this play, Ryley unsuccessfully mixed farcical elements with a serious theme.

At the center of *A Coat of Many Colors*, Esther Gunning (Effie Shannon), a young California lawyer in her father's firm, has been sent to New York by her father to locate a woman long estranged from an early lover. Her mission is to "bring about reconciliation and a belated marriage—for the daughter's sake." Not until after she accomplishes what she sets out to do does "she discover that the lover is her father and she is the daughter herself." Herman Walboys (Herbert Kelcey), a bachelor lawyer who is nicknamed "Joseph" because he has "consistently repulsed the Mrs. Potiphars of this world," is hired to help Esther; in several instances, he puts himself in a false light (hence, the coat of many colors) for Esther in order to keep her father's secret but lends his assistance, which contributes to a growing affection between them.[63] But, there are far too many deceptions in this play, according to Dithmar, who feared that Ryley's fondness for this sort of device was "constitutional and incurable."[64] Neither did Metcalfe mince words, calling the play "an illustrated rebus," where "every incident proposes a fresh riddle to the innocent spectator.

A mixed-up telegram, a misdelivered letter, an ambiguous child of hazy parentage, all jumbled together with a lot of irrelevant, incompetent and immaterial personages."[65] The *Tribune* suggested that the woman-with-a-past character had her day in "more earnest drama"; her presence in a play which was "nearly half farce" only posed "a worriment and a distress."[66] Although Ryley tailored the play for Shannon and Kelcey, Albert White Vorse in *Illustrated American* found it difficult to accept either actor in their roles: "Miss Shannon is the essence of blond-haired femininity. Her law business seems like farce. Mr. Kelcey is a finished portrayer of refined character, [but] no more like a brute of a misogynist than Miss Shannon is like a new woman."[67] It appears that Ryley pushed too hard to include too many elements in this play, and *A Coat of Many Colors* closed after only twenty-four performances.

It is unfortunate that after such a poor showing with *A Coat of Many Colors*, Shannon and Kelsey would then opt three years later to produce Ryley's *My Lady Dainty*, which turned out to be one of her weaker plays. Set in England and America, the plot centers on Jemima Jeffreys (Shannon), a virtuous young English governess who marries William Oglethorpe (Kelcey), a "caddish" young man estranged from a well-to-do father. He takes her to New York City where they live in a modest apartment and encounter financial difficulties; and while Jemima secretly gives French lessons to pupils to help supplement their income, her husband takes up with an unsavory American, Barry Selters (William Boag), to whom he goes deeper into debt. Oglethorpe, who has not told his father of the marriage, receives word that the old gentleman is ill and seeks reconciliation; the father's stipulation for any inheritance, however, is that Oglethorpe marry his stepmother's daughter. Leaving his inconsolable wife, Oglethorpe hurries back to England. While she pines for her husband, Jemima begins to rely on their composer friend, Bob Rocket, for moral support; on New Year's Eve, Selters drops in to tell her that her husband is filing for divorce. Jemima rejects Rocket's affection and returns to her aunt and uncle Folger in England. Like the first act, the fourth occurs in rural England amid the eccentric Reverend Francis and Mrs. Folger and their lively offspring, all of whom provide most of the comic elements in the play. A contrite Oglethorpe shows up to talk with the clergyman, telling him of his change of heart, and by the end of the play Jemima and husband are reunited.

Other than to acknowledge the actors' hard work, reviewers found little to compliment in the production. Of the Brooklyn tryout in December, a critic railed: "A more lugubrious play than this it has seldom been our lot to see. The hero and heroine get married in the very first act and are unhappy ever after." He complained not only about the copious tears Effie Shannon sheds throughout the play but also harped on "the entire family of five brats," who all have speaking roles. The review concluded with a warning to the actors that tempting fate on Broadway in *My Lady Dainty* "would be foolhardy, to say the least."[68] In spite of this warning, however, the play opened on Broadway the following January at the Madison Square Theatre. The *New York Times* reported that *My Lady Dainty* was much better acted than it deserved and stated that it was "quite the feeblest production" of Ryley's "frequently diffusive and incoherent but generally lively and entertaining pen."[69] Considering the inherent weakness of the central characters, along with other flaws in the play, it is a wonder the production survived thirty-nine performances.

In less than five years, between 1895 with the New York opening of *Christopher, Jr.* and 1899 with London's first showing of *An American Citizen*, Madeleine Lucette Ryley became established as a professional dramatist on both sides of the Atlantic. In fact, three plays—*The Mysterious Mr. Bugle*, *A Coat of Many Colors*, and *An American Citizen*—opened on Broadway in April, September, and October of 1897; with *The Mysterious Mr. Bugle's* weeklong engagement at the Harlem Opera House in September, Ryley may have had three plays running simultaneously in New York, possibly setting a record for a woman dramatist.[70] At any rate, her success for that year remains outstanding for any dramatist, let alone a woman.

TRANSATLANTIC HUMOR IN *AN AMERICAN CITIZEN*, *THE ALTAR OF FRIENDSHIP*, AND *AN AMERICAN INVASION*

Ryley drew on both her perspective as an Englishwoman and her experience of living and touring in America for twenty years when creating several comedies. Many of her plays contained both British and American characters, contributing to contrasting viewpoints and humor; in addition, as a playwright, she often worked with both British and American actors who interpreted her work. And, as previously mentioned, the differences between British and American critical reception of her work makes for fascinating comparisons. *An American Citizen* received a long life with Nat C. Goodwin and Maxine Elliott, who also performed five years later in Ryley's *The Altar of Friendship*. And *An American Invasion* gave J. E. Dodson and Annie Irish, both British-born actors working in America, their first opportunity to fill starring roles.

During a stay in London in the summer of 1895, Ryley wrote *An American Citizen* for American comedian Nat C. Goodwin.[71] Goodwin, with Maxine (his future wife) and Gertrude Elliott in his company, set sail for Australia and toured for three months, performing five plays, among them *An American Citizen*. When they reached Chicago in January 1897, large and friendly audiences welcomed Goodwin's company for two weeks at Hooley's Theatre. *An American Citizen* did so well that, at the request of actors playing in Chicago, "an extra matinee for the theatrical profession and the public" was given on a Thursday afternoon.[72] A week after the closing of *A Coat of Many Colors*, on October 18, 1897, Madeleine Lucette Ryley saw *An American Citizen* open in New York at the Knickerbocker.

Comparing *An American Citizen* with Ryley's previous plays, the *New York Tribune* called it, in some respects, "decidedly the best of all"; however, the critic added snidely that "if Mrs. Ryley goes on improving, she may sometime write [a really good comedy]. But she needs to control the flights of her imagination." He seemed to contradict himself by saying that Ryley's creation was not just amusing, but "ingenious, delicate and extremely funny."[73]

Generally, other reviewers agreed with the *Tribune* that Ryley's dialogue was well done and clever, her plot "oddly and whimsically contrived."

In *An American Citizen*, Beresford Cruger (Nat Goodwin), along with his partner, Peter Barbury, discover that Brown, a third partner, has absconded with funds entrusted to their law firm. By way of a letter from Sir Humphrey Bunn, it is revealed that Cruger has recently turned down a 60,000-pound bequest from an English uncle due to its conditions: that Cruger marry an Englishwoman before his thirtieth birthday (two days hence), become a British subject, and adopt the family name Carew. Furthermore, the uncle, who has disowned his own daughter Beatrice for becoming engaged to an American, stipulates that Cruger not share any portion of the legacy with his cousin. If Cruger refuses the legacy, the money will go to an Archaeological Society. But when Beatrice (Maxine Elliott), who is traveling with Sir Humphrey and his wife, pays a call at Cruger's office, it becomes clear that both cousins are sorely in need of money. At Barbury's suggestion, they elect to marry in order to fool the court, giving Cruger an English bride and Beatrice a means of support— each is then free to go his or her separate way.

A year after the marriage (Act Two), Beatrice and Cruger, who now goes by the name Carew, meet accidentally on the Riviera, falling headlong in love with one another. News arrives on the ship, however, that Beatrice's former fiancé, thought to have died in the Swiss Alps, is alive, so Cruger naturally assumes she still loves her former lover—who, coincidentally, turns out to be Brown, the missing partner. Beatrice, however, sees Cruger with a young American woman (Gertrude Elliott) and hears falsely that they have been engaged for years. But to make matters even worse, the Archaeological Society calls into question the cousins' bogus marriage and wins a suit against Cruger and Beatrice. In London, eight months later (Act Four) Cruger resides in simple lodgings attached to a stove polish business he operates with the assistance of a young lad. On this snowy Christmas Eve, Cruger learns through a telegram that a land speculation in Wyoming has paid handsomely. Beatrice shows up because she has discovered that Cruger, despite impoverished circumstances, has nobly continued to support her, and all misunderstandings become resolved.

Vorse in *Illustrated American* called the final scene "exquisitely treated" for the way it was underplayed, its subtly carrying more weight "than the embrace of affianced lovers, usual in last acts."[74] Beatrice rises and begins putting on her hat:

> BEAT. Oh, dear, see how it is snowing again, and I promised Lady Bunn I would be home in half an hour.
>
> CRU. (reproachfully) Home?
>
> BEAT. (smiling) Forgive me. (he leads her down to arm-chair, takes off her hat and removes the boa from her neck; the fire begins to blaze up; he places hat on mantelpiece; she sits in arm-chair, and he seats himself on the arm, he is facing her and he extends his arms)
>
> CRU. Home![75]

Some of the more far-fetched aspects of the play did not go unnoticed; Vorse, for example, stated that "a British court is not so stupid as to forget that Beatrice Carew is still Cruger's cousin, though she has become his wife." And while he affirmed that Cruger "is, by design, an incarnation of Americanism," he called into question the Englishness of Beatrice: "She has no more British young personishness, or British matronliness, than Mrs. Grover Cleveland."[76] Dithmar declared Ryley's *An American Citizen* "as frail as her other plays, and by no means of even merit." And yet, like other reviewers, Dithmar cited the strength of the dramatist's dialogue, enhanced by "the effervescent humor of Goodwin," which lent "new sparkle to old jokes" and had an ability to be "excruciatingly and irresistibly funny."[77] Indeed, most critics glossed over the improbabilities of the story due to a smooth, briskly paced production and the comedic talents of Nat C. Goodwin, whose company enjoyed a successful New York run of ninety-six performances.

Goodwin presented Ryley's play in June 1899 at London's Duke of York, after two unfavorable weeks in Clyde Fitch's melodrama, *The Cowboy and the Lady*. Whereas American reviews had treated the play as a straight comedy with farcical elements, English reviews adamantly maintained the play was

> a farce with an occasional tinge of sentiment and a more than occasional tinge of burlesque. "My lover was killed on a glacier ten months ago," says the heroine sadly. "Nice cold place," replies the gentleman who is conversing with her, and humorously alludes to the deceased as "on ice." He even gently banters the lady on her interests being all below zero! It is vulgar, of course, but funny enough for those who like this kind of thing. Only it is not comedy any more than that pleasant melodrama, *The Cowboy and the Lady*, was comedy. American dramatists should really be more careful about their theatrical nomenclature.[78]

Although American reviewers found the last scene touching, the *Athenaeum* disparaged its "tawdry Dickens-like effects" and "Christmas sentimentality." Rather, suggested the critic: "If played throughout in the vein of farcical comedy in which most of it is written, 'An American Citizen' would take London by storm." The *Times* reviewer, however, disapproved of "the satire on English manners and customs, which probably helped its success in the States, [and] seems to us inadequate, not to say inept." Interestingly, Max Beerbohm asserted that other than the slang in its dialogue, the play contained "no racial character: it might have been written by any of our own playwrights. I do not know whether the author, Mrs. Ryley, is an American. American or English, she is a very crude dramatist." Nevertheless, he urged readers to "see the play, in order that they may see Mr. Goodwin in it. Mr. Goodwin is an American of the Americans, and a comedian of the comedians."[79] *An American Citizen* fared well in London, playing for a month in the summer and again in September, chalking up sixty-nine performances. Goodwin not only kept the play in his repertoire, but in 1906, with a different supporting cast, played a week at London's Shaftsbury Theatre. Onscreen in 1914, *An American Citizen* provided a notable motion picture debut for John Barrymore in the role of Beresford Cruger.[80]

An American Invasion, posits Gerald Bordman, "attested to a persistent undercurrent of bad feelings between American and England," specifically noted in the resentment of some Englishmen toward the central character, an American engineer, who goes to India with better methods for draining a swamp.[81] J. E. Dodson and Annie Irish, in their first staring vehicle, were supported by both British and American actors. Initially scoring a success in Baltimore at Ford's Opera House in October 1902, the play opened soon after in New York at the Bijou Theatre, running three weeks.[82] According to the *New York Tribune,* J. E. Dodson's portrayal of John Brainard, an American engineer, carried the play. The location of the first three acts is Calcutta, and all of the characters are English, with the exception of Brainard, who is pitted against Colonel Strahan (Henry Hart). Strahan makes the beautiful widow, Lucy Penruddock (Annie Irish) his instrument for stealing the engineer's plans of an invention for draining swampland. By appealing to Lucy's affection for her brother, who may lose his position if the American deal succeeds, and her grudge against one of Brainard's investors, Sir William Bond, who snubbed her socially, Strahan manipulates the young woman. At a social gathering at Brainard's cottage, she filches the documents and puts them into her music folder but has a change of heart, lays them on the piano, and leaves. Her brother, recognizing the folder as Lucy's, thinks she has forgotten it and takes it. Not until the end of Act Four does the misplaced folder again turn up.

A major fault of *An American Invasion* is that pivotal points become based on feminine jealousy, hatred, duplicity, and happenstance. Indeed, Lucy, the attractive widow, while admired by all the men and adored by her stepdaughter, falls into exchanging unpleasantries with her sister-in-law and the snobbish social climber, Mrs. Norreys. The *New York Times* reviewer suggested that the wit of Ryley's often clever repartee became overbalanced by the ill nature of the characters, particularly the women, "so that the effect sometimes seem[ed] like a continuous performance of catfighting."

The strength of the work lies in the wit of her often epigrammatic lines. One critic even went so far as to state that "it would not be surprising if several of her rockets of conversation passed into current use."[83] When Mrs. Norreys hears about Lucy's motorbike mishap involving the American engineer, for instance, she remarks: "And the American—do tell us about him. Did he say 'I guess' and swear he was going to 'quit' driving? My first husband was an American, you know. And he always would talk about 'quitting' things." To which Lucy says: "And he kept his word finally, by quitting you, eh?" When pressed into describing the motorbike incident, Lucy dramatizes the event with American clichés: "Well, my Yankee man, having jerked his prancing steeds to their haunches with one iron-like wrist, raised me from the ground with the other. Then, regaining his bowie knife and pistols, which had been scattered by the collision, he waved his sombrero to the breeze, and we drove home whistling the 'Star-Spangled Banner.'"[84]

Most of the "tart turns of phrase," however, are delivered by the sterling-charactered Brainard;[85] when Lucy comments that he has "no ear for music," he quips: "Oh yes, I've an ear, but it's punctured. Must be. The sounds run out so quickly. I only know just two tunes. One is the 'Swanee River' and the other—the other isn't."[86] Later, Lucy flippantly remarks that he must be "a man with a past," to which he replies "Prefer to regard myself as a man with a future. Fifteen years ago I was tried and convicted of—of—poverty. Was sentenced to fourteen years' hard labour. I have served the full term, with no reduction for good conduct. A man who works with his hands all day and his head at night hasn't time to get into mischief."[87] One critic even quoted Brainard's: "The British mind finds it difficult to dissociate the wholesale use of electricity from thimble rigging and three card Monte."[88] Another reviewer stated that it is as a melodrama that *An American Invasion* makes its biggest appeal, while still another thought the plot "sufficient enough," and "set off with several pretty situations." Generally, however, Ryley's attempt to blend social comedy with melodrama does not work; her villain conveniently disappears in the third act (dodging the law for another crime), and she portrays Lucy as initially vain and shallow, having her "reform" in the fourth act by taking up nursing. Interestingly, critics agreed that Brainard, the American—as portrayed by a British actor—was the most interesting and palpable character in the play.

Madeleine Lucette Ryley again fell into similar patterns of mixing her elements with her next play, *The Altar of Friendship*; "bathos," Max Beerbohm termed it, where "her comedy and her melodrama do equal mischief to each other."[89] Even so, the mix of comedy and drama in this play fared better than did *An American Invasion*, most likely aided by a stronger scenario and the acting ability of Nat C. Goodwin. Goodwin and Maxine Elliott had been looking for a play to last through the end of 1902, and because they toured so successfully in *An American Citizen*, they contacted Madeleine Lucette Ryley to see whether she might have something. Ryley told them about *The Altar of Friendship*, which had two good "starring roles" but that the play had been tried out by "John Mason in a few Eastern cities, and since shelved. They took the rights from Mason, planning to put it in their bill when the Christmas season approached." Ryley returned to New York in the fall of 1902 to direct *The Altar of Friendship* herself.[90] After John Mason's previous mediocre production, it is no wonder the dramatist wanted a hand in this production of *The Altar of Friendship*.

Set in London and Wimbledon, *The Altar of Friendship* concerns English author Richard Arbuthnot (Goodwin), whose sister, Florence, plans to marry Arnold Winnifrith, a clerical student. The first act reveals that Winnifrith has just broken off a secret involvement with a typewriter girl, Mary Pinner, employed by Richard when her father was sent to prison. The central interest of the play revolves around the romantic relationship between Richard and Sally Sartoris (Elliott), a single American woman, soon to reach the advanced age of twenty-nine and a longtime friend of the family. Because Sally's father has given her an ultimatum to hasten her search for a husband or he will cut her off, she has led her father to believe she is engaged. Colonel Sartoris arrives, looking for Sally, and begins prying her with questions about her "intended" when Richard steps in and assumes the role of the fictitious fiancé. Their bogus engagement soon takes on aspects of a real attachment, and as Sally and Richard engage in jocular banter and carry on the pretended betrothal in front of others, they begin to fall in love.

A crisis arises, however, when Mary Pinner's father shows up just after Florence and Winnifrith are married; when the rough-cut man wrongly accuses Richard of ruining his daughter, Richard, to shield his sister's husband, does not deny the accusation. His attachment with Sally now in jeopardy, Richard confronts Winnifrith, who fears that telling the truth will destroy his marriage. Nevertheless, Florence ends up learning of her husband's previous affair while talking with Mary Pinner, and she then informs Pinner's father to clear her brother. In the meantime, Winnifrith has had a change of heart and confesses the truth to Sally, after which she apologizes to Richard, allowing their pretend engagement to become a real one.

Despite the melodramatic ingredients of the wronged typewriter girl and her revengeful father, the growing relationship between Richard and Sally and their ongoing banter, which becomes increasingly more charged with meaning, as well as the play's likeable characters, all lend interest and humor to the plot. Lady Chalmers, Richard's grandmother, for instance, is an eccentric dowager in her seventies, accompanied by a little dog and a young male protégé. At one point Lady Chalmers declares: "Once established a reputation for eccentricity, and you can enjoy all the benefits of society without any of its disadvantages. It is a sort of perpetual Lord Chamberlain's license, minus restrictions."[91]

New York heartily welcomed Nat C. Goodwin and Maxine Elliott after a two-year absence. The *Tribune* critic called Goodwin's unobtrusive drollery "a sort of facetious sapience touched now and then with sentiment" that always gives pleasure; and he observed

Elliott's "arch demeanor and brilliant beauty" with delight.[92] The play provided Goodwin with ample opportunities for comedy, yet several situations for more serious work—"he did not disappoint in either." The *Tribune* also stated that "Mrs. Ryley's comedy, which is so contrived as to blend a somewhat farcical frolic with a serious story, and parts of which are vivaciously written, affords a pleasing illustration of the ancient adage that it is dangerous to play with edged tools."[93] *Theatre*, however, handed Goodwin the full credit for the success of the play, since "he knows a play when he sees it."[94] New Yorkers found favor with the production, supporting it through fifty performances. Goodwin's company took the play to Washington, DC, and toured New York, New England, and the Mid-West, after which, having performed seven seasons together, Elliott and Goodwin parted ways.[95]

In the spring of 1903 for yet another production of *The Altar of Friendship* in London, Ryley hurried back from Italy for rehearsals.[96] Opening in March at the Criterion Theatre, with Paul Arthur as Richard and Ellis Jeffreys in the role of Sally, the play ran for a month to conflicting reviews. Although Americans apparently thought little of it, a main grievance of English critics focused on Richard Arbuthnot's willingness to sacrifice his honor on "the altar of friendship." *Athenaeum* could not accept "the idea that a man should immolate himself at that [shrine] of brother-in-lawhood . . . even though in so doing he may be to some extent protecting his sister."[97] Grein agreed, suggesting "Mrs. Ryley does not know men"—a good man might "consent to a sham engagement with a fair American lady," but would not silently submit to a charge that "affects his honor, his happiness, and his future." In addition, he took offense over the use of Winnifrith, a divinity student, as the errant character: "I am surely not squeamish, but it repels me to find a clergyman not merely a moral weakling, such as he is here depicted, but a misdemeanant of the most irredeemable kind. It is in bad taste to reflect discredit upon the cloth for mere theatrical purposes."[98] Max Beerbohm had trouble accepting the entire premise of *The Altar of Friendship*, stating that a novel based on this same story "would not be put on the market" and called the play "of the stage stagey." He advised the dramatist: "to shun melodrama in the future, and to devote herself wholly to comedy. She has a keen sense of humour—not a verbal or intellectual humour, but that dramatic humour which is, of course, the most effective on the stage. And this gift she ought not to waste."[99] By now Ryley must have grown accustomed to such mixed reactions of British and American critics and audiences.

CONTINUED DILIGENCE MEETS MIXED REVIEWS

Reflecting continued diligence on the part of the dramatist during this period, *The Voyagers* was produced in October 1898 at Chicago's Grand Opera House by Roland Reed who was described by the *Chicago Tribune* as being "a comedian of the Goodwin school," although "terribly behind his master." At the center of the play, Dr. Elwyn Tobias Bodkin (Reed), traveling about the world with an artist friend, becomes involved in the family affairs of a young girl with whom he is acquainted onboard a steamer. Through an innocent and "unintended act of imposture, he has become nominally her cousin, when suddenly the property on which she and her mother live reverts to him in his assumed character." If, however, he declares his true identity, the property (without a male heir) will go to the government of Honolulu—the location of the second and third acts. And since the villain of the play suspects him, neither can he continue the pretense. Dr. Bodkin "makes a clean breast of it" before setting out to find a genuine male heir, searching the globe, only to discover that the heir is none other than himself.[100] Unfortunately, the reviewer in the *Chicago Tribune* pounced on the play, calling Ryley's first act dull, the second weak, her dialogue "wonderfully vapid," and the characters "strangely without interest." The critic gave Ryley credit for amusing and natural dialogue and commended her handling of incidental situations, but the play, as did the actors, failed to impress Chicago critics and theatregoers.[101]

Opening in New York the same month, *On and Off*, an adaptation of a French farce, is mentioned in Ryley's obituary and in *Who Was Who in the Theatre* as one of her plays.[102] The play, an adaptation of Alexandre Bisson's *Controleur des Wagons-lits*, was listed in the program as being "by some person or persons unknown." Rather than being publicly associated with a spicy French farce declared as "not food for children," Ryley very likely requested her name be omitted, since her reputation rested on creating wholesome, clean comedies.[103] The farce centers on a bored husband (Edmund M. Holland) who pretends to be an inspector of sleeping cars to escape his in-laws and get away from home several days a week; when the real inspector (Fritz Williams) hears of the misuse of his name and office, the fun begins. In *On and Off*, however, Ryley had another success, since Frohman's production ran for eighty performances, with a week in January 1899 at the Harlem Opera House and again in March at the Grand Opera House.

Ryley's one-act "comedietta," *Realism*, served as a suitable vehicle for the author herself. As a curtain raiser to J. M. Barrie's *The Wedding Guest*, it was produced at the Garrick Theatre in London in the fall of 1900. Ryley had not performed on stage for a number of years, so her appearance created "special interest" in the play; the *London Times* reviewer called it "smartly-written" and declared Ryley "pleasing and natural" in the role of Mrs. Cimfel. The setting of *Realism* is a flat in Bedford Street, Covent Garden, the home of Harry Cimfel (James Erskine), an editor, and his wife, Josephine (Ryley), a successful dramatist. Mrs. Cimfel encourages her husband to lend his criticism to a piece she has just written, and after listening to her description of a scene, he expresses his opinion as "Rotton. It won't do, Joe."[104] The situation in Mrs. Cimfel's play concerns a husband who returns home unexpectedly to find his wife in the arms of another man. The man tells his wife to leave the room and "in a fury seizes the disturber of his domestic peace." When Mrs. Cimfel's asks her husband to explain his severe criticism, he replies that though the scene may be dramatic, "it is certainly not real, and realism is wanted in the present day." He believes that in real life a husband, rather than resorting to violence, would put everything in the hands of his solicitor.

Cimfel soon takes his leave, but as she brushes his coat, his wife lifts his letter case, resolved to carry out a scheme of her own. Once he is gone, Mrs. Cimfel sends a note to an actor of her acquaintance, Vincent Palgrave (Henry Vibart), requesting him to call upon her. Palgrave, a good-looking young man who considers himself a "lady killer," quickly arrives from the nearby Green Room Club. He is to play a part in her new play, she tells him, and in due course she also gives the impression that she would make an easy conquest. When Palgrave makes his move and takes the lady in his arms, the door opens and Mr. Cimfel appears, having returned for his letter case. What transpires becomes a repetition of the scene in her play: the husband assaulting the young Lothario, who departs threatening vengeance. When her husband suggests that she leave her scene as it is, Mrs. Cimfel has realized the point of her scheme—proving her husband wrong, as well as paying off a grudge she owed the conceited actor.

Realism played between October 4 and November 20, 1900, for a total of forty-one performances. As a curtain raiser, it received only scant critical attention, although William Archer did note: "Mr. Barrie's play is now preceded by an amusing comedietta, *Realism*, in which the authoress, Mrs. Madeleine Lucette Ryley, plays the leading part very brightly."[105]

ATTEMPTING THE HISTORY PLAY IN RICHARD SAVAGE

History plays remained popular at the turn of the century, and well known actors seemed eager to embrace meaty roles of historical figures, particularly English—as did Richard Mansfield with Clyde Fitch's *Beau Brummell* (1890), E. H. Sothern as Richard Brinsley Sheridan in Paul Potter's *Sheridan; or, The Maid of Bath* (1893) and Stuart Robson in August Thomas's *Oliver Goldsmith* (1900), not to mention Robertson's *Garrick*, which various actors tackled over the years.[106] Thus, Madeleine Lucette Ryley gave a play to Nat Goodwin to consider, "an historical tragedy based upon the life of

Richard Savage, the vagabond poet and author." It was a play she researched, spending "weeks in the old book shelves of the British Museum acquiring the atmosphere of Savage's time." Ryley stated that she felt it was "a strong character work, but must have an expensive production and heavy scenery.[107] Making no pretense of historical accuracy, she used a biography written by Samuel Johnson on Richard Savage for the basis of her melodrama. The plot centers on Savage and his claim of being the son of a former countess, who, when confronted by Savage, denies his claim and proceeds to estrange Savage from all his friends. He becomes wrongly accused of murder, thrown into prison, and condemned to hang. The publication of a poem he has written, however, changes public feeling in his favor; everyone abandons the countess and Savage's friends secure a pardon for him, but his health has been undermined by the ordeal and when the two women who love him rush to his prison cell with the pardon, he dies.[108]

When the play was produced in February 1901 at the Lyceum Theatre, it was not with Nat C. Goodwin in the title role, however, but Henry Miller. While a notice on the Rochester, New York, tryout indicated that the play was a "hit," apparently Broadway audiences found the five-act melodrama tiresome.[109] One reviewer lambasted the play's construction, situations and "wearying monologues," stating that the Savage role did not display Miller's best talents.[110] Three days later another critic pointed out that the play "is worse than weak in its motive"; Ryley, as in *My Lady Dainty*, "wastes her energies on the useless and the impossible" and fritters away "her good talent."[111] The following Sunday, Dithmar commenting on the actors in the production, expressed that it was a pity Miller's new role was so deficient in genuine dramatic motive." The critic wondered if Miller, a decidedly popular and likeable actor, took himself seriously enough, relating that on opening night: "He made a speech after the penultimate climax of the play in which he jested about the death scene which was yet to come. This is not so much bad taste as bad policy. A death scene that lasts nearly a quarter of an hour—such a bad quarter of an hour—is hard enough to bear when it is approached without a joke."[112] William Winter took an opportunity to air his views in the *Tribune* on the real Richard Savage by describing at great length what a scoundrel the man really was, a far cry from Ryley's literary, heroic stage image.[113] Lasting only twenty-six performances, *Richard Savage* may have served as a marked departure for the playwright, but in the future she focused on her strong suit, comedy.

MICE AND MEN

Increasingly, England drew Madeleine and J. H. Ryley. They were settled enough in London by the fall of 1899 to offer Gertrude Elliott a home with them while the young American actress took roles in London theatres. Diana Forbes-Robertson, Gertrude's daughter, recorded that the Ryleys "took Gertrude to live with them, assuring Maxine [Gertrude's sister] that they would treat her as their daughter and protect her every moment of her waking day."[114] From the Ryley's residence at No. 3 Clements Inn that November, Gertrude wrote in a letter: "I am living here with Mrs. Ryley, author of the 'Citizen.' She is a dear and we are as comfy and congenial as never was."[115] Thus, a life-long friendship developed between Madeleine Lucette Ryley and Gertrude Elliott. In December 1900, when Gertrude married leading actor Johnston Forbes-Robertson, J. H. Ryley gave Gertrude away, and an "hilarious wedding breakfast took place at the Ryleys' house, nearly causing the newly-weds to miss their train."[116]

Sometime in 1901 after nineteen years of living in America, the Ryleys officially made London their permanent residence. This is stated in a 1903 interview with Ryley, in which Curtis Brown called upon the playwright in her home, "a little house in St. John's Wood—a quarter of the metropolis that is famous for the number of its resident authors, artists, and playwrights." Brown described her "cozy" house with "its portrait of George Washington in the hall, its drawing room crowded with pictures and mementoes of famous stage folk both in England and America, and its bright attic, which the playwright had converted into a "den."[117] The Ryleys, who did not have children, enjoyed traveling, taking a trip around the world in 1906; in addition, Ryley's involvement in most of the productions of her plays, from meeting with managers and actors, to directing rehearsals, and attending openings, necessitated frequent transatlantic travel between the United States and Great Britain.

Mice and Men became ultimately, Ryley's most enduring play and was written specifically for Gertrude Elliott and Johnston Forbes-Robertson. The Forbes-Robertson company tried out the romantic comedy at Theatre Royal in Manchester on November 27, 1901. The actor-manager wrote in his memoirs of *Mice and Men*: "We played it in Manchester with so much success that I felt emboldened to venture London, and nothing could have been more cordial than its reception. Peggy, played to admiration by my wife, took the hearts of the public, and we had a very long and prosperous run with Madeleine Lucette Ryley's graceful and ingenious play."[118] When *Mice and Men* opened at London's Lyric Theatre the following January critics were quick to point out that the plot had already been seen upon the stage, comparing the play to Garrick's *The Country Girl* and Barrie's *The Professor's Love Story*. "There is no more favourite stage-figure than the middle-aged guardian who falls in love with his girl-ward, only to resign her in the end to a gallant of her own age," began the *London Times* review.[119] And, indeed, *Mice and Men*—the title taken from "The best laid schemes o' Mice 'an Men gang aft a-gley" of Robert Burns—foreshadows (or inspires) Shaw's *Pygmalion*.[120]

Events occur in a country setting at Old Hampstead in 1786. Mark Embury (Forbes-Robertson), a reclusive scholar in his early forties, jilted by a woman some years earlier, tells his friend and neighbor, Roger Goodlake: "If women are in general feeble in body and mind, it is the fault of our modern education; we encourage a vicious indolence, which we call delicacy. We teach them useless arts. We breed them to insincerity, and then we wonder at their fickleness and duplicity."[121] In response to Goodlake's inquiry, Embury details his own "required attributes" of the ideal wife: "She must have a taste for the sciences; be chaste, but not prudish; simple as a mountain maid; fearless as the Spartan wives—in short, with all the virtues of her sex, and none of its weaknesses."[122]

In order to fulfill his contribution in perpetuating the race, therefore, Embury plans to locate a simple girl and train her for a fitting wife. He carries this out by adopting a foundling from a local home, one of ten girls brought by a matron for his inspection. The foundlings, ranging from eleven to sixteen years of age, line up in Embury's study, each calling out her own name—ascribed by the location in which she was "found" (such as Stepney Green, Clare Market, Highbury Barn, Charring Cross, and Ivy Lane). The girl who catches Embury's attention is Little Britain (Gertrude Elliott), a sixteen-year-old he considers "straightforward and simple." Immediately, he christens her Peggy and assigns her to reciting multiplication tables as he goes outside and leaves her in the care of Mrs. Deborah, his housekeeper. When the housekeeper momentarily leaves the room, Peggy cannot unlatch the door and begins crying into her apron; at the same time George Lovell (Ben Webster), Embury's nephew, slips in by a window to look for a miniature he has lost. Lovell, described as a handsome fellow of about twenty-three, clad in regimentals, engages in a friendly exchange with the girl. The miniature he has lost is one given him by Joanna, the flirtatious younger wife of the middle-aged Goodlake. Now the gallant is being sent off for two years' service by his uncle as penance for "running with a petticoat."

A couple of years later finds Peggy a naturally charming young woman and Lovell due to return. It becomes apparent they have been corresponding, but because of what Joanna Goodlake tells her, Peggy believes Lovell is in love with someone else. It also becomes clear that Mark Embury, realizing he must soon inform Peggy of his marriage plan, is losing objectivity of the situation by falling in love with his ward. Everything becomes overshadowed by the excitement of a masquerade ball being held that evening on a neighboring estate. Kit Barniger (J. H. Ryley), a fiddler, comes in from London for the occasion and stops to visit his cousin, Mrs. Deborah; Peggy asks the quaint little man to escort her to the ball and presses him to play a tune so she might practice the dance steps. Confusion and mistaken identity occur in the third act at the masquerade ball, where Peggy has gone without her guardian's consent. The gown she wears is Joanne Goodlake's, which causes a confrontation when Roger Goodlake and Embury see her, masked, with the dashing Captain Lovell. And when Joanne appears, Peggy covers up the woman's intrigue in order to protect Lovell. In her confusion over events which transpire (and since Joanne divulged Embury's marriage plan to her), Peggy throws herself into the arms of her guardian, pledging her devotion to him. Momentarily enraptured, Embury accepts her at her word.

Six weeks later in Act Four in the garden of the cottage which Embury has built and furnished for himself and his bride, Embury asks Peggy to encourage his nephew to attend their wedding, set for the next day, and gives her a note for him. When Captain Lovell arrives and they are alone, his and Peggy's mutual feelings are obvious, but she dutifully hands him Embury's letter—in it, Embury informs his nephew that he is giving the two of them the house, along with his blessing. After Peggy rushes off in tears, Lovell retrieves Peggy and they timidly kiss before going into the cottage hand in hand. Embury slowly enters

> with hands linked behind him; as he reaches the house the harpsichord is heard playing the old melody, "My love is like a red, red rose"; he halts a moment, and then listens, while the two voices take up the refrain . . .; then he proceeds on his way, and goes slowly up the centre path; when he comes to the little wicket gate, he passes it and closes it behind him, turns and facing the audience, he fastens the latch, gives one more glance at the cottage, then continues along the path and out of sight.[123]

Nightly, theatregoers dabbed their eyes, and without exception, critics praised the play, its author, the actors, and the production. *Mice and Men*, stated, J.T. Grein, is "a good example of what a romantic play should be."

It is neither too sweet nor too sentimental. It creates
an atmosphere of pure imagination without flying
into the regions of the impossible or the bombastic.
It strikes the right note of pathos and the right note
of joy. The grown-up world will see it with as keen a
pleasure as the younger generation.[124]

In the same vein, Max Beerbohm wrote that while "Mrs. Ryley has
a genuine talent for sentimental comedy," what prevents the
sentiment from becoming maudlin and keeps it "airy and
wholesome" is her humor. Moreover:

she can write. What a relief . . . to find dialogue that
is really like human speech, yet terser and more
distinguished than human speech! Even by mere
reason of its literary style, "Mice and Men" is
delightful, and rare among plays. But the chief
ingredient of its delightful rarity is that it is a fairy-
story conceived in a sincere spirit—a fairy-story in
which I can believe.[125]

At the center of the play is the girl-woman, Peggy, "as pretty a
picture of girlhood as the stage can show." Offering a glowing
appraisal of Elliott in the role of Peggy, the *Times* critic described:

The charm with which the part is written is matched
by the charm with which Miss Gertrude Elliott looks
it and plays it. "Tell him," she says to her guardian,
speaking of the gallant, "I don't love him—but oh!
don't let him believe it." In little passages like
this—and there are many such passages in the
part—Miss Elliott last night provoked that gentle
murmur of satisfaction from the audience which is
really better worth having by an artist than the
loudest "thunders of applause."[126]

Similarly, J. T. Grein describes the role as fitting Elliott "like a glove."

> Yet she enlivened it with so much intelligence, with such wealth of gesture and piquancy of speech, that the attraction was irresistible. Nothing was mechanical, nothing forced, nothing done for effect. Miss Elliott, young by the grace of nature, turned her recollections of yesterday to the best account; we believed her statement of age sixteen. She looked, she acted it, and we ourselves enjoyed it in temporary rejuvenescence.[127]

The *Athenaeum* declared, as well, that the play "revealed in Miss Gertrude Elliott gifts of archness and pathos which advance her to a foremost place in her profession," noting that the love scenes between her and Forbes-Robertson "had much witchery."[128]

That Forbes Robertson "had left the lion's share of the play to his wife" did not pass without comment. But Grein also made the point that although the actor did not have many opportunities to display his fine acting gifts in *Mice and Men*, there were occasions in the play where Forbes-Robertson spoke "volumes in moments of silence, and then his gestures and his eyes revealed a world of unexpressed emotions. His wordless farewell at the gate, when he had dreamed his dream and returned to his home a lonesome man, was unforgettable. And he is a fine actor, indeed who, without uttering a word, can stir his audience as did Mr. Robertson in this memorable scene."[129] Dithmar deemed Forbes-Robertson "the great Othello, the peerless Hamlet of his hour, in the esteem of thousands of English playgoers."[130]

The playwright expressed her delight over the unanimous praise of *Mice and Men* and revealed that Forbes Robertson "made arrangements to remain at the Lyric until Christmas."[131] Although the run ended on December 10, the company continued to give matinee performances of *Mice and Men* into the new year for a total of 365 performances. Almost the same cast reprised the play during three weeks in June of 1904; and in 1913 Forbes-Robertson revived the play for ten performances in London between April and June, using a different cast, with the exception of Forbes-Robertson, Elliott, and J. H. Ryley. *Mice and Men* was also one of eight plays presented by Forbes-Robertson and Gertrude Elliott during a season of revivals at the Shubert Theatre in New York, September through December 1913.

The first American production of *Mice and Men*, produced by Charles Frohman, starred Annie Russell at the New National Theatre in Washington, DC, in December 1902.[132] A "characteristic Frohman story" is related in a 1915 clipping in connection with *Mice and Men*: "Charles Frohman ordered this play from Madeleine Lucette Ryley for Maude Adams. When he read the manuscript, he sent it back to Miss Ryley with the laconic comment, 'Worst yet.' The author showed it to Gertrude Elliott, who immediately bought it for England. When Charles Frohman heard of this, he immediately accepted it, and it proved to be a success."[133] The production was greeted warmly in Washington, but apparently the reception at New York's Garrick Theatre in January 1903, while friendly, was not especially enthusiastic. Even so, a *New York Times* reviewer pointed out that "not for many a long day have we seen a play in which the stock materials of the stage were used to such fresh and lively effect." And he predicted that the second night's audience would be more favorable.

Annie Russell was an appropriate choice for the role of Peggy. Despite her age—she was thirty-eight, while Gertrude Elliott was twenty-eight— she possessed the right attributes for the role—small, winsome, "eternal freshness, and surprise." The *New York Times* found her sixteen-year-old Little Britain believable and her older, half-tamed Peggy skillfully displaying the variances of the part. Supporting roles were played by John Mason as Embury, Orrin Johnson as Lovell, and Mrs. G. H. Gilbert, a well-known character actress, as Mrs. Deborah, the housekeeper.[134] William Winter, reviewing the two-week reprise of *Mice and Men* the following February at the same theatre, stated the "gem of the acting is Mr. John Mason's embodiment" of Embury, "technically, a fine example of simplicity and truth in the dramatic art." [135] In spite of the positive reviews during the 120 performances at New York's Garrick Theatre, the play did not seem to have as huge an impact upon American audiences as it did with the English. Nevertheless, the play remained in the public eye for some time through stock company productions—Maude Fealy, for instance, played Peggy at one of Denver's productions of *Mice and Men* in 1905.[136]

Thus, Madeleine Lucette Ryley, while still in her early forties, reached the apex of her dramatic career with the huge sensation of *Mice and Men*. Not only did the romantic comedy serve as her longest running play in both London and New York, but *Mice and Men* had major revivals in both cities and was toured by numerous American and British stock companies. A film version by Daniel Frohman, released in 1916, placed the location in Virginia before the Civil War. While the plot remained essentially the same, Captain Lovell (Marshall Neilan) was now a hero of the Mexican War and the role of Molly, the kitchen maid, became a "colored mammy." Marguerite Clark, distinguished in stage roles prior to film, played a charming Peggy, according to *Motography*, and Charles Waldron provided an impressive Mark Embury. *Mice and Men*, stated the reviewer, "is a picture whose delicate charm cannot be denied and one that can be recommended heartily." [137]

Although little information appears in print detailing Ryley's earnings, considering how lucrative playwriting was at the time and how thrifty she was with her earnings, it would not be surprising if royalties generated from *Mice and Men* alone provided financial security for the rest of her life.[138]

LATER DRAMATIC WORK

Ryley did not rest on her laurels, but continued to write and stage her work. Indeed, 1902 proved a demanding year for the playwright. After *Mice and Men's* January opening, she found time in the spring to organize two companies of *Mice and Men* to tour the provinces. In June the London production of *The Grass Widow* opened, along with yet another revival of *Jedbury Junior*. In

September, she sailed to New York to rehearse two new works, *An American Invasion* and *The Altar of Friendship*.[139] Indeed, as *Theatre* commented in February 1903, it would seem that "Mrs. Madeleine Lucette Ryley [was] writing all the plays that Clyde Fitch ha[d] not written already."[140]

Ryley not only produced, but also directed *The Grass Widow*, a comedy she described as "quite as much a farce as *Charley's Aunt* . . . a light entertainment of two hours' duration, to begin at 9 and end at 11, and its only object is to amuse." She also related the impracticality of even attempting anything serious in June, "especially the June of the Coronation year."[141] First performed in Devonshire Park Theatre, Eastbourne, in May 1902, *The Grass Widow* opened at London's Shaftesbury Theatre the first week of June.

The play concerns a woman married to a Russian "with a hearty appetite for cutlets and a fierce thirst for human gore." Since they both want a divorce, a scene is arranged "wherein the lady shall be discovered in a comic flirtation with a Paris cabman, who is not really a cabman, but an American wine merchant on a business trip to Paris." There occurs a burlesque duel that is "interrupted by a reporter with notebook and camera, who is not really a reporter, but a detective in the Russian's employ."[142] Despite the author's intention to create a farce, reviewers agreed that *The Grass Widow* fell short and, for that matter, failed to entertain. The *London Times* called the play a "farce of sheer fantasy, wherein what people do at any moment seems only less premeditated than what they say." And, apparently, a sense of strain on the part of the acting afforded little, if any, spontaneity to the piece.[143] Grein began his review with "axioms" of the farce in order to show how, in *The Grass Widow*, the playwright "offended" them; Ryley was not a humorist, but a sentimentalist at heart, suggested Grein, and had she written the play as such, it would have worked.[144] After only five nights, the manager of the Shaftesbury Theatre cut his losses and closed *The Grass Widow*, putting up a quickly-mounted, cordially received two-week revival of *Jedbury Junior*.

Mrs. Grundy, presented by Forbes-Robertson and Gertrude Elliott, represents a domestic play with comic elements. London theatregoers of 1905, the year Ryley's play was produced, would have understood the title, since "Mrs. Grundy," according to the playwright's introduction, "was an ancient village gossip, who constituted both mentor and censor among her terrorized neighbors." Over time, her name "passed into a proverb, and 'Mrs. Grundy' thenceforward became synonymous with all that is narrow-minded and bigoted in so-called public opinion." She added that Grundyism is particularly rampant in small country towns.[145] Essentially, this notion forms the theme of Ryley's play, the scene of which is laid in a Midlands community in a small provincial town. A new vicar, Edward Sotheby (Forbes-Robertson), has arrived, but parishioners soon learn that he is an unconventional parson. An ex-Army chaplain, Sotheby not only possesses humanitarian ideas, but also indulges in tobacco, declines using the vicarage because it is too expensive to maintain, and brings with him an old soldier, Joe Puddiford, who acts as a servant; from his marriage to the "wrong type of woman," who is now deceased, he has a ten-year-old son, Jack.

Act One opens in the Jevons' drawing room where Kitty, an "emotional girl of twenty-two," helps two younger Jevons children with lessons. Before long, it becomes apparent that Mr. and Mrs. Jevons are disapproving and snobbish, and that Kitty, their poor relation/servant, and Will, a young man from a nearby respectable family, are in love, despite the fact that he has an "understanding" with the Jevons' oldest daughter, Amelia. Edward Sotheby rents a cottage from Mrs. Patullo (Elliott), described as a "pretty, vivacious woman of about twenty-eight," who first appears in a bicycle dress stained with mud; as in *An American Invasion*, Ryley has the two principals meet via a bicycle accident. In brief, Kitty impulsively runs off with Will on a train to Edinburgh, but changes her mind and returns, only to be scorned by the narrow-minded Jevons and others in the town. The parson takes her in, but gossip runs rampant in the small community and, although he is in love with Mrs. Patullo, he proposes marriage to Kitty to rectify the situation. Mrs. Patullo, motivated by her growing affection for Sotheby, confesses to him that she is only posing as a "grass widow" to avoid fortune hunters and has now "killed off" her imaginary Australian husband in the bush. Kitty learns of their feelings for one another and secures a job that takes her away to another town, leaving Sotheby free of any obligations toward her.

The *London Times* summed up *Mrs. Grundy* as a "harmless little story, of quite harmless little conventionalities."[146] But Max Beerbohm's comments in Saturday Review bordered on vicious, calling the protagonist a fool and most of the characters "conventional stage daubs"; he described the child who played Sotheby's son, Jack, as having "a peculiarly fixed smile, and a peculiarly squeaky voice, and, sitting stiffly beside Mr. Forbes-Robertson, it squeaked a string of precocious questions which were parried in a deep, sonorous baritone.[147] But the critic in the *Athenaeum* put "the responsibility for comparative failure" of the production "upon faults of interpretation [rather] than upon inherent weaknesses of conception or construction."[148]

The most interesting character in the play, according to most commentary, was Joe Puddiford, the servant of the clergyman, played by Sydney Brough. And it appears this production would have benefited by more rehearsals before the November 16 opening at the Scala Theatre, since the *Times* indicated: "The acting, if not very good, is perhaps good enough. Mr. Forbes-Robertson may make something of the quixotic vicar, but we can only speak conjecturally, for last night he had to resign much of his part to the prompter."[149] The *Athenaeum* critic concurred: "The breath of the prompter was constantly and vainly expended, and the good things with which …. Mrs. Ryley had provided the characters passed unappreciated and unheard.[150] The production must have improved, however, since *Mrs. Grundy* continued for a few more weeks.

J. H. Ryley filled the minor character role of Josh Harmony, one of the parishioners with whom Sotheby makes a deal to stop smoking his pipe, if Harmony will stop betting on horses. Although the play had its moments, there were simply not enough of them to carry the production. Several notices in American papers mention that Madeleine Lucette and J. H. Ryley docked in New York in November 1906 onboard the Teutonic; pausing in New York for two weeks, they were on a trip around the world, bound for San Francisco and on to Australia, Japan, China, the Mediterranean and back to London. Ryley told reporters that she had brought two scripts, one which had been accepted by Ellis Jeffreys and another intended for Forbes-Robertson.[151] Her only other disclosure about the scripts was that one was a comedy, while the other a drama.[152] Evidently, she did not secure the interest of managers in either script, and plans for the play designated for Forbes-Robertson apparently did not materialize, while a comedy for Ellis Jeffreys, *The Sugar Bowl*, opened in London the following year.

Ryley was not given credit for the American production of *La belle Marseillaise* when it opened in New York in July 1906 with Virginia Harned, but an account in a Chicago paper suggested that it was she who adapted the French play for Charles Frohman.[153] Since Pierre Berton, the playwright, was in attendance and the play had been so highly successful in Paris, perhaps Frohman was being diplomatic in giving him sole credit, even though it had been translated for an American audience. At any rate, despite a relatively short New York production of twenty-nine performances, Frohman mounted an elaborate production in London, March 1907, and called it *The Great Conspiracy*, giving Ryley full credit for the adaptation. Briefly, the plot contains a quasi-historical background, with Napoleon (John Hare) at the center, beginning at a point just before he becomes Emperor. Others central to the plot are a royalist, the Marquis de Tallemont (Aubrey Smith) who, under the pseudonym of Lacaussade, has become proprietor of the restaurant La Belle Marseillaise, and Jeanne de Briantes, his beautiful landlady, with whom he is married (in name, at least). Although the restaurant serves as a base of operations for directing plots against Napoleon, Jeanne (Irene Vanbrugh) is in love with Captain Roger Crisenoy (Henry Ainley), one of the Emperor's devoted adherents.[154]

There are many plot twists and, as the *Athenaeum* stated, while the play begins "in fairly commonplace melodrama, it ends in something like a comedy, and even in what, in the days of Scribe, might have been regarded as vaudeville."[155] Containing a large cast, *The Great Conspiracy* offered four substantial roles, with particular interest given to Hare's interpretation of Napoleon. Produced at the Duke of York's Theatre, *The Great Conspiracy* ran for sixty performances.

The Sugar Bowl opened the new Queen's Theatre in October 1907 and marked Madeleine Lucette Ryley's return to the genre for which she became known, light social comedy. Although the play occurs in the present, a reading of the script lends the impression of a world and situation of a decade or so earlier.[156] The play opens in a reception room at Lady Andover's in Belgrave Square, London. Grace Pemberton (Ellis Jeffreys), despite being, as one critic stated, "so attractive a creature, at once so blithe and full of sensibility, that it is hard to see why she should ever have lacked suitors," is in her tenth season and harassed by a match-making mother.[157] Mrs. Pemberton reminds Grace that all the other girls at the party are dancing—"Girls with half your attractions, who have dozens of men dangling after them." And when her mother speaks of her own humiliation, Grace reaches her limit: "And what about *my* humiliations? My snubs? *My* disappointments? (with tears in her eyes) Hawked about here and there—made to smile at this man and be grave with that. Spreading my net in accordance with the habits of the prey—but always casting—always pursuing (with a burst) Mother, I am tired of it—tired to death of it all!"[158] Shortly after the outburst with her mother, Grace notices Sir Basil Loring (Frederick Kerr), a diplomat recently returned to England and considered to be the "catch" of the season. When Grace intentionally bumps into a plant and knocks it over, Sir Basil comes to her rescue, and the encounter leads to a dance.

"There is a tremendous lot expected of us now-a-days," Grace tells him, "and when we don't come up to the mark, we—well, we suffer for it." Sir Basil, taken with Grace's honesty, presses her to continue, and she confesses to him that, socially, she is considered a failure. When he encourages her to extrapolate on what constitutes a woman's success, Grace explains: "Well, in the first place, when she's poor, to marry *early*, and if necessary *often*. You see, if a woman happens to divorce her first husband, she can always have her choice of the next. Divorcees are always interesting."[159] Since the diplomat has been out of the country for a number of years, she continues to educate her skeptical listener about society and suggests he let her prove it to him. Grace proposes to Sir Basil that he devote the next five weeks to her exclusively to boost her social standing, during which time she promises never to take him seriously. The good-natured Sir Basil agrees, and the act ends with the two of them going into dinner arm in arm, while Lord Fraylingham who had snubbed Grace earlier looks on.

When Act Two opens, Grace has become in demand within their social sphere, due to the attentions of Sir Basil. "Is he serious?" a Dowager Countess asks Lady Andover, a friend of Sir Basil's. "Well, serious or not, it seems to be extraordinarily catching." Lady Andover agrees: "It *is*. Have you never noticed the flies round a sugar bowl? The first one alights out of curiosity—or to satisfy his appetite. The flies that follow, come simply because *he* is there."[160] But for Grace, things are getting out of hand, as expectations begin to rise about her supposed relationship with Sir Basil; indeed, she learns that her brother has secured a position in Africa based on her aspect of marriage to Sir Basil and even her mother's creditors are holding off on their demands. But when Sir Basil actually declares his love and proposes to her, Grace becomes visibly upset, believing he does so out of obligation. To free the man from any sense of duty toward her, she accepts Fraylingham's proposal. Misunderstandings continue, so that by the end of the third act, even though by now she has turned down Fraylingham, Sir Basil gains the impression that she is only toying with the other man. In Act Four at the office of the solicitor, Grace arrives to collect 1,000 pounds of her dowry to pay off some of the family debts, only to learn that her brother's 3,000 pound note is coming due. After she departs, Sir Basil drops by to sign some papers and learns of the

Pembertons' financial problems through the money lender and takes care of the loan. Grace returns, and Sir Basil discovers that she is not engaged, after all, and thus each is free to disclose their true feelings.

Calling into question the accuracy of Ryley's colloquy, the *London Times* critic devoted almost half of his review to criticizing her representation of the upper-class residents of Belgrave Square. An Ambassador, for instance, is not called His Excellency, and a young Englishwoman would not describe herself as a "popular society belle" nor use dictionary words like "relegate" or "jeopardize." But while the play was not a "very enthralling story," stated the critic, it nevertheless made for a "harmless evening's pastime." The *Athenaeum* believed the play had one too many acts, but the ending contained a "scene of genuine and appealing emotion." Indeed, "Mrs. Ryley's main story is charming enough to justify Mr. Vedrenne's choice of it for the opening of his handsome new theater."[161] *The Sugar Bowl* ran for a month, marking Ryley's last opening in London.

PERFORMANCES AND SUFFRAGISM

Whether Ryley quit writing plays after 1907 or simply could not interest anyone in her later work is not known. *New Idea* sums up her situation in 1909: "She has written twenty-seven plays, some of them having been exceedingly popular, and she is considered to be very well off. She has a handsome home in London, where she prefers to live and do her work, for although she spent many years in America, like Mrs. [Frances Hodgson] Burnett she is an Englishwoman by birth."[162] Despite being semi-retired, Ryley remained active within the theatre community well into the 1920s. Occasionally, she returned to performing, most notably for a charity production in 1904 and the suffrage cause in 1909. At the Garrick Theatre on July 19, 1904, for one matinee performance to aid the Busheyheath Cottage Hospital, two plays by W. S Gilbert were performed, *The Fairy's Dilemma* and *Rosencrantz and Guildenstern*. The latter, in which Ryley performed, was a "tragic episode in three tableaux," "founded on an old Danish legend"—essentially a clever spoof on *Hamlet*. The *London Times* described: "there is more brilliance of merely verbal wit in this little play than in anything else of Mr. Gilbert's." He also called it:

> a very subtle piece of criticism, sometimes of Shakespeare's play, sometimes of the commentators, sometimes of the actors who have played the great part. When Guildenstern asks what Hamlet is like, Ophelia replies: "Alike for no two seasons at a time./Sometimes he's tall, sometimes he's very short,/Now with black hair—now with a flaxen wig," and adds that he "always dresses as King James I.[163]

It is no wonder that the performers of such verbal wit would consist entirely of dramatic authors. Gilbert played Claudius with Lady Colin Campbell as Gertrude and Madeleine Lucette Ryley as Ophelia, while Robert Marshall played Hamlet; Leo Trevor served as Rosencrantz and Paul Rubens, Guildenstern; among the players and courtiers were Sir Francis Burnand, G. B. Shaw, Anthony Hope, Max Hecht, Edward Rose, Alfred Sutro, Gladys Unger, and Margaret Young.

Another significant appearance for Ryley was in *A Pageant of Great Women* held by members of the Actresses' Franchise League and the Women Writers' Suffrage League on November 12, 1909, at a matinee at the Scala Theatre. While *A Pageant* served as the last event in a matinee presentation which lasted over four hours, the *Times* critic assured readers that it was "four hours of real and sustained interest." Three new one-acts were performed, each giving a different slant on the suffrage cause. *A Pageant*, written by Cicely Hamilton and arranged by Edith Craig, consisted of forty-six women representing famous women throughout history. As Woman (Adeline Bourne) appeals to Justice (Lady Grove) against the tyranny of Prejudice (Kenyon Musgrave), various women are called upon as witnesses: the Learned Women, the Artists (including Ellen Terry as Nance Oldfield), the Saintly Women (with Ryley portraying Catherine of Siena), the Heroic Women, the

Rulers, and the Warriors.[164] It was "a picturesque appeal" that for those present, regardless of their political views, remained an afternoon long remembered.[165]

Madeleine Lucette Ryley served as one of several vice presidents of the Actresses' Franchise League from its formation in November 1908 until the League was dissolved in 1918 with the passage of the Woman Suffrage Act.[166] Ryley spoke regularly for the League at open-air meetings and at "At Homes"; she donated the blinds for the League's office, "beautifully embroidered by Miss Madeline Roberts [her niece], and the badge cleverly sewn on by her, whilst Mr. Ryley gave a roll top desk."[167]

Gertrude Elliott served as the president of the AFL throughout its duration, while Forbes-Robertson, a strong supporter of women's rights, spoke at one of their first meetings at the Criterion Restaurant in December 1908, along with theatre critic, J. T Grein. A lengthy account in *Era* describes: "Mrs. Lucette Ryley and Miss Cicely Hamilton made very bright and witty speeches in support of the movement."[168] Several other notices on AFL meetings note Ryley as being among those present.[169]

Ryley again tried her hand at producing in 1920, with *Come Out of the Kitchen*, a domestic upstairs-downstairs type comedy in which Gertrude Elliott toured; Elliott's eleven-week run began at the Strand on March 15, 1920, with, noted the *Times*, "their Majesties and the Prince of Wales" in attendance.[170] That Ryley continued writing in later years is suggested by poems appearing in *English Review* in 1923 and 1924. "Watching the Crowd" includes the lines:

> Hither and thither, thronging the street,
> Whence are you bound, all you hurrying feet?
> Bearing your forms, both the frail and the strong,
> Eager and hasty you scurry along . . .
> Anxious expectancy marked on each face,
> Lending an impetus quickening the pace.
> The spirit of contest grows ever more warm,
> For each would be first in the curious swarm.[171]

While it was not made public, it appears that the Ryleys were not together toward the end of his life. Although he had been retired from comic opera for quite some time, J. H. Ryley carried small roles in several of his wife's productions, appearing as late as 1913 in Forbes-Robertson's last revival of *Mice and Men* and making forays into film—seen as the Gravedigger in a silent film version of Hamlet in 1913.[172] According to a notice in the *London Times*, J. H. Ryley died on July 28, 1922, at the age of eighty; the address given is 216 Portsdown Road, N.W., which is not the same as Madeleine's in St. John's Wood. He is cited only as "the beloved father of Marie W. Verden, of Pinnercote, Pinner, Middlesex," with no mention of his wife.[173]

Twelve years later, after a long, incapacitating illness in which she was partially paralyzed, Madeleine Lucette Ryley died on February 17, 1934.[174] Her estate was ample enough to leave bequests of 1,000 pounds each to her surviving sisters Anna Roberts and Kate Bradley, and to her niece, Madeleine (Roberts) Tearle, along with 500 pounds to her housekeeper with a life annuity of 104 pounds per year. In addition, she gave 300 pounds each to five charities, including the Actors' Benevolent Fund and the Actors' Church Union. She bequeathed all of her personal belongings to Madeleine Roberts Tearle, who used the stage name Jane Comfort.[175] Ryley's will designated as co-Executor and Trustee, her long-time friend, Lady Gertrude Forbes-Robertson.[176]

Indicative of Ryley's renown in the United States, the write-up on her in the *New York Times* is much longer than that accorded her in the *London Times*. Reviewing her performing and playwriting careers, the obituary ends by citing a *Boston Transcript* article of 1901. Referring to a group of her later plays, the *Transcript* states: "These were all clean, wholesome comedies, and she scored heavily, for she proved, in contradistinction to many of her contemporaries, that American audiences could be entertained and amused by Anglo-Saxon themes and witty comedy as readily as by those of Latin origin with their salacious plots and suggestive dialogue. Indeed, as far as women playwrights are concerned, she now has the field almost to herself."[177]

As demonstrated in this chapter, for a brief period, from

about 1897 to 1903, Ryley ranked at the top of her field as a professional dramatist. Her romantic comedies, above all, were enjoyed by thousands of theatre-goers in New York, London, Paris, and throughout both England and America. She not only supported herself and her husband, but invested her money and became quite comfortable. As a professional dramatist, she exercised control over her work, and often took an active role in productions by directing rehearsals herself.

Although Ryley's ability for writing a certain style of comedy remained her strong suit, in the long run, her inability to shift with the demands of the public abbreviated her career as a dramatist. When other playwrights began writing lyrics for musical theatre or tackling substantial, realistic themes or "problem plays," Ryley turned to domestic or sentimental comedy that succeeded in *Mice and Men*, but failed in *Mrs. Grundy*. Indeed, whenever she veered too far from a light, farcical vein reminiscent of the comic opera in which she trained, Ryley's plays did not work. Other than the historical play, *Richard Savage*, she did not venture into serious themes, nor did she attempt critical commentary on women's or social issues, other than in a lighthearted way, despite being highly visible and vocal in the suffrage movement. She did, however, poke fun at both English and American sensibilities in much of her work, employing puns, satire and epigrammatic language to humorous effect. Adept at creating viable roles for star comedians, among her most memorable were those of Mark Embury and Little Britain in *Mice and Men*. Madeleine Lucette Ryley industriously applied herself to her craft and ultimately earned the high regard of critics and audiences on both sides of the Atlantic.

A 1910 INTERVIEW WITH
"MRS. MADELEINE LUCETTE RYLEY"[178]

There are few women dramatists of the present day with such a long list of successes behind them as Mrs. Madeleine Lucette Ryley. In America, she went on the stage at an early age, and, being the possessor of a fine voice, she quickly came into prominence as *prima donna* of several of the well-known opera companies, marrying Mr. J. H. Ryley, comedian, in 1890. Later, her literary bent became apparent, and she took to writing short stories and sketches for the American magazines; finally, with a ripe knowledge of stage technique, gained in a practical way, she turned her attention to dramatic work. Independence, initiative, and a constructive imagination, combined with a rare knowledge of humanity, are the characteristics of her work. Her men and women are human and delightful, and not facile automata. In America she is as well known as in Great Britain, and her plays, notably "An American Citizen" and "Jedbury Junior," have had runs of as great length as "Mice and Men" had here. Her cosmopolitan acquaintance with human nature has made her one of the most convinced feminists of our time.

Recently, at the Women Writer's Suffrage League her appeal for funds was one of the features of the afternoon.

"Why do you think that women should have the Vote?" she was asked.

"Looking at it from the standpoint of commonsense, I think it necessary for the progress of humanity—necessary as the mean to an end. Women must be educated to their responsibilities, and as long as the Vote is denied them they will remain uneducated. My point of view is impersonal and altruistic. For my own part I can exist without a vote," she added, smiling.

"Perhaps women at the present time are mentally undeveloped, but to argue from that that they need to be educated up to their responsibilities before possessing them is nonsense! The Vote will help to educate them! It is a mere matter of logic."

"Why do you say it is a matter of logic?"

"When you want a puppy dog to learn to carry a stick, you don't sit down and theorise [sic]; you don't say to him, 'Not now; but later on, when you have thought out the matter of carrying sticks, then you shall have this to carry!' Instead, you save all the labour [sic] by giving him the stick, and his pride in the sense of possession teaches him to carry it."

"You think that a sense of responsibility, then, will do all the teaching necessary for the exercise of the Vote?"

"It will do much, and the educational service alone would be worth the experiment, and would be sufficient reason, even if there were no grievances to redress. As a sex, women are helpless for lack of authority, but when they have the Vote they will grow accustomed to power and will become less self-conscious.

"I believe, though, in taking the Anti-Suffrage premises, and arguing from them," went on Mrs. Ryley. "You can always get an excellent result. They say only 10 percent of the women of Great Britain desire the Vote. Granted that that is so, why should that 10 percent be denied its privileges? In politics, as in other matter, the minority has its rights. And this, while often forgotten, cannot be too strongly insisted upon. What has that 10 percent done that it should be denied common justice? The other 90 percent need not exercise the Vote if they do not choose."

"What do you regard as the causes of Anti-Suffrage agitation?

"First, overwhelming ignorance; second, overwhelming ignorance, third, overwhelming ignorance!"

"And fourth?"

"Fear. Fear that they may lose something—esteem of their male kind. Fear also that they may have to think for themselves. The prospect is not a pleasant one. They dislike thinking. And, if you want a fifth, indolence. They are too indolent to put themselves out; they hate any kind of mental exertion."

"As a woman wage-earner, what is your opinion of the income tax?"

"That it is iniquitous! I pay income tax three times over. First, as my husband's chattel, I have it paid for me—it is included in his returns; secondly, as a wage-earner, I pay on what I make; and, thirdly, I pay on my investments, for being a thrifty woman I invest a portion of my earnings. But I only pay income tax in order to spare inconvenience to others. If I were unmarried I certainly would not pay it.

"I do not mind fighting," said Mrs. Ryley, in answer to a question regarding militancy. "If it were not for the fighters we could not exist; someone must do the rough work. If there were no grievances and no one to remedy them, the fabric of society must fall to the ground.

"The trend of this movement is revolutionary; it affects and will affect every woman born into the race. It will raise the status of the sex. No great reform can be thought of apart from it. To every great movement the enfranchised women will bring a new point of view—a new stimulus and a new blood."

"When did you become a Suffragette?"

"I have always been a Suffragette without knowing it. Since the agitation commenced five years ago, I have formulated my views, but I had always held them unconsciously. The other day I was turning over an old play of my own (written twelve years ago), and there I was amused to see that I had made a man and woman take the same views of sex equality that I hold today."

"Have you written a Suffrage play?"

"No; I have thought of doing so several times, but the difficulty is not to miss the broad issues in dwelling on one of the irritations. And that is what one would have to do in taking up a single point in which there is sex disability and writing a play round it. It is because I regard the whole question as so vital and so great, and so cumulative in its possibilities as a whole, that I think it dangerous to dwell on one of the little flies in the ointment—a little fly which in itself it might not be impossible to eliminate. Remedying small disabilities is the insidious method of delaying the great result, and it is the great uplifting, that the responsibilities of full and perfect citizenship will give us, that we are waiting for!"

WORKS OF MADELEINE LUCETTE RYLEY

[Includes date and length of most significant American and English productions, source material, collaborators, leading "star" performers, publisher, and, if not published, where the typescript may be located. If no location is noted, the work is likely not extant. See legend at the end.]

1890
Lady Jemima, three-act comedy
  Produced outside of New York by Minnie Maddern
The Junior Partner,* four-act comedy

1891

Valentine's Day,* three-act comedy
The Merchant of Pongee, unproduced musical c. 1890s
  Typescript, SA

1893
The Basoche, musical (adapt. from French)
  Casino Theatre, February 27–March 11, 1893
The Promised Land,* 1893 (four-act play)

1894
The Golden Calf,* 1894 (four-act drama)

1889
Christopher, Jr. (John Drew / Maude Adams)
  Empire Theatre October 7, 1895 (64)
  as *Jedbury Junior* (Frederick Kerr)
  Terry's Theatre, London, February 14, 1896 (105)
  Globe Theatre, London, December 21, 1896 (51)
  (New York: Samuel French, 1917)
  Typescript JRL

1896
The Time of Strife, one-act
  Empire Theatre School, January 27, 1896 (1)

1897
The Mysterious Mr. Bugle (Annie Russell / Joseph Holland)
  Lyceum Theatre, April 19, 1897 (56)
  Strand Theatre, London, May 29, 1900 (18)
  Typescript, JRL
A Coat of Many Colors (Effie Shannon / Herbert Kelsey)
  Wallack' Theatre, September 13, 1897 (24)
  Typescript, JRL
An American Citizen (Nat Goodwin / Maxine Elliott)
  Knickerbocker Theatre, October 11, 1897 (96)
  Duke of York's, London, June 19, 1899 (69)
  (New York: Samuel French, 1906, 1923)
  Novel (New York: G. W. Dillingham, 1898)

Film, Famous Players Film Co., January 1914 (w/John
Barrymore) Typescript, JRL, BR

1898

The Voyagers (Roland Reed)
   Grand Opera House, Chicago, October 10, 1898
   Typescript, JRL
On and Off, adapt., Alexandre Bisson's *Controleur des Wagons-lits*
   Madison Square Theatre, October 18, 1898 (80)

1900

Realism, one-act (Madeleine Lucette Ryley)
   Garrick Theatre, London, October 4, 1900 (41)
   Typescript, BL

1901

My Lady Dainty (Effie Shannon / Herbert Kelsey)
   Madison Square Theatre, January 8, 1901 (39)
   Typescript, JRL, BR
Richard Savage, based on Dr. Johnson's *Lives of the Poets*
   Lyceum Theatre, February 4, 1901 (26) (Henry Miller)
      Typescript, JRL
Mice and Men (J. Forbes-Robertson / Gertrude Elliott)
   Theatre Royal, Manchester, November 27, 1901
   Lyric Theatre, London, January 27, 1902 (365)
   Garrick Theatre, New York, January 19, 1903 (Annie Russell) (120)
   (New York / London: Samuel French, 1909)
   Film, Famous Players Film, January 1916
   Typescript, JRL

1902

The Grass Widow
   Shaftsbury Theatre, London, June 3, 1902 (5)
   Typescript, JRL
An American Invasion (J. E. Dodson / Annie Irish)
   Bijou Theatre, October 20, 1902 (24)
   Typescript, JRL

The Altar of Friendship (Nat Goodwin / Maxine Elliott)

Knickerbocker Theatre, NY, December 1, 1902 (50)
Criterion Theatre, London, March 24, 1903 (26)
Typescript, JRL, BR

1905

The Lady Paramount (Margaret Anglin)
California Theatre, San Francisco, April 9, 1905
Typescript, JRL
Mrs. Grundy (J. Forbes-Robertson/Gertrude Elliott)
Scala Theatre, London, November 16, 1905 (32)
(London: Stage Play Publishing Bureau, 1924)
Typescript, JRL

1906

La belle Marseillaise adapt. from P. Berton (*The Great Conspiracy*)
Knickerbocker Theatre, July 22, 1906 (Virginia Harned) (29)
Duke of York's, London, March 4, 1907 (John Hare) (60)
Typescript, JRL

1907

The Sugar Bowl (Ellis Jeffreys)
Queen's Theatre, London, October 8, 1907 (36)
Typescript, JRL, BR

* Listed in *Dramatic Compositions Copyrighted in the United States, 1870 to 1916*, 2 Vols. (Washington, DC: Government Printing Office, 1918). Three additional works may be Ryley's earliest efforts, written under the pseudonym Noel Grant. They are listed in *Dramatic Compositions*, copyrighted by J. H. Ryley: *Fairy's Fortune*, 1886 (three-act comedy); *Blue Blood*, 1888 (three-act domestic comedy); *Lady Jemima*, 1888 (three-act comedy).
    BL   British Library, Lord Chamberlain Play Collection
    BR   Billy Rose Collection, New York Public Library, Lincoln Center
    JRL   John Rylands Library, Manchester University
    SA   Shubert Archives, New York.

Beulah Marie Dix & Evelyn Greenleaf Sutherland

COLLABORATORS AND FRIENDS: EVELYN GREENLEAF SUTHERLAND (1855-1908) AND BEULAH MARIE DIX (1876-1970)

> Blue eyes once ruled men's hearts, Fame says, / But now 'tis shocking! / The maid my heart is fain to praise / Wears a blue stocking.
> —Evelyn Greenleaf Sutherland, 1884[1]

> "I fancy I should have written books, even if I had not gone to Radcliffe, but I do not believe I should have written plays, if I had not found a little stage that demanded plays.
> —Beulah Marie Dix, c. 1920[2]

THE COLLABORATIVE RELATIONSHIP OF Evelyn Greenleaf Sutherland and Beulah Marie Dix fittingly demonstrates how, during the early 1900s, women often joined forces to create successful plays. Sutherland worked as a drama critic for several Boston newspapers before she began writing plays, while Dix, twenty years younger, wrote plays and novels during her years at Radcliffe. Both were included in "Boston's Great Array of Literary People" in August 1902, Sutherland described as an "author, collaborator, and playwright," while Dix was deemed "the young writer of promise."[3] Early in 1901, the two began collaborating, eventually creating over seventeen plays, most of which were historical romances or "costume" plays, often based upon Dix's student plays and novels. They enjoyed success with *The Breed of the Treshams*, performed by John Martin Harvey in London and throughout Great Britain. *"Matt" of Merrymount*, produced by Fred Terry, and *Young Fernald*, a vehicle for Evelyn Millard, also achieved moderate British success. Dix and Sutherland's most well-known American work became *The Road to Yesterday*, a "comedy-fantasy" in which a romantic young woman is transported back three hundred years on Midsummer's Eve to encounter familiar people in other incarnations and finds her true hero. During the seven years Dix and Sutherland collaborated, they regularly attended theatre together and traveled abroad several times to see productions of their work. Their partnership ended abruptly with Sutherland's accidental death in 1908, after which Dix went on to marry, move to Hollywood, and establish a career writing for the movie industry. This chapter gives an overview of each woman, discussing her early years and her individual creative achievements, before focusing on their collaborations.

EVELYN GREENLEAF SUTHERLAND, SIXTH-GENERATION BOSTONIAN

Born in Cambridge, Massachusetts, on September 15, 1855, Evelyn Greenleaf Sutherland was the only daughter of James Baker, a prominent wholesale merchant and Rachel Greenleaf Baker, a fifth-generation Bostonian. James Baker, a "devoted anti-slavery worker," died when Evelyn was only three. She received schooling via her mother, public schools, girls' schools, and two years' study in Geneva, Switzerland. Evelyn began writing "little rhymes and tales" as a child and at the age of fifteen was awarded a prize by *St. Nicholas* magazine for an essay, "What is a Gentleman"; early writings appeared in *Puck*, *Life*, and *Cosmopolitan*, among others.[4] "In 1894, under the name of Dorothy Lundt, a *nom de plume* she used for twenty years, she won one of the prizes offered by *McClure's Magazine* [for] an army tale, 'Diccon's Dog.'"[5]

When she was twenty-four, Evelyn Greenleaf Baker married her childhood friend, John P. Sutherland on March 10, 1879, after his graduation from Medical School of Boston University. Immediately following the wedding, they toured Europe for several months, returning to Concord, Massachusetts, where he practiced medicine for a year. In 1881, they settled in Boston where Dr. Sutherland took up medical practice and became identified with Boston University School of Medicine as an instructor, a full professor of anatomy, and then a dean, a position he held from 1899 on.[6] A description of Dr. Sutherland can be seen from Beulah Marie Dix's daughter, Evelyn Scott's memoir, *Hollywood When Silents Were Golden*: "Mrs. Sutherland was married to an eminent doctor, a wiry Scott marvelously energized by what we now call health food, of which he was a pioneer. (He, too, wrote—a formidable volume called *Malnutrition: The Medical Octopus*.)"[7] According to Evelyn Scott, the Sutherlands had an adopted son, Allan Rowe, who became a doctor in endocrinology.[8]

Evelyn Greenleaf Sutherland joined the staff of the *Boston Transcript*, contributing book reviews and dramatic criticism. Trained as a critic by Francis Jenks, dramatic editor of the *Transcript*, she filled in as dramatic editor during 1889–90, writing most first-night reviews. As "Dorothy Lundt," Sutherland also wrote a column, "Library and Foyer," for the *Transcript* for seven years. Suffering from "acute nervous prostration, she retired in 1894 from active life for eleven months, living out of the city."[9] When she returned to work in 1896, she wrote for a number of Boston area newspapers and served for a while as drama critic for the *Daily Journal*.

Letters to Evelyn—housed in the Boston Public Library—provide an impression of her social connections, as well as her influence as a drama critic. An 1893 communiqué from playwright James Herne, for instance, thanks Sutherland for her positive comments in the *Boston Transcript* on his play, *Shore Acres*, and includes: "It seems to come from one who had sat beside me during the writing of the play. You have looked into my very soul, it seems—taken what of good you found there and published it to the world—"[10] David Belasco, unaware he was writing to a woman, addressed a note "My dear sir," thanking her for criticism of *The Girl I Left Behind Me*.[11] A letter from actor Alexander Salvini in 1896 tells that since Chicago reviews were "condemning" and he was "treated unfairly by critics," he hopes to conclude his upcoming two-week engagement of Othello in Boston "on a high financial note"; thus, he asks Sutherland "for her kind assistance to help in swelling the receipts"—perhaps a positive word "that you might give me the benefit of either in your paper or among your many friends of the Boston four hundred where I know you to be most influential."[12] A note in the spring of 1897 from William Gillette, a well-known playwright of the era, accepts a dinner invitation and tells he would "be happy indeed to meet your husband," but "please let this be between ourselves—I am refusing all invitations— and do not go out at all."[13] Some ninety-four letters in all include chatty missives concerning dinner invitations, holiday greetings, or various matters from theatre personalities who include May Robson, Minnie Dupree, Harry Woodruff, Mary Mannering, and Blanch Walsh. Jay Benton, a Boston Correspondent with the *New York Dramatic Mirror*, refers in casual notes to Sutherland as "Dorothy," while Rudyard Kipling congratulates her in a letter on her change of address to Commonwealth Avenue and gibes her about living in such an affluent part of Boston.[14]

Echoed in many of her letters, a number of sources refer to Sutherland's hospitality and describe her home as a refuge for college students, actors, and playwrights. "The Sutherlands kept open house for an enticing group of friends," states Scott.[15] And in 1904 Julia Ward Howe wrote: "Her [EGS] Sunday evenings are the property of her 'boys,' not only of Boston University, but of Harvard and Tech also. At her home they find on Sunday nights a 'picnic supper,' a warm welcome, and an 'open parliament,' whose leader is often the honored and beloved Dean."[16] Even while vacationing in Nantucket, Sutherland interacted with theatre people. A 1902 feature story in *Cosmopolitan* revealed that in the summer many in the acting profession preferred to go to Siasconset, a "quaint" village on the coast of Massachusetts and the location of Sutherland's family place. That summer Mrs. Sutherland was joined by Minnie Dupree, recently cast in Sutherland's new play, *The Rose of Plymouth*. Stated the article: "'The Auld House,' as Mrs. Sutherland has christened her island home is one of several big homesteads running from the moors to the long narrow lane we call Broadway."[17] Another summer residence the Sutherlands owned was "Clans home," located in Marlow, New Hampshire. They also traveled periodically to Dr. Sutherland's native Scotland.[18]

Sutherland was involved with a number of organizations, including the New England Woman's Press Club (charter member), Boston Authors Club, New York Professional Woman's League and the American Dramatists' Association. While it was Beulah Marie Dix who helped to organize the Boston Authors Club in late 1899, Sutherland joined in 1903.[19] Sutherland may not have had the time or inclination to carry banners for woman suffrage, but she was "much in sympathy with the cause." Around 1897, she expressed confidently in a published Boston symposium that "women have obtained most things that they seriously have wanted in this world, and so it will be until the end of time."

> I see no reason why, in the day of woman suffrage that is so surely coming, a woman may not follow a career in the political field just as properly as today she enjoys a place in the counting room, business office, or newspaper world. Her intuition, womanly tact, good breeding, and integrity eminently fit her for such a position, and the day will come when she is admitted by the world to be the political equal of man, as she is now acknowledged to be his intellectual and social equal.[20]

Evelyn Greenleaf Sutherland's opinion reflected her own status as an educated woman with a career, married to a man who, from all appearances, treated her as an equal.

SUTHERLAND'S ONE ACT-PLAYS

While in her mid-thirties, Sutherland began writing theatre pieces, initially preferring the one-act play, a form which served her well. Between 1892 and 1900, she saw sixteen or more short plays performed in various venues, from amateur productions for clubs and benefits, to professional showings in New York theatres. The premier of one of her earliest efforts, *Drifting*, in collaboration with actress Emma Sheridan Fry, marked no small event; it was the first production of the short-lived Theatre of Arts and Letters. More social than theatrical, this event had some 600 "well-known society and literary men and women" in attendance.[21]

Drifting, shown as a curtain raiser, featured Nelson Wheatcroft in the role of Ralf Guion, an experienced man of the world who has spent a summer trifling with the heart of Maida, an eighteen-year-old. "The girl's aunt knows she loves Guion and tries to prevent their final interview, but to no avail."[22] In their meeting Guion comes to say goodbye and "thanks the girl for having allowed him to admire her" and cruelly "reads her a lesson upon the folly of flirting with a man twice her age."[23] In the process of rejecting her, "he discovers that he actually loves the girl, but she learns enough of his character to send him away, though she has a fainting fit after he has gone."[24] Critics had few positive things to say about *Drifting*. According to one, there were no "clever lines of any sort." While Nelson Wheatcroft "played the man's part with all the skill of a veteran actor" in contrast, Kuhne Beveridge in her stage debut as Maida, was only "an amateur full of good intentions."[25] Even so, *Drifting* faired better with the critics than did the accompanying full-length "dramatic impression," *Mary Maberly*, by novelist J. S. Stimson.

Four years later Sutherland and Emma Sheridan Fry's *Mars'r Van* enjoyed a longer run at the Empire Theatre as the curtain raiser for *Marriage*, a three-act play by Brandon Thomas and Henry Keeling. *Mars'r Van* centers on a southern belle who "scorns her lover for joining the Union army, then relents and accepts him."[26] While reviewers focused on the full-length play and called the one-act merely a "trifle" or "novelty," the *Post* did mention that the story appealed "to romantic and patriotic sentiment," thus, winning "passing favor." Among the characters, noted the critic, was "Miss May Robson, as a little negro servant of the Topsy variety, with an excruciating laugh [which] caused some of the heartiest merriment of the evening."[27]

Henry Woodruff was one of Sutherland's Harvard "boys" mentioned earlier.[28] In fact, Sutherland appears to have been partial toward both Henry Woodruff and Minnie Dupree, young actors who played in several of her one-acts and full-length plays. For Woodruff, Sutherland wrote the role of Drent Dury, the main character of *Po' White Trash*, described as "a study of a little-known phase of American life."[29] Set in Georgia, the scene is the exterior of Suke Dury's dilapidated cabin at the edge of a swamp in mid-July. The play opens with the sounds of locusts and Zep Poon, a "burley negro" snoring under a tree. Sal Hankers, a neighbor, dressed in gaudy, cheap calico," appears, calling out for Suke. Described in the script as a more vivid version of Sal, with deep red hair, Suke stands in the doorway, knotting together the ends of a frayed rope. Conversation between the two women discloses that Suke and her nephew, Drent, have recently returned to the old cabin that was boarded up twenty years before, having left after Suke's sister, Pen, became pregnant. Suke expresses concern that Drent may have the same condition that caused the sudden death of her sister.[30]

Indeed, from the moment he enters, pale and listless, Drent Dury presents a fascinating and pathetic character. Carrying a shotgun and a "dilapidated game bag" slung over his shoulder, he is dressed in "ragged brown jean trousers, a dull blue shirt, open at the throat, and a ragged hat."[31] His long monologue to Dr. Payne describing how he and his dog tracked down a raccoon in the swamp reveals Drent's sensitive nature:

> An' then, Doctor, I saw that coon's eyes.—I saw that coon's eyes. Doctor, I—I never saw a coon's eyes befo'. I reckon—I reckon—thar wouldn't be so much hurtin' done in this world ef jes' befo' yo' hurted yo' saw the thing's eyes! An' I looked at him—an he looked at me—, an' his eyes said, "Be yo' goin' to kill me? Be yo' goin' to kill me?"

Thar worn't no trees— no sky—no nothin'—jes' only that coon's eyes... An' I flinged my gun's far's she'd flew, an' I sez, "No, yo' mean, scared, hunted critter, yo'! I'll be damned if I kill yo'!"[32]

Drent secretly pines for Carol, who's engaged to Judge Page's son. Carol comes by to ask Drent to sing at her engagement party, but misunderstands his actions when he forcefully pushes her aside. The Judge appears and as Carol describes Drent's "abuse," they realize he has been bit by a copperhead snake that meant to bite her, prompting Carol to rush off for the doctor. It is then that the secret of Drent's parentage comes out in the conversation between the Judge and Suke, who waves a marriage license proving Drent is his legal son with her dead sister, Pen. Drent overhears and snatches the document, stuffing it into the fire pot with the branding iron. "It takes mo'n a paper to make quality out o' po' white trash," he declares. When Drent falls ill from the snake poison, the Judge runs off for help and Suke rushes into the house for a torch, only to find upon her return that her nephew has died in the middle of his song.

After an initial showing in Boston, Henry Woodruff portrayed Drent at the Lyceum Theatre in 1898 in a special matinee that included two other Sutherland plays, *A Comedie Royall* and *A Bit of Instruction*. While the *New York Herald* critic had nothing positive to say about the other two plays, he expressed genuine surprise that in *Po' White Trash* Woodruff "suddenly revealed himself as an actor of exquisite poetic feeling. Of all the things he has ever done here this part of Drent Dury is incomparably the best." The critic also credited Sutherland for creating a play of "uncommon merits."[33] Indeed, the *New York Times*, too, commented that the "piece has character as well as appreciable humor and pathos to commend it."[34] Despite the praise he received for the role, Woodruff does not appear to have continued with Drent Dury much beyond this production; however, he did reprise *A Bit of Instruction* in which he played a man of society, Mertoun Newbury, in an "extended vaudeville tour in the autumn of 1898."[35] Today, *Po' White Trash* can be noted as a strong example of the early American folk-play, predating the folk-plays of Lula Vollmer.[36]

Sutherland utilized a variety of themes in her one-acts, seen in her theatrical settings in *A Bit of Instruction* and *In Far Bohemia*, and in the use of self-sacrifice on the part of a social inferior in both *Po' White Trash* and *The End of the Way*—where Robin Hood's Will Scarlett loves but leaves the married Lady Jacqueline Werewood.[37] In *A Song at the Castle*, set in Ireland in 1798, an heiress, Eileen Fitzgerald, champions several suitors, including Desmond O'Moirne, a young Irish singer. When he defiantly sings "The Wearing of the Green" and risks arrest by her English guardian, Lord Cornwallis, Eileen demands as her birthday boon Desmond's life and liberty, stating: "where he goes, I go with him." Cornwallis then grants "the free gift of a soldier to a soldier's deed."[38] Susan Croft points out that while most of Sutherland's protagonists are male, courageous women characters appear in *At the Barricade*, set in Paris during the Commune of 1871—strong women in the *pétroleuses* not only fight the soldiers, but are also sexually assertive.[39]

Several of Sutherland's one-act plays include "negro" characters, most often for comic effect, as seen in *Mars'r Van*, *Po' White Trash*, and particularly in *Aunt Chloe's Cabin*, a minstrel piece performed by the Women's Professional League.[40] But *His Own*, first performed in 1908, stands out as significant because it "marked a departure in the treatment of the negro as stage material."[41] Although the piece is not extant, one can glean a sense of the play from James Metcalfe's description of a Brooklyn production in *Life*:

> The characters were impersonated by white artists, but the story dealt with a domestic tragedy, the parties to which were all negroes. The same plot might have been used powerfully if its *dramatis personae* had been represented as white persons in conventional surroundings. Located in the Black Belt and its characters credible natives of that district, it gained different sidelights, different motives and different trends of thought, which made it more than usually interesting as a play and gave its scenes and dénouement a vastly increased force.[42]

Metcalfe points out that this "interest-compelling little tragedy," along with several other plays "dealing with purely American conditions," demonstrated that American dramatists no longer had to go outside of the country to find dramatic topics. "The racial problems arising in the new conditions of this country should furnish valuable material to replace the exhausted social perplexities which we have imported from abroad to supply our stage with dramatic situations." Stated Metcalfe: "'His Own' opens up possibilities of comedy and tragedy to the life of the negroes, viewed from the inside. ... Its strength as a play is evidence ... that the American playwriter [sic] has no need to seek abroad or to confine himself to the conventional to find novel and powerful dramatic material."[43]

It is not known if the play was actually ever produced with an all-black cast. A February 1913 notice in an Indianapolis paper announced: "A drama of negro life, 'His Own,' written by Evelyn Greenleaf Sutherland, will be presented this season by Louise Randolph, late art director of the Marlowe Players in Chicago. The characters in the play are all negroes."[44] In 1926, the play was used as a curtain raiser by the Lena Ashwell Players at the Century Theatre in Bayswater, England; however, the program suggests that rather than being "a drama of negro life," the play was interpreted as a southern drama with white characters, affirming Metcalfe's opinion that the plot could be applicable to any race. [45]

SUTHERLAND'S EARLY FULL-LENGTH PLAYS
FT. FRAYNE, BEAUCAIRE, AND JOAN O' THE SHOALS

An interesting passage in Julia Ward Howe's discussion of Sutherland notes the dramatist's fascination for the military: "Many of Mrs. Sutherland's writings have dealt with army life, and she has many friends in both the army and navy. She has spent much time 'in garrison.' At one time when some especially dear friends were stationed at Fort Warren, she had a den fitted up for herself in one of the old casemates which was used as a prison during the Civil War."[46] Thus, it naturally followed that Sutherland should choose a military theme for her first full-length play, *Fort Frayne*, collaborating with Emma Sheridan Fry and Captain Charles King, a published author who still held the rank of Adjutant General in the Wisconsin militia.[47] *Fort Frayne* was written around 1893, but due to Sutherland's illness, could not be completed at that time. King, in the meantime, secured his collaborators' permission and turned *Fort Frayne* into a novel that became serialized in the *New York Times* in 1895. The authors then reconstructed the story as a play, receiving an initial showing by the Actors' Society of America in New York in March 1897; the presentation at the Broadway Theatre included well-known actors, Mary Shaw, J. H. Gilmour, W. J. Le Moyne, James A. Herne, and Minnie Dupree.[48]

After this round-about beginning, *Fort Frayne* opened for a run in Chicago at the Schiller Theater on August 30, 1897. Advertisement for the play in the *Chicago Tribune* boasted: "Introducing the NEW DRAMATIC STOCK COMPANY in the Original Production of a New American Play, FORT FRAYNE"— prices for seats ranged from 25 cents to $1.[49] The significance of this production was the fact that the new dramatic stock company, headed by Miss Proctor Otis, was not under the control of the syndicate and was opening its first play in Chicago. It did, however, afford a good opportunity for Charles King and Evelyn Greenleaf Sutherland, who rehearsed the play themselves, to see their play realized on stage. A few days before *Fort Frayne* opened, a *Chicago Tribune* writer described Sutherland as "a woman of immense energy and nervous force; her training as a dramatic critic for twelve years has given her a keen eye for stage effect, and her knowledge of garrison life is almost as extensive and accurate as Captain King's."[50] Relating that Sutherland was pleased with the cast and the way the production was going, the writer· added revealingly: "which is saying a good deal for a playwright who has not been able to exercise her choice in any single direction."[51]

Briefly, the play concerns Helen Daunton, whose "scapegrace" husband has died somewhere in Mexico, or so she believes. Helen is in love with Captain Leale at Fort Frayne, when her despicable husband turns up alive as a private in his father's old regiment. The melodrama centers on how the husband is eventually "removed" and how Helen "finally achieves happiness."[52] At the end of Act Two, Helen describes the abuse she suffered from her husband, relating that the death of her child was caused by a blow from its drunken father. A critic in the *Chicago Daily* claimed that Miss Proctor Otis's "most important scene [was] conceived in such bad taste that her whole performance [was] necessarily somewhat tainted." Apparently, he objected to the realistic gestures the actress used in her description of the tragic event: "Even supposing that the time and place were suitable for such a revelation, we cannot possibly conceive a woman telling her story in such a manner. The suggestions of the child's presence at her breast was inexpressibly distasteful, and was due, it is hoped to the misguided ideas of those who conducted the rehearsals rather than the intelligence of the actress."[53]

By the second week a number of cuts and alterations improved the play—"the changes have performed miracles," stated the *Chicago Tribune*.[54] The *Tribune* also noted that during the second week "General Wheeler and staff and several officers of the Wisconsin National Guard occupied boxes at the Schiller" one night.[55] By the fourth week, cooler weather brought in larger audiences, making the four-week Chicago run at the Schiller Theatre a moderate success. Although the play apparently had a showing on the West Coast, nothing much came of *Fort Frayne* following this initial production.

Evelyn Greenleaf Sutherland, however, experienced far more success with her next full-length collaboration. When Booth Tarkington, a young novelist from Indiana, published his novelette, *Monsier Beaucaire*, in 1900, actor Richard Mansfield lost no time in securing the stage rights.[56] Mansfield then charged Booth Tarkington and Sutherland with dramatizing the novel for the stage, intending the play to be a companion piece to Stephen Phillips' *Herod*. However, the public reception of *Beaucaire* was so enthusiastic that he gave the play top billing for the season. Interesting to note is that when *Beaucaire* opened in New York at the Herald Square Theatre in December 1901, Adolf Klauber pointed out in the *New York Times*, "no less than seven 'dramatic versions' of stories of novels" were showing that week.[57] Indeed, with the ready-made publicity of best sellers, it is no wonder that theatre managers favored dramatized novels.

Tarkington and Sutherland decided to write a story different from the novel, keeping only some of the situations and, of course, the central character. The play concerns "Beaucaire," the Duke of Orleans, cousin of the king of France, who has gone to England disguised as a barber to escape a political and loveless marriage. At Bath he falls in love with the lovely Lady Carlyle, and his attempts to win her hand without disclosing his identity bring him into many difficulties, including sword play. The dashing lead role in *Beaucaire* offered opportunities for an actor to speak French, engage in sword fights, and play the amorous lover. The initial review in the *New York Times* related that although Mansfield as an actor "must always command respectful attention," because of his high ideals and "technical excellence," that his impersonation of Beaucaire disclosed "nothing new in his accomplishments." On stage the character of Beaucaire, stated the critic, "is a somewhat anemic personage, who talks very prettily, dances very gracefully, and fights very recklessly."[58] Nevertheless, most audience members enjoyed Mansfield's performance; after opening night at a trial run at the Colonial Theatre in Boston, Beulah Marie Dix recorded in her theatre journal: "A workmanlike performance. Rather thin, rather tenuous . . . but altogether charming. The spirit of the book was kept in character and atmosphere, and there was a finish to the phrasing. Of course it was all Mansfield (Beaucaire) and nothing else, but that was enough."[59]

Although the play provided Mansfield with a profitable season, some critics pointed out that its chief fault lie in the fact that the playwrights had stretched Tarkington's short novel into five acts. Indeed, James Metcalfe considered the piece "too attenuated" and that Mansfield had too little to do that was "worth serious consideration."[60] William Archer felt the English production had "considerable merit," but also pointed out its "willful dragging-out" of the plot toward the end and found no "necessity for 'Monsieur Beaucaire's persistence in keeping his secret even from Lady Mary Carlyle." However, the English critic did state that the play was "moderately entertaining" and described his "little thrill of emotion" when Beaucaire's identity becomes revealed at the end of the play. "The mere imagination of this sudden and splendid reverse of fortune, helped out by the roll of the high-sounding titles, gave me a moment of real, undeniable pleasure, and set me wondering once more at the persistence, even in the most rugged and case-hardened bosoms, of the relish for romance."[61] Where Mansfield's impersonation of Beaucaire tended to be "studied," English actor Lewis Waller enlivened the role, playing it with "a lightness, an ease, a humour which [made] the character really charming."[62] Tarkington and Sutherland's play ran 316 performances in the first London showing, and returned for nine London revivals, remaining widely popular with English audiences. By the time Waller brought *Monsieur Beaucaire* to New York in 1912, the English actor had played Beaucaire "nearly 900 times in London" as one of the best parts in his repertoire.[63]

Sutherland's *Joan o' the Shoals*, her only produced full-length play written sans collaborator, resulted in box office failure and perhaps some hard-earned lessons for its creator. The play attracted the interest of Henrietta Crosman, who rose to stardom in 1900 playing Nell Gwyn in George C. Hazleton's *Mistress Nell*. While touring in the fall of 1901 with *Mistress Nell* and *As You Like It*, Crosman began rehearsing *Joan o' the Shoals* with Sutherland traveling along to aid with rehearsals and make revisions.[64] *Joan o' the Shoals* "takes place before the Revolution and the scenes are laid in the New Hampshire village of Portsmouth and the Isle of Shoals lying off the entrance to the harbor." It concerns a "free-born race of seafaring people, who have never acknowledged either the sovereignty of the British King nor the Colonial Congress, with whom Joan's lot has been cast."[65]

Joan Seastrawn is an "untamed" fisherwoman who lives with her grandmother and "not only helps her shy local minister court the young lady of his dreams, but also lands for herself an exiled British peer" (Henry Woodruff) from the Court of King Charles II.[66] As related by the *New York Sun* critic, a dramatic snag between the latter two lovers occurs when, because of Joan's free and liberated manner, he "couples a declaration of love with a suggestion that they may be intimate without marriage. Her grief at that is heartbreaking, but her resentment is energetic. She [harangues] him so spiritedly that he feels his guilt and becomes an honest suitor." The critic declared this moment to be the play's "best dramatic incident among many that are not sufficiently correlative for the purpose of the drama."[67] Heightened interest during the play occurs when Joan opposes the riled fishermen who extinguish a beacon with the intention of wrecking a ship and she relights the lamp and saves the ship.

Because of considerable changes in the script during rehearsals and possibly bad advice from management, the play went into production with a number of deficiencies.[68] Although reception was cordial during Philadelphia's two-week run, New York reviewers panned the play. The *New York Times* critic, for example, felt that there were too many disparate threads in *Joan o' the Shoals*, and that the playwright had included "feeble, cardboard lords and ladies who pose in popular novels of Colonial times" and who were "as pointless, witless, and childish as possible."[69] Described as a "quaint tale of the sea," the play contained a few shore scenes with "fisherfolk," but, stated the critic, these scenes are "enacted by people who have the sea neither in their action nor their speech. Even Mrs. Crosman does not savor of the ocean." What is more, claimed the critic, Crosman's acting was forced, "too noisy and strenuous throughout."[70] The *Sun*'s ambiguous description of the character of Joan, may reflect some of the inherent problems in the play, as well: "Her ready ingenuity, cool courage and sincere devotion made her a character at once familiar and unusual, theatric and naturalistic, old in a general way but new in particulars."[71] The opening night audience, initially enthusiastic and "kindly disposed toward Miss Crosman," became by the end of the evening, "tired, disappointed and in a derisive mood."[72]

Unfortunately, *Joan o' the Shoals* did not get an opportunity to develop through production as did most Broadway productions. Henrietta Crosman announced two days after the February 3rd opening at the Republic Theatre that she had decided to revive *Mistress Nell* the following Monday, giving *Joan o' the Shoals*— according to Sutherland—"no opportunity to win a verdict, favorable or otherwise, from the New York theatergoing public."[73] Sutherland wrote a letter to the *Dramatic Mirror* refuting claims that she was "disgusted" with the reception of the New York press; she also denied reports that she had refused to make changes in the script, when, in fact, she had made many changes suggested to her by the management team, some against her better judgment. Concluded Sutherland: "I respect the laws of our common craft too deeply to in any public utterance resent the judgment my brother critics may see fit to express on my work, and that I hold it not the least of an author's privilege to learn from those competent to teach, where the faults and weaknesses of her work lie, both before and after that work has been given to the public."[74] Indeed, despite her disappointment, Sutherland quite likely gained valuable experience through the production process of *Joan o' the Shoals*.

BEULAH MARIE DIX, NOVELIST AND PLAYWRIGHT

Born December 25, 1876, Beulah Marie Dix was the younger of two daughters of Maria (Mason) Dix and Henry Dix, a factory foreman. An article in *The Chelsea Evening Record*, ca.1932, states that she was remembered as a somewhat "retiring and very charming girl, who often wore a cap like those worn by the boys in their battalion drill."[75] Dix's daughter, Evelyn Scott, writes that when she was young Beulah wished she had been a boy and rejected "girlish things."[76] By all accounts, Dix was very bright and studious. In early grades she would take an apple to school and during recess, while other students socialized outside, she would "make a dash for the dictionary and stand there all during recess, munching her apple and pouring over the dictionary."[77] Dix related one of her most vivid memories of growing up in Chelsea was walking down Washington Avenue to school and "fishing a few copper pennies" out of her purse to buy a paper in order to read the latest developments in the Sawtell trial, a sensational 1889 murder case. "That's the sort of blood-thirsty brat I was, she confessed. "No wonder I took later to writing swashbuckling novels!"[78]

Although her father could scarcely afford tuition, Beulah entered Radcliffe in 1893 at the age of 16, assuming she would pay her father back though teaching—for women in the 1890s "the respectable and logical result of a degree."[79] During her first three years at Radcliffe she boarded in Cambridge with relatives, after which time her father changed jobs and the family moved from Chelsea to Cambridge.[80] Always an avid student of history, Dix had early success during undergraduate years selling college themes and short stories to journals like *Lippincott's*, *Short Stories*, and *Godey's Magazine*. Dix's titles reflect her interest in historical themes: "The Cavalier's Sister" (1900), "A Daughter of the Puritans"(1902), "A Dead Man's Boots" (1899), "The Honor of a Gentleman" (1898), "The Measure of Justice" (1897), and "A Spoil of War" (1897).[81] She graduated from Radcliffe with an A.B. degree in 1897, "summa cum laude, with highest honors in English and the George B. Sohier Prize given for the best thesis... offered by a candidate for English honors," "winning even over Harvard graduates."[82] She followed the next year with her master's degree in English.

Theatrical opportunities at Radcliffe encouraged the budding playwright by providing venues in which to produce student plays. Her first play in 1895, *The Wooing of Mistress Widdrington*, was set in the period of knickerbockers to circumvent a school rule that forbade girls to wear pants upon the stage. Stated Dix: "We tried camouflaging the male characters with long overcoats or gymnasium bloomers. However, in the summer of 1895 some forward-looking spirits suggested that we write our own plays, and synchronously came the brilliant thought: why not lay them in a knickerbockered period and thus solve the vexatious problem of male costume!"[83] After several productions with the Radcliffe student theatrical club, The Idlers, as well as the Cambridge Dramatic Club, Dix presented her first full-length play upon the Idler stage, *Ye Lustie Man of Wessagussett*. Another "costume play" followed in 1899, *To Serve for Meat and Fee*." Both works later served as material for full-length plays written with Sutherland.

In 1896 when the Walter Baker Company offered Dix $15 to publish her play *Cicely's' Cavalier*, she sought the advice of Professor George Pierce Baker.[84] "I remember how kind he was in going over the manuscript of an unknown student, and how helpful were his suggestions upon sundry other dramatic scripts that he encouraged me to bring to him."[85] Along with Professor Baker's advice and encouragement, Dix found in Radcliffe a stage, fellow actors, and "a small but very friendly audience, whose approval engendered in the embryonic playwright confidence and the courage to go on. I fancy I should have written books, even if I had not gone to Radcliffe, but I do not believe I should have written plays, if I had not found a little stage that demanded plays. I did my bit to supply that demand."[86]

Throughout her writing career, Dix tackled several genres including novels for both younger readers and adults, with many of her most enduring works set in the seventeenth century. Dix's novels reflect a proclivity for historical accuracy and for themes centered upon war, military matters and settings that are generally more "masculine" than those usually dealt with by women of her generation. In her second year at Radcliffe, she became "keenly interested in the period of the Cavaliers and Roundheads and the battles between King and Parliament" and began writing a novel with a young red-headed hero; later, while studying for her Master's Degree during the week, she worked on weekends to complete the novel. After more than one rejection of the novel, Macmillan published it in March 1899. Originally intended as a boy's book, *Hugh Gwyeth, Roundhead Cavalier* was, according to a reviewer in the *New York Saturday Review*, "so strong in its description, so ingenious in its incidents, and so exciting in its situations that it is rightly rated as a novel." The reviewer commented on both Dix's gender and her youth: "It is a rather extraordinary fact that one of the successful works of fiction of a season should have been written by a young woman barely twenty-two years of age and just out of college. It seems the more extraordinary when we consider that it is the peculiarly masculine story of *Hugh Gwyeth, the Roundhead Cavalier*."[87] Indeed, another reviewer stated of Dix's writing in 1901: "her stories have spirit and 'go' in their incidents, her style is virile and stirring."[88]

In 1932 Dix stated that she had written about thirty books in all: "some novels, some juveniles, some historical, some modern. Paradoxically, the books that have lived longest and are best known are my historical juveniles, such as 'Merrylips' and 'Soldier Rigdale,' and 'Little Captive Lad.' They have gone through many editions and entertained successive generations of children."[89] Indeed, Dix's most popular novel with little girls was *Merrylips*, published in 1906, featuring an eight-year-old girl as the central character. The story's heroine is Sybil Wenner, known as "Merrylips," a nickname bestowed by her father. Merrylips is quite the tomboy and detests everything feminine; she wants to go off to the war with her brothers who are staunch supporters of the King. When she gets into trouble for fighting with her younger brother, her mother sends her to stay with godmother Lady Sybil to improve her manners and decorum. As it turns out, godmother is involved in Royalist activities and must flee when Roundhead troops arrive. Due to becoming ill, Merrylips cannot travel and stays behind as an in-house captive of the Roundheads. After she is rescued by her older brother, she takes on the disguise of a boy and goes through a series of adventures before eventually reuniting with her family. Once she has arrived at home after all her experiences as a boy, Merrylips decides that being a girl is not such a bad thing, after all. Dix dedicated *Merrylips* "to every little girl who has wished for an hour to be a little boy." Reviewers were enthusiastic, if not ecstatic, including a writer in the *New York Sun* who stated: "If the tale is not read with deep interest by a multitude of little girls we shall be greatly mistaken." Since *Merrylips* was regularly reissued between 1906 and 1951, it appears the reviewer was not mistaken.

Beulah Marie Dix met her husband, George Flebbe, a German immigrant, through the Sutherlands. George Flebbe studied at Munich, Oxford, and Göttingen, where he met Allan Rowe, the Sutherlands' adopted son. When George left Germany for Boston to take a position as junior partner in a book firm, he became a part of the circle of young people who frequented the Sutherland home. Evelyn Scott relates that once George Flebbe arrived, "Mother suddenly stopped acting like everybody's younger brother, seventeenth-century type."[90] Dix and Flebbe were married in 1910. They lived in Brookline, Massachusetts, where their only child was born, Evelyn Greenleaf Flebbe, named for their dear friend, Mrs. Sutherland.

For a number of years, from 1889 through 1916, Dix kept theatre journals in which she recorded impressions of plays.[91] In her journals, one gains an impression of an ardent theatregoer with a critical eye toward plays and actors—far more studious than a typical "star-struck" matinee girl of the period. In May 1892, for example, sixteen-year-old Beulah recorded seeing Alexander Salvini in *Monte Cristo* in Boston with "Papa, Momma, and Jaime"; she wrote that the production was not as good as Salvini's production of *The Three Guardsmen* and "the actors were not very enthusiastic." "A fearful and wonderful production," she wrote in 1899 of *The King's Musketeer* in which E. H. Sothern was "of course, interesting" as D'Artagnan. More often than not, she wrote exactly what she thought, as shown in her assessment of well-known actress Virginia Harned in *The Song of the Sword*: "Miss Harned excruciating. A snub-faced, fat woman, intolerable in all her gowns, but especially in her boy's clothes which suggested burlesque."[92] In the spring of 1901 in Boston, Dix went with a friend to see Sarah Bernhardt and Coquelin in the French production of *L'Aiglon*. She found the French style of acting strange—"they stood still and waved their arms, then said and did something. . . the action and speech never coincided as in our English work." Even so, Dix wrote favorably of Bernhardt: "Graceful, a fascinating face, perfect self-control and restraint and power of expression, the one voice in the world."[93] Of David Belasco's production of Charles Klein's *The Music Master*, she recorded: "Rotten. Material for a 20-minute turn stretched over 2 hours and 1/2." Upon seeing *Hedda Gabler* in 1906, Dix responded: "Mrs. [Minnie Maddern] Fiske played the first three acts as comedy, waiting for laughs—Heaven knows why! The audience gave them to her. A full house—but mostly people who came because it was "the thing" and were much bewildered by what they saw." On the other hand, she thoroughly enjoyed Barrie's *Peter Pan*, calling it: "A very exquisite fancy, kept to its own light level throughout. A memory of childhood, that brought laughter near to tears. Maud Adams was delightful—fantastic, light elvish, sexless, at times even boyish. She gave a remarkable performance such as no other English speaking actress could equal."[94] Overall, Dix's journals and her candid impressions of theatre of her day offer interesting and entertaining reading for anyone interested in the era.

DIX'S ANTIWAR PLAYS: *ACROSS THE BORDER* AND *MOLOCH*

Dix wrote few significant plays on her own following the death of her friend and collaborator, Evelyn Greenleaf Sutherland. Two notable works, however, are *Across the Border* (1914) and *Moloch* (1915), both which effectively depict the horrors of war. With little sentimentality and sensationalism, Dix showed the senselessness of war and effectively demonstrated how human nature becomes altered, even perverted during wartime. *Across the Border* and *Moloch* were written and produced before America's 1917 entry into World War I, but the war in Europe was certainly a topic occupying many Americans; an article in the *New York Tribune* in September 1915, for example, reported that "more than ten thousand people were turned away" at the opening of *Motion Pictures of German Battlefields*.[95] In addition, being married to a German must have greatly contributed to Dix's interest in the war and her pacifistic beliefs.

Across the Border was one of four one-act plays presented on November 24, 1914, by Holbrook Blinn at New York's Princess Theatre—a small house that began as a "home for one-act plays."[96] Only one of the plays was a comedy, *Nellie*, by George Ade, but critics seemed to find the more somber tone of the evening a welcome change from usual light-hearted fare. Of the four plays, Dix's *Across the Border* was the longest and appears to have received the most attention and praise. Hector Turnbull in the *Tribune* stated: "'Across the Border' is a real achievement. It is one of the few pleas for peace that touch both the heart and the intellect at the same time. And by virtue of its remarkable blending of stark realism with extravagant fancy it strikes home in a fashion that defies analysis."[97] Although *Across the Border* was last on the program, the *New York*

Times called the piece "the first in importance," deeming it "as elaborate and ambitious a work as it has fallen to the Princess to present since this small playhouse opened its doors."[98]

Dix placed the action of the play in a non-specified country, explaining in both the published version and the program: "The people in the play speak English, but they are no more meant to be English than they are meant to be Austrian, French, German or Russian."[99] Four episodic scenes take place in abstract locales: The Hut in the Wood, the Place of Quiet, the Place of Winds, and the Field Hospital. The play opens in a hut where soldiers are pinned down by enemy forces. The junior lieutenant volunteers to attempt to reach reinforcements and slips out after giving his fellow soldiers the last of his supplies and rifle; after a while, the soldiers listen helplessly to distant gunshots, which signal he did not make it through the enemy line.

The scene that follows is somewhere "across the border" where the Junior Lieutenant is now in another realm—a warm and inviting atmosphere with flowers, a warm hearth, a starry sky, and "gentlefolk who have chosen the simple ways of peasants."[100] The Master of the House (Blinn) serves as a guide for the young man; The Girl appears, as does The Old Woman, The Little Boy, The Woman with the Baby, and The Dark Man, who restrains the combative Lieutenant when he draws his revolver. These simple folk question the Lieutenant's conviction that he and his countrymen are "saving humanity" by engaging in war with their enemies. In his defense, the Lieutenant insists: "We do not kill unless we are forced to. As I told you, we are the most civilized of nations. In proof of that, we have the greatest army that the world has ever seen." War, continues the young soldier, has come about because of the "outrageous actions of other nations" that are "jealous" because "my country is so rich and enlightened."[101] But when the officer gradually realizes that he is, in fact, dead, and asks to stay in this peaceful place, the others turn from him because, as The Girl states: "The smell of blood—it clings!"[102]

When the Lieutenant continues defending his actions and his country, the guide takes him to The Place of Winds where the harsh coldness and sounds of war finally penetrate his consciousness. Like Virgil in Purgatory, now the Lieutenant "hears the wails and awful cries of the battle" and sees "the fearful wreckage of war's bestial work."[103] Realizing the errors of his ways, he asks the Master of the House for an opportunity to return to "the other side" to convince someone, if only one person, of the senselessness of war and killing. Back in a field hospital, dying on a cot, he tries to communicate with The Surgeon, The Orderly, The Man Who Prays, The Man Who Curses, and even his Senior Lieutenant. Although he is unable to make anyone listen to his insights about war, he has attempted to redeem himself and can now join The Girl in The Place of Quiet.

The *New York Times* described *Across the Border* as "a voice raised in the theatre against the monstrous horror and infamy of war." Burns Mantle in the *Chicago Tribune* called it "an impressive combination of stark realism and poetic fancy."[104] The *New York Herald* commented favorably on the play and the production as a whole, however, the critic summed up: "as an evening's entertainment" the piece was so gruesome "that it makes General Sherman's description of Europe's present pastime sound pale and uninteresting."[105] The leanness of Dix's writing, the expressionistic aspects of the play, as well as the universality of her theme combine to make *Across the Border* seem quite modern and applicable to any period.

Less than a year later, Dix earned mixed reviews for *Moloch*, her full-length play produced at the New Amsterdam Theatre. In *Moloch* Dix showed war as not only senseless, but a force of evil— the word "moloch" used metaphorically to stand for a god of war (or devil) who exacts a terrible tribute to those who follow his ways. In this work Dix did not hold back in her depiction of man's inhumanity to man, creating scenes where soldiers torture prisoners and kill townspeople; Robert (Holbrook Blinn) the central character, actually shoots a young soldier because he will not fight. As in *Across the Border*, there are no specified countries, other than "our people" and "the foreigners," but the play is more realistic, containing a prologue, three acts, and an epilogue.

Moloch centers on a loving and close-knit family—Robert; his wife, Katherine; their young son, Roland; his mother, Lydia; his uncle, the Old Professor; and his brother and sister, Basil and Gertrude. The Prologue establishes the characters within their "shabby, homelike" country-house and the warm relationship of family members. Also revealed is that Robert's younger sister Gertrude is admired by Philip, a doctor working in a nearby laboratory; although Philip works to seek a cure for cancer through his medical research, he is nevertheless regarded as a "foreigner." At the end of the Prologue, Philip and Gertrude make it known they are betrothed, but war breaks out between their two countries and now Philip is viewed as an outcast—the enemy.[106]

Dix demonstrates how war quickly divides friends and families and destroys homes. The able-bodied men go off to serve in the army and the women left behind have their home commandeered by the enemy. The ever-maternal Katherine feels sorry for a young Lieutenant in charge and shows him kindness by encouraging him to rest in the same room as her son. Gertrude learns that the officer is a cousin of Philip's and begins penning a letter for him to deliver. But when a Corporal comes in to check on his commanding officer, he discovers in the inner room the dead Lieutenant with his throat cut. A frightened Roland reveals that it was their servant Martha, distraught over the loss of her own family members, who killed the officer; the soldiers then drag Martha out of the house and execute her, order the family to leave, and burn the house.

Life worsens for Robert and Katherine as their only child dies and they both become occupied with the war effort—he is a colonel in the infantry and she a Red Cross nurse. Katherine comes to a farmstead occupied by Robert's company where they are questioning an enemy pilot. Before long, it becomes clear that the badly burned and blinded pilot is actually Philip. Left alone with Katherine, he begs her to give him "medicine" that will put him to sleep and out of his misery. Her sense of humanity and friendship with the man motivate Katherine to grant him his request. Although the Epilogue unites the surviving family members in their old home, there is no tidy finish to this play, for yet another war is declared where allies fight among themselves and soldiers now tramp by outside on their way to new skirmishes. "Moloch is hungry still," declares Katherine. "If only they'd stop that damned noise!" Robert says. "Marching—marching—marching—" states Katherine as the "March-out is at its fortissimo."[107]

One of the producers of *Moloch*, George C. Tyler, writes in his memoir that for a while it appeared the play was "going to be a real success." Before coming to New York, *Moloch* opened at Powers' Theatre in Chicago, "the most prominent house in town, but of shaky, old-fashioned wooden construction." Tyler describes: "When the machine guns of the big battle scene started barking away under the stage in that rattly old theatre, they jarred every seat in the house and sent electric shocks up audience's spines. It was a tremendous realistic effect—people came out of it as white as sheets—and it bade fair to make *Moloch* a sensation."[108] In New York, however, the play opened in the New Amsterdam theatre, "a concrete-built house that an earthquake couldn't jar, and the machine-guns weren't any more exciting than so many Chinese firecrackers." Although the play did run for a month, the end result, according to Tyler, was that audiences found the play "ungodly depressing" and far too pacifistic when "pacifism wasn't the intellectual fad then that's it's become since."[109]

In *Moloch* Dix accomplished her purpose of preaching the "cult of peace by showing the horrors of war," and although some critics had favorable comments, others argued that the playwright did not explain *why* her characters were engaging in war. For example, The *Bookman* pointed out that in *Moloch*: "We behold a nation suffering all the afflictions of frightfulness; but we are never told the reason why it chooses so to suffer. Yes some reason there must be. Men do not die for nothing; but only for an idea, whether truthfully conceived or not, that lives within their souls and is destined to survive the darkest iniquity of suffering. This is the truth of war; and, with this truth eclipsed, the facts mean nothing."[110] As an entertainment, *Moloch* failed to draw in crowds, but it certainly left an impression on those who did see it. Retrospectively, a 1940 article in the *Chicago Tribune* referred to *Moloch* as "the most nerve-wracking play we have ever seen" and "medicine too strong for pleasure seekers."[111] Another article in the *Boston Transcript* reflecting on Radcliffe playwrights referred to Dix's *Moloch* as being "so far from 'pretty-pretty' that people were carried out in a faint after nearly every performance! Mrs. Flebbe was called 'coarse' and 'hysterical' for being the first to get away from the idea of war as a chocolate soldier musical comedy. Today, rather belatedly, many critics say her 'Moloch' was the best thing in America to come out of the World War."[112] Indeed, as a playwright Dix made her mark with *Moloch*, demonstrating that women could tackle so difficult and unpleasant a topic as war. She continued writing antiwar themes with other venues such as one-act plays for the American School Peace League, but *Across the Border* and *Moloch* remain Dix's most controversial antiwar plays.[113]

SUTHERLAND AND DIX'S FIRST SUCCESSFUL COLLABORATION: *ROSE OF PLYMOUTH TOWN* WITH MINNIE DUPREE

Among Sutherland's letters, a note dated April 13, 1901, from Beulah Marie Dix indicates that their first collaborative project might very well have been an adaptation of Dix's third novel, *The Making of Christopher Ferringham*. Although Dix states that she had made a synopsis of the first act and found it read "quite prettily," it does not appear the play came to fruition—no extant copy is listed among Dix's inventory of her papers in the Knight Library at the University of Oregon.[114] As it turned out, their first produced collaboration was *A Rose o' Plymouth Town*, an adaptation of Dix's college play, *Ye Lustie Man of Wessagussett*.[115] Despite the setting of Plymouth and pilgrims, the authors claimed there was nothing historical about this romantic comedy, "but the atmosphere and the Indians."[116]

Rose o' Plymouth Town concerns Rose de la Noye (Minnie Dupree), an impetuous Huguenot who, with her brother Philippe (Douglas Fairbanks), lives in the household of Miles Standish in Plymouth, New England, in 1622. In the first act, Rose meets Garrett Foster (Guy Bates Post), "a well-favored young dare-devil of twenty," who lunges headlong through the open window after tossing in an armful of corn he has just stolen. When the young man begs her to hide him from John Margeson, the town constable, she impulsively does so. Garrett Foster, as it turns out, is one of "those lusty men of Master Weston's," staying in the colony "till they plant their settlement at Wessagusett."[117] Rose and Garrett begin a flirtation as she gives him bread, but when family members come in, he hides behind a high-backed wooden bench, a settle, near the fireplace. Amusing moments follow when the family gathers at the dining table for dinner and Rose secretly interacts with Garrett off in the corner. When his presence becomes revealed to everyone, Rose claims it was she who stole the corn, forcing Garrett to speak up and admit to the crime. A stern Captain Standish passes punishment "that Garrett shall sit on the settle by Rose until the corn is roasted and he has eaten it."[118] In the second act there is a duel between Garrett and Margeson, who has been courting Rose, during which her brother Philippe, becomes seriously wounded. Rose and Garrett quarrel in the third act and he tells her he is going back to England, so out of spite, she accepts Margeson's proposal. Garrett does not go to England, but appears at the Standish House (fourth act) to confront Rose, prompting Margeson to follow with a warrant for his arrest; Standish insists that Garrett be "paroled" to remain inside the Standish house. But when Indians attack the settlement, Garrett slips out of the house and holds off Indians at a breach in the stockade until others come to help. Later when everyone learns of Garrett's heroic act, it becomes known that Margeson actually ran for the woods during the attack; the discovery of Margeson's cowardice releases Rose from her pledge to Margeson, so she can accept Garrett, the man she really loves.

The part of Rose de la Noye was created for Minnie Dupree, who embraced it as her first leading role in a play.[119] The *New York Sun* stated that the playwrights "had given the new star every possible opportunity to show herself most agreeably... they have placed her as roguish, hoyden, coquettish, vivacious, yet possessing a depth of feeling beneath it all."[120] Dupree was about twenty-seven when she tackled the role of the teenage Rose, but her personality and diminutive frame contributed to a convincing performance— she was called "little Minnie Dupree" by the press. New York audiences were familiar with the actress from a number of earlier supporting roles. As was the case in many "star vehicles," the star received more favorable comments than did the vehicle. The measured commentary of the *New York Times*, related that *A Rose o' Plymouth Town* did not "prove to be quite as even and plausible as Miss Dupree's acting." The reviewer felt that the collaborative effort "proved to be a novel wrenched into theatric form," citing Dix's ability in writing seventeenth-century novels and Sutherland's "talent for theatrical effects." But he goes on to state that the strength of the play was a number of character sketches as seen in Dupree's Rose, as well as Augustus Cook's "humorous, racy and virile" Miles Standish and Mrs. Sol Smith's portrayal of Standish's aunt, Resolute Story.[121] When complaining about how uneventful it was living in Plymouth, for instance, Aunt Story shocks Barbara Standish by declaring: "I came to your little Plymouth in the hope that I might find in the wilderness one last new sensation; and for a new sensation I would go to—[Rises excitedly, points downward.]"[122]

When the play tried out in the playwrights' hometown, the *Boston Transcript* called *A Rose o' Plymouth Town* "a very good play; not a play to shiver over, but a well-constructed, well-written, and steadily interesting drama."[123] However, when it moved to New York, drama critics such as the *Herald* did not mince words, calling the play "crude," "insipid," and "infantile."[124] In a lengthy examination of the play in the *New York Times* a week after opening night, John Corbin cited the construction of the play as one of its inherent deficiencies. He managed to belittle the playwrights' gender in saying: "Any competent playwright can construct a plot and situation, but properly to construct the motives and the characters of a play requires nothing short of a dramatist—a man of letters who is also a man of the stage."[125] *A Rose o' Plymouth Town*, nevertheless, served as a respectable first effort for Dix and Sutherland, playing three weeks in New York before touring. Perhaps an Ohio critic summed up the worth of the play best: "The play is not a great one, nor will it place its authors, Beulah Marie Dix and Evelyn Greenleaf Sutherland, on the top rung of the ladder of fame. But it is interesting, bright, clean, pure and affords pleasing diversion for an evening. Mothers may take their daughters and not be afraid to talk of the play afterward, and that is certainly unique in these days."[126]

"COSTUME PLAYS" FOR MARTIN HARVEY:
BREED OF THE TRESHAMS AND *BOY O'CARROLL*

English actor Martin Harvey's first starring tour to America in the fall of 1902 included in his repertory *The Only Way*, Freeman Wills' adaptation of Dickens's *Tale of Two Cities*, in which his impersonation of Sydney Carton was widely acclaimed in England. Describing him as "the only important new-comer," of the season, John Corbin enthused: "Mr. Harvey is a young actor of consummate grace and ideal sentiment, who will be of interest to everybody and may be relied upon to cause a flutter in the dovecote of matinée girls. He has an ideal carriage and handsome brown eyes."[127] When Harvey was playing in Washington, DC, an agent gave him a copy of Dix and Sutherland's *The Breed of the Treshams*. The authors thought him ideal for their central character of "Reresby the Rat." Dix and Sutherland put the name of "John Rutherford" on their script, feeling that the masculine milieu of *The Breed of the Treshams* merited a male pseudonym "better suited to so much leather and steel."[128] Martin Harvey described in his autobiography his initial reaction to *The Breed of the Treshams* as positive, although he did not like killing off the hero at the end, "and quite gratuitously!"

> Yet here in this play was an astute knowledge of "theatre" and (what was much more rare) it was combined in places with "style" of some distinction, *and* a knowledge of English history. These last elements were seldom at that time found in American historical plays; yet this was obviously by an American because of a characteristic element of "grit," which in such work the English generally lacked.[129]

Harvey arranged to meet "John Rutherford" while playing in Ottawa, Canada, "and in walked a pair of very handsome American ladies!" related the actor. Sutherland and Dix accepted the actor's criticisms of the last act and went to work making changes, although agreement did not occur overnight. "It was many a long day before we got this last act shapely and avoided unpardonable tragedy on the one side and mawkish sentimentality on the other," Harvey wrote. The first showing of *The Breed of the Treshams* took place in Newcastle, England, on September 28, 1903, to "instantaneous success."[130]

Set during the English Civil War in 1644, *The Breed of the Treshams* centers on the doings of a swashbuckling, drinking, not altogether scrupulous lieutenant of guards, Reresby, known as "The Rat," stationed with the Royalist garrison at Feversham Castle. He is the illegitimate son of Lord Tresham and half-brother to Cornet Francis Tresham, a newcomer to the company. Reresby holds a hatred of his father, "who has been a *roué* of the worst type," and offers his opinion to that effect, offending young Francis and prompting a duel between the two in which Reresby wounds his opponent.[131] In the outcome, the half-brothers become friends, drawn together by their mutual affection for Margaret Hungerford, Francis Tresham's *fiancée*; Reresby's feelings for Margaret are due to her likeness to another Margaret he once loved. Although he resolves to become a better man in the future, Reresby, as a "soldier of fortune," is involved in treasonable intrigue with Colonel Hungerford (son of Viscount Dorsington and brother to Margaret) in which the colonel plans to give up the town to the army of the Parliament. In the meantime, affairs in the garrison at the castle become exacerbated by the hard-drinking officers and men who mutiny and seek to kill Reresby; the latter saves himself by pretending drunkenness and stalling for the arrival of loyal troops. Later, during a dance at the castle, the charge of treason is pushed forward against Reresby, but despite being tortured, he does not break; ironically, among those who torture him is the real culprit, Colonel Hungerford, but because of Margaret, Reresby does not reveal the truth. Eventually matters are cleared up by Batty (played by Harvey's wife, Nita da Silva), a boy whom Reresby has befriended, who places in the viscount's hands papers proving the real conditions of affairs and implicating his own son, even as they exonerate Reresby. Now brokenhearted, the viscount consents to a marriage between Margaret and Francis Tresham and restores "The Rat's" sword to him.

A cable sent to Evelyn Greenleaf Sutherland from Newcastle after the play's opening, stated: "Tresham's was enthusiastically received. Company called after each act. Is an undoubted success. 3rd needs cutting, 4th changes. Have splendid company. Staging good."[132] Dix and Sutherland traveled to Great Britain the following month to see their play for the first time in Dublin. In her usual terse style Dix wrote in her theatre journal, expressing disappointed in many of the actors. She felt, for instance, that Frank Vernon in the role of Viscount Dorsington was "too ecclesiastical. He played the Pope in *Eternal City* last year, and throughout Act Four excommunicated Reresby. Never for a moment a soldier. In delivery he fulminated." Percy Anstey, who played Clement Hungerford "did sufficiently well. His Clement had no brains, "a . . . fool who was garrulous and scared at the least provocation." In his role of Lieutenant Willoughby, Dix considered Montague Curry, "vile—an effeminate trying to swagger. He gave the effect of a girl in boy's clothes." Milton Rosmer, who played Tresham, "was boyish, ingenuous, but stood badly." Neither was Dix happy with Amy Coleridge in the role of Margaret, who she felt was "too old and her reading falsetto and bad. She did best in II and in IV—Harvey carried her though both scenes, but she was never right to look at." In spite of her dissatisfaction with some cast members, however, she considered most of the cast "flawless," including Mrs. Harvey as Batty, "a bad, hot-tempered and crudely passionate boy." "As to Harvey," stated Dix, "he *was* "Rat" Reresby!"[133] And, indeed, Harvey himself writes of their initial reaction to "their beloved play" as being "rapturous."[134]

Martin Harvey's account of the "evolution" of "Reresby the Rat," however, demonstrates how a character, once turned over to a star actor, can take on a life of its own. Harvey related that initially he did not put a great deal of thought into Reresby or even his costume—as manager/producer of his own production, he paid more attention to characters other than his own. "But Reresby could not long be content with being a mere 'romantic abstraction,'" confessed Harvey in his memoirs.

> He was fretting to come alive. He began to feel his feet when I got an exact reproduction of a pair of seventeenth-century Cavalier boots, which encouraged the gait of a man accustomed to horseback. When Reresby got into a real buff coat, made with proper rider's flare to its skirts, and threw on the plumed hat which he wore hind part before to give his feathers a raffish angle, the man began to live. Thereafter, there was no holding him. [135]

"'The Rat' became like a Callot drawing," recorded Harvey, "with the raffish habits of the stable and the guard room in which he had lived during the Thirty Year's War." [136]

Three years later when Dix and Sutherland returned and saw the play in Edinburgh and then Newcastle, they were, as Harvey related, "shocked to their souls" upon seeing "what Reresby had grown into! They went so far as to say that I had 'prostituted' their play, and threatened to forbid my performances of it." It was Harvey's wife, Nita de Silva, who mediated between her husband and the playwrights, although Harvey does not appear to have altered his interpretation of Reresby. "My wife implored me to moderate my reading of the character, but that was a physical and psychological impossibility. There was his habit of mind and there was the expression of it. The authors had builded [sic] better than they knew. I could not control the man. He was a living creature, independent and most emphatic." [137] Apparently, Dix and Sutherland had other grievances with Harvey's production, as well. Records Dix in her journal of the 1906 production: "A deplorable spectacle. The text garbled and cheapened. Rashleigh's scene in II cut out. A silly unauthorized scene written into IV. The whole vulgarized by word and gesture and over played to the pitch of cheap melodrama."[138] Although Dix now felt that Coleridge was "much improved as Margaret," she found "Batty very tired, careless and feminine." And "Reresby no kin to the part we wrote and Harvey used to play," calling him "a vulgar, drunken . . . buffoon."[139]

But perhaps Martin Harvey better understood the preferences of English audiences than did the creators of Reresby. Critical reception was almost always favorable toward *The Breed of the Treshams* during all four revivals brought to London and during the thirty years the actor played the role throughout the provinces, even after the genre had passed out of favor. Audiences simply enjoyed seeing Martin Harvey in the role. Of his last London showing in 1921, now as Sir John Martin-Harvey, the *London Times* stated that Harvey's "performance of Reresby the Rat must be seen to be appreciated."

> It is impossible to explain the delicious *abandon* of which, single-handed, he slays hordes of his opponents. He puts to flight an army with a couple of pistols, and deals with the stragglers with his sword in the "chop to the right, chop to the left" fashion practised by the brothers Crummles.[140]

The Breed of the Treshams was produced as a film in England, October 1920, with Martin Harvey as Reresby. His last performance of the role on stage was on November 20, 1934, at Brighton.[141]

Martin Harvey took on another play created by Sutherland and Dix which they had originally given to English actor/manager Fred Terry, entitled *The Rapparee Trooper*. Previously, he had received *Matt of Merrymount*, a play dealing with Puritan days in New England, when Terry had already put into rehearsal *The Rapparee Trooper*. But Harvey reveals that the two actors, neither particularly content with their properties, decided to switch. Harvey felt that the "dour surroundings" of the puritans would "fail to attract the sympathy of British audiences," while *The Rapparee Trooper* struck him "as a most charming romantic comedy, verging on farce." The play did not measure up to the success of *The Breed of the Treshams*, but for a while it offered Harvey a completely different character.

The play was christened *Boy O'Carrol* after the principal character following its initial opening in Newcastle in April 1906.[142] The lighter vein of *Boy O'Carrol* reflects a genuine Irish wit which gave Harvey, as well as others in his company, an opportunity to play something other than "heroic sentiment." Brian O'Carrol, an Irish lieutenant in the King's Army during the Parliamentary Wars, has "a very rich brogue, unbounded impudence, and a wonderful power of getting out of difficulties."[143] Essentially, O'Carrol begins this complicated plot by snatching a letter from an officer who boasts of his conquests to fellow officers—the letter is from the officer's cousin, Lettice Yarington, who only asks him for escort for safe passage, but O'Carrol feels compelled to defend the unknown woman's honor and means to return the letter to her. This prompts several challenges between the men, but O'Carrol is hurried away by his captain to take dispatches to Upper Lowcombe. Confused by the names of English towns, O'Carrol, ends up in Lower Upcombe and is taken prisoner by Parliamentarians under the command of Major Yarrington. When the major discovers his niece's letter on Brian, he jumps to the worst conclusions about the devil-may-care Irish soldier and his niece, bundling them both off to a parson for a quick marriage ceremony. Afterward, Brian gets sent to London en route for Barbados and Lettice is packed off to a strict aunt.

It ought to be mentioned that O'Carrol is in love with a bewitching Irish widow, Lady Honoria Vere who has given her heart to Captain Hebblethwaite, "an obtuse, unimaginative, unimpressionable Englishman."[144] Thus, in the third act, it is at Armitage Manor, Lady Honoria's home, where Brian is taken by Roundhead troops and Lettice is discovered by Lady Honoria in an oak chest. Captain Hebblethwaite is now Brian's fellow captive and the two men become handcuffed together in an upper-story wardrobe room—a situation ripe with comic effects as they struggle to get a key from a loaf of bread provided by Lady Honoria. They manage to escape, but Brian later turns up at Marbrook Hall, where Hebblethwaite, Lady Honoria, and Brian's horseboy Paudheen (played by Nita de Silva) have been recaptured. Brian bluffs the major into thinking the house is surrounded with his troops and takes over the house. The curtain falls on Lady Honoria's engagement to Captain Hebblethwaite and on Brian O'Carrol's discovery that he has fallen in love with his own wife.[145]

True to form, Martin Harvey made changes to the original script, some of which Dix noted during the trial performances in Newcastle and Liverpool in April and May 1906. While the play "just managed to steer round disaster at Newcastle," the end of Act Three was rewritten before Liverpool. "The sets were extremely fine and full of imagination and well studied detail," noted Dix with her historian's eye. And although the costuming was excellent on the whole, she felt Brian O'Carrol "looked as if he were bound to a fancy dress ball and Paudheen [the horseboy] was dressed to emphasize every feminine line of the figure." With the opening of the London production, the first night audience was kindly and the "actors were nervous, as was natural to a company that in the main was rawly provincial." Dix's judgment of Harvey was much harsher than any of the reviews, indicating that the authors held a different vision of the central character from that of the actor. She wrote in her journal: "Harvey not good in part. Lacks comedy. Played a dark, melancholy, lowborn, *sexless* youth, at times disagreeably effeminate. His Irish accent extremely bad. Spoke English at times, and at others "slapstick" Irish."[146] Even so, critics remarked favorably on the play and of Harvey's part in it. The *London Times* called it a farce "from beginning to end" providing the audience with familiar incidents where "the natural man cannot help laughing."[147] Quite likely audience members enjoyed seeing Martin Harvey in a role that contrasted with previous ones, demonstrating his versatility in playing the devil-may-care Irishman."[148] Harvey revived the show during a later provincial tour, but found audiences "puzzled at seeing situations which they were accustomed to take seriously treated in this instance in a farcical spirit." While it was never "substantially supported," by English audiences, stated the actor, "I think I have never heard laughter louder or more spontaneous than in certain situations in this play."[149]

MODERATE SUCCESSES IN ENGLISH PRODUCTIONS,
YOUNG FERNALD AND *MATT OF MERRYMOUNT*

American actress Margaret Anglin, wrote to Evelyn Greenleaf Sutherland on 15 March 1906: "I liked the title 'Young Fernald'— but I don't think Mr. Miller did quite so much—I am most interested in the play." Originally titled *The Conversion of Carrick*, this play had an initial American showing in Boston with Anglin and Henry Miller. While reviews of the production seem so-so, other than perhaps some performances on the road, the play did not catch on in the United States. Several years later, however, the same play received new life in England as "A Modern Romantic Comedy" with Evelyn Millard. At the center of the play is Derrick Lowne, a misogynistic writer who wants nothing more than to be alone in his workshop at Moorfield Lodge, in Yorkshire, working on his historical book. When the play opens, however, he must contend with women relatives who have shown up unexpectedly and who insist on tidying up all the time and interfering with his work. When his brother's new wife throws five chapters of his book into the fire, mistaking the pages for trash, Derrick explodes. Thus, the "weeping bride," the "uxorious" husband, and the "meddlesome" aunt take themselves off "in high dudgeon," with the housekeeper tagging along.[150] Derrick, now despondent over his chapters, is left with his brother Robert and his man Bennett in the house. He has forgotten about the newly hired secretary due to arrive; earlier he had been enormously pleased to have found someone as highly qualified and published as young Carey Fernald. The trouble is, when the new secretary arrives through the developing snowstorm, Carey Fernald turns out to be a woman; as described in the script, she is "dressed in substantial tweeds, and a heavy hooded cloak. Her face is alert and vivid, and she radiates an atmosphere of entire womanliness and wholesomeness. There is absolutely no suggestion of the 'strong-minded woman' about her anywhere."[151]

    In the ensuing conversation, Derrick claims he cannot work with her because she is a woman despite Carey's reasonable assertions that she can do the work. When Carey then leaves, against the protests of the men, they follow her to get her in out of the snowstorm. What occurs, of course, is that she is the one who helps Robert return with an injured ankle. Carey's competence takes over, as she prepares an omelet and coffee and then proceeds to stay up all night with Derrick, taking dictation on a chapter of his history, thus convincing him that here is one woman who can do a man's work. The next morning, however, the women-folk return, initially misconstruing Miss Fernald's presence; thereupon, she again flees to escape insult. Derrick, by now a converted misogynist, follows her to the train station, refusing to accept her protests, and takes the train with her to York, presumably for matrimonial purposes. *Young Fernald* contains a simple plot laced with old-fashioned notions that come up against a subtle New Woman theme. Reviewers did not heartily embrace the play, nor did they dwell too long on its deficiencies. However, the production with Evelyn Millard and Norman McKinnel pleased most audiences. Perhaps the *Times* spoke for most who enjoyed the play: "But there is something fresh and tonic in the play, a certain ingenuousness, and plenty of humour, too, of a hearty simple kind. Its people are caricatures rather than characters. The whole affair is artless and, to speak the truth, rather absurd. Yet for its vigour and originality it is better worth seeing than many a deft, smooth, conventional play."[152]

Interestingly, *Matt of Merrymount*, the play which Fred Terry "swapped" for *Boy O'Carrol*, ended up with a longer London run for Terry than Harvey had with *Boy O'Carrol* and provided a role well-suited for him. The playwrights had based this play on the early history of New England, using a real person, Thomas Morton, as their model for Matt, the central character. He is, according to *Era*, "one of those irresistible adventurers who win all hearts by their amiable qualities and their ill-luck and end, of course, by reforming and reinstating themselves." Matt, who calls himself a sailor, is really a gentleman of birth, but has fled England because he thinks he has killed his "rascally" cousin in a duel. The cousin turns up at Edgemouth, ironically, to marry Diantha, the woman Matt now loves. Matt then travels to England to regain his position and fortune, returning to Edgemouth on the eve of Diantha's wedding, in time to save her and "discomfit" his enemy.[153] The *London Times* remarked that the play was "compact of situations," and "received with great approval" in large measure because the role was "precisely suited" to Fred Terry's talents.[154]

THE ROAD TO YESTERDAY WITH MINNIE DUPREE

The Road to Yesterday represents Dix and Sutherland's most successful play in America and quite likely served as their most gratifying theatrical experience; at any rate, this "comedy of fantasy" served as the pinnacle of their collaborative career. The play centers on Elspeth Tyrell, a romantic young American woman visiting London with her Aunt Harriet. Elspeth has passed a whole day visiting sights with her friend, Dolly, and arrives back at the Levensons' studio where they are staying, ecstatic but exhausted. While her cousins and aunt have awaited her return, Will Levenson's American college chum, Jack, arrives and gets coaxed into posing for Will's painting of a seventeenth-century chap in costume as a "Bulwark of England." Early on, conversation touches on aspects of reincarnation from Malena, Will's wife, who jokes that she was a gypsy three hundred years earlier. And Norah, a superstitious Irish maid, comes out with: "Saints 'fend us, Miss Lena! Don't be wishin' me ill—and it Midsummer Eve!" Why not? Malena wonders. "Because, acushla," declares Norah, "wishes wished on Midsummer Eve come true and hold fast—ay, year-fast!—for you can't unwish them till it's Midsummer Eve again!" And it is Norah who emphasizes that Elspeth needs to be careful about wishing she were back in another time, or "she might be takin' the road to yesterday."[155] But Elspeth *does* make the wish to her aunt and Will's friend Adrian: "I've wished all day—Oh, how I've wished!—in the midst of those splendid old-world places, that I was living in them again and was a part of them! . . . And that I might see, right before my eyes, coming to meet me, one of those big, splendid lads coming out of the time when men were men—a lad in doublet and hose." Just then Jack, in costume reenters, seen only by Elspeth, who rises in terror, thinking she is hallucinating, causing Jack to hastily retreat. Overwrought, Elspeth lies down to rest at the urging of the other women.[156]

Once she falls asleep, she travels the passageway of time back three hundred years and finds herself on the porch of an inn where she is assisted by "Reformado" Jack who brings her into the inn. There she sees Aunt Harriet, only it is not her aunt, but Goody Phelps, the landlady and Adrian is now Tomkin the tapster. And she soon learns that she is no longer Elspeth, but Lady Elizabeth Tyrrell, who has run away from her guardian, Kenelm Pawlet, Lord Strangevon, who intends marrying her, despite already being married to Elinore Tylney. It then occurs to Elspeth that she is the heroine in a real romance, so she looks about for her hero. Reformado Jack has some attributes, but, alas, he eats with his fingers and calls for help when attacked by six men. No one understands that she is dreaming except Mother Gillaw, an Irish witch and a thief. Elspeth must hide from Lord Strangevon, so she borrows a suit of boy's clothes from Tomkin; the clothes do not fit nearly as well as they do in books, and so no one is fooled by her disguise. As Strangevon and his men drag her away, she calls to Jack, "If you were a man you would help me!" "If I were six men, I would," he answers and jumps from the window. Thus, at the end of Act II, Elspeth, tearing loose from Kenelm, runs after Jack, yelling: "You coward! Oh, where is the hero? Where is the hero?"[157] Eventually, after more confrontations with the dreaded Lord Strangevon, Elspeth remembers that it is again Midsummer Eve and with all her might she wishes herself back into the studio and the twentieth century. When she wakes up with a start in the studio where Jack Greatorex, still in his model's costume, is opening wine for the midnight supper, she falls into his arms, thankful that he is still alive. Jack gladly goes along with the situation and everyone from their past lives now resolves some issues in the present.

The play was an immediate "hit" when it opened in Chicago with all of the elements working to bring the story to life on stage. Dix's theatre journal confirm that the sets were good and "well studied" and the cast was excellent. Of Minnie Dupree as Elspeth,

Dix wrote that she was "charming, both in comedy and pathos." She concludes with: "Play has made very good and is booked for about 19 weeks." In New York *The Road to Yesterday* opened at the Herald Square Theatre on December 31, 1906, and moved to the Lyric Theatre on April 15, where it was still playing a year after the initial opening. The two aspects of the play most discussed in the reviews were the play and Minnie Dupree, the play often compared with Barrie's *Peter Pan* and the diminutive Dupree compared favorably with Maude Adams. "A play of greater poetic charm and real poetic imagination has not been seen on the boards for many years," declared *Town and Country*.[158] The *New York Evening Post* called it "cleverly imagined, dexterously wrought... and furnishes a liberal measure of genuine entertainment." The *New York Herald* acknowledged the authors' craft: "Miss Beulah Marie Dix and Miss Evelyn G. Sutherland are the authors and, despite their sex, they have contrived cleverly enough to interweave with the daintier phases of the work not a little of the virility and force which is supposed to be, and so often as not, a part of the swashbuckling drama that had a vogue not so long since."[159] Criticism aimed at the play concerned the promise of fantasy and satire at the beginning of the play not fully played out, so that by the end of the third act, the play became romantic melodrama. Critic Alan Dale stated that in *The Road to Yesterday* "Fantasy evaporated very early in the game. Women—practical minded, substantial women—cannot tackle fantasy. It needs the delicate touch of the 'sterner' sex."[160] The *New York Times* reviewer also discussed the lack of satire in the play and noted: "Mrs. Sutherland and Miss Dix tell you at the outset that they are having a joke with serious romantic melodrama, and then proceed to explain the joke in the romantic seriousness of Anthony Hope himself."[161]

Nothing but praise came forth about Minnie Dupree in the role of Elspeth, which fit her splendidly, as she embodied the character in a truthful and natural way. One critic stated that her acting "involves impersonation rather than the more familiar and more easily accomplished exhibition of mere personal idiosyncrasy, which on the part of so many actresses nowadays passes for histrionic accomplishment."[162] Another stated, "It is difficult to describe the charm of Minnie Dupree's acting in the role of Elspeth as it is to indicate the charm of the play."[163] Indeed, the play not only had a long run in New York, it continued in revivals and stock for many years following. In 1925, Cecil B. de Mille paid Dix and Sutherland (posthumously) $15,000 for the film version.

A PUBLIC FAILURE IN THE LILAC ROOM

After the huge success of *The Road to Yesterday*, *The Lilac Room* must have been a real let down for the two collaborators. A comedy used as a starring vehicle for Amelia Bingham, the production ended badly for both playwrights and the actress. Initially, when Dix and Sutherland traveled to see Bingham's staging of *The Lilac Room* at the Academy of Music in Norfolk, Virginia, in the fall of 1906, they were pleased with the play and quite positive. Dix recorded in her journal: "Bingham herself vital, hearty, rather Western, but quite girlish, and really charming in her scenes with the little girl." Dix comments mostly favorably on all the actors and concludes with: "The play started a 7-weeks tour in the South and is making very good."[164] Unfortunately, by the time the play arrived in New York the following April at Weber's Theatre, the production had deteriorated and the authors were dismayed. According to Dix, Amelia Bingham "had seen fit to keep many of the interpolations we had forbidden, including her silly love scene in IV and the ineffective monologue. Also had added an entirely new ending to Act III." The collaborators also felt the scenery was shabby and were unhappy that the production used the same set from the road production, other than "a new library set which was cheap and garish." "A poor cast," states Dix, "Miss B with her bumptiousness and her vulgarities destroyed any illusion that her support built up." Critics "damned the piece heartily and deservedly."[165]

When seen in New York, the plot was melodramatic with a variety of elements—"comedy, drama and farce commingled." The play concerns an American girl who visits an English family, subdues the choleric and domineering father, "rescues a girl from a scheming young man" and exposes his character as a thief when he comes to the haunted room to remove some counterfeit plates, and marries the son of the house.[166] The *Sun* rated the play as "far too slender and improbable and far too clumsily acted," while the *New York Times* dubbed it "a howling farce."[167] Despite negative comments directed at the play, the dramatists, however, were vindicated in the *Evening Post*, which stated that the "extraordinary theatrical hotch-potch" presented in *The Lilac Room* was "by Miss Amelia Bingham" and that it was "scarcely credible that the authors of such a bright and fanciful piece as 'The Road to Yesterday' could have been responsible for more than a fraction of it."[168] In the end, the authors decided to close the play in New York after only four performances, declaring the contract cancelled because of violations.

COLLABORATION ENDS WITH SUTHERLAND'S DEATH

The Lilac Room "fiasco" did not detour Sutherland and Dix, who continued working diligently on various collaborations. Eva Unsell provided a story, which became *Stigmata*, called a tragedy or "miracle play"; very little happened with the play until 1924 when it was toured in England by Phyllis Nielsen Terry. Various unproduced plays by the two women reside in Dix's archives: *The Other Side of It, Phyllida*, a four-act romantic comedy, *State O'Maine* (also Pendleton Place), and *Supernumeraries. The Arnott Will*, while produced, did not progress beyond the Shubert's try-out in New Haven, Connecticut, at the Hyperion Theatre in June 1908. Dix and Sutherland may not have actually seen a production of their last successful play, *The Substitute*, a star vehicle that well suited the talents of actor-comedian Max Figman.[169] From various clippings of performances of the play, from early in December 1908 in San Francisco at the American Theatre, through the fall of 1909 in the South and Midwest, Figman appears to have done quite well touring with this light-hearted comedy with melodramatic overtones.

The Substitute centers on James Smith, described by one critic as a "sporty, successful young lawyer," who rushes off to a small country town to fill the pulpit for his pastor-brother.[170] Initially, the situation lends itself to farce, but then Smith not only falls for Celia, daughter of the former clergyman, but gets involved with a court case and ultimately saves the old man from a false charge of misappropriation of funds and uncovers the villainess who took the money. There are numerous opportunities for comedy set up by the dramatists, and reviewers all rave over Figman's comedic ability. In Act Four, when Smith defends Celia's father in a trial, he uncovers the evildoers and saves the day. At one point, when Celia becomes faint from hunger, Smith turns to Minnie, his secretary (who has come in to help with the trial), and says: "Minnie, haven't you something for her to smell? One of those green bottles for pale people?" "A vinaigrette?" replies Minnie, "No, being a new woman, I never faint."[171] All of the reviews of The Substitute refer to the amount of laughter generated throughout the play; indeed, Max Figman helped to end the dramatists' collaborative career on a high note.

Evelyn Greenleaf Sutherland's death came as a shock for everyone. She died on December 24, 1908, as a result of burns when her dressing gown caught fire from a bathroom gas heater. It was a cold New England night and her husband was away at the time. Beulah Marie Dix's daughter, Evelyn Scott, wrote that her mother "somewhat blamed herself. She often spent the night at the Sutherlands' when the Doctor was gone, and if she only had been there, perhaps she could have helped!"[172] Dix's personal diary records on Wednesday, December 23, 1908: "Mrs G very badly burned. Spent most of day at 302." Thursday, December 24, 1908, states simply, "Mrs. G died at 3 o'clock this morning. Her heart failed. I was at the house all day."[173] The loss of her close friend and collaborator must have been difficult for Dix, as well as for all of those who regularly socialized with the Sutherlands. Jacob North described in Sutherland's obituary: "So many players have enjoyed her hospitality that there is great sadness and sympathy expressed everywhere that actors congregate. Prominent upon the stage and in public life are many who owe much to her help and encouragement."[174]

Dix and Sutherland became known for their collaborative work in America, primarily from the popularity of *The Road to Yesterday*. Although their work was certainly known in England with varying degrees of success, they remained "John Rutherford" for *The Breed of the Treshams* and "B. M. Dix" and "E. G. Sutherland" for the other three works—*Boy O' Carroll*, *Matt of Merrymount*, and *Young Fernald*. By 1910, with the London performance of *Young Fernald*, some reviewers seem to be aware of their identities, but one critic continued to refer to them as "Messrs. Sutherland and Dix."[175] It is only conjecture, but one wonders if their identities had been more widely known, would their unproduced work have attracted more attention from producers and actors? Nevertheless, Dix and Sutherland wrote in a particular genre that became popular at the end of the nineteenth and into the twentieth century, but which declined around 1910 as both American and English theatre began to produce contemporary-themed plays and far more musicals. As demonstrated in *Beaucaire* and *Breed of the Treshams*, once certain historical plays with fascinating central characters became popular, they remained so for decades through revivals. With Beulah Marie Dix's knowledge of history, particularly the English Civil War, and Evelyn Greenleaf Sutherland's technical expertise from her years of being a drama critic, the women combined their resources to create entertaining theatre of their day, culminating in *The Road to Yesterday*, their most successful achievement.

WORKS OF EVELYN GREENLEAF SUTHERLAND

[The following lists for Sutherland and Dix include date and length of most significant American and English productions, source material, collaborators, leading "star" performer(s), publisher, and/or where typescript may be located. If no location is noted, the work is likely not extant. See legend for sources at end of chapter.]

1892
Drifting, one act, w/Emma Sheridan Fry (Nelson Wheatcroft)
   23rd Street Theatre, December 15, 1892

1895

Fort Frayne w/ Gen. Charles King and Emma Sheridan Fry
  Serialized novel in the *New York Times*, 1895
  Actors' Society of America in New York, March 1897
  Schiller Theatre, Chicago, August 30, 1897 (4 wks) (Minnie Dupree)

1896

Mars'r Van w/ Emma Sheridan Fry, one-act
  Hollis Street Theatre, Boston
  Empire Theatre, February 17, 1896 (curtain raiser, 24 perf.)
Rohan the Silent, w/ Emma Sheridan Fry, one-act (Alexander Salvini)
  Tremont Theatre, Boston, 28 May 1896

1897

Po' White Trash, one-act (Henry Woodruff / Minnie Dupree)
  Bijou Theatre, Boston, March 25, 1897
  Toured by Daniel Frawley 1898-1899
A Comedie Royall, one-act (Henry Woodruff / Minnie Dupree)
  Bijou Theatre, Boston, March 25, 1897
  Lyceum Theatre, April 22, 1898

1898

In Far Bohemia, w/ Emma Sheridan Fry, one-act (Minnie Dupree)
  Bijou Theatre, Boston, January 18, 1898
A Bit of Instruction, one-act (Henry Woodruff)
  Lyceum Theatre, April 22, 1898, & toured
In Aunt Chloe's Cabin, a negro-comedy sketch, one-act
  Woman's Professional League, NY, May 12, 1898
  at their "all women's" Minstrel Show, Hammerstein's Olympic Theatre
  Published (Boston: Walter H. Baker, 1925)
The End of the Way, written for Robert Ederso
  Bijou Theatre, Boston, 1897; Lyceum Theatre, 1898
At the Barricade: An Episode of the Commune of '71, one-act
  (Emma Sheridan Fry / William Farnum)
  Hollis Street Theatre, Boston, April 28, 1898
  American Academy of Dramatic Arts, December 14, 1899

1899

In Office Hours, one-act
   Boston University School of Medicine, April 7, 1899
A Quilting Party in the Thirties, sketch for music
   Boston Theatre, April 10, 1899
The Story of a Famous Wedding, sketch for music and dancing
   Boston Theatre, April 10, 1899
On the Arcady Trail, one-act
   Empire Theatre, October 26, 1899

1900

Po' White Trash and Other One-Act Dramas
   (Chicago: Herbert S Stone & Co, 1900)
   Includes *Po' White Trash, In Far Bohemia, The End of the Way, A Comedie Royall, A Bit of Instruction, A Song at the Castle* w/Percy Wallace Mackaye, *Rohan the Silent, At the Barricade* and *Galatea of the Toy-Shop.*
Cinderella and the Telephone, one-act, written for Minnie Dupree
   In Office Hours and Other Sketches for Vaudeville or Private Acting
   (Boston: Walter H. Baker & Co., 1900)
   Includes *In Office Hours, A Quilting Party in the Thirties, In Aunt Chloe's Cabin,* and *The Story of a Famous Wedding.*
Beaucaire, adapted from novel by /w Booth
   Tarkington (Richard Mansfield)
   Herald Square Theatre, February 12, 1901 (64)
   Comedy Theatre, London, October 25, 1902 (316) (Lewis Waller)
   New York revivals, 1904 & 1912
   Opera, New Amsterdam Theatre, New York,
   December 1919 – April 1920
   Typescript, BR; IBDB

1902

Joan o' the Shoals (Henrietta Crossman, Henry Woodruff)
   Republic, February 3, 1902 (8)
A Rose O' Plymouth Town, w/Beulah Marie Dix (Minnie Dupree)
   Manhattan Theatre, September 29, 1902 (21), IBDB
   (Fortune Press, 1903) (Chicago: Dramatic Publishing, 1908)
   As *Stolen Fruit*, a comedy in one act, adapted by Paul Moffett

1903

The Breed of the Treshams, as John Rutherford w/BMD
   (Martin Harvey)
       Newcastle, September 28, 1903
       Lyric Theatre, London, June 3, 1905 (48)
       London Revivals 1907, 1915, 1925
       Astra Films, London, October 1920
       Typescript, KL

1906

Boy O' Carroll (also *Rapparee Trooper*) w/BMD (Martin Harvey)
   Imperial Theatre, Liverpool, May 19, 1906 (29)
   Typescript, KL
Young Fernald w/BMD (Henry Miller, Margaret Anglin)
   Majestic Theatre, Boston, May 28, 1906
   New Theatre, London, September 28, 1910 (Evelyn Millard)
   Typescript, KL
Matt of Merrymount, w/BMD (Fred Terry, Julia Neilson)
   Theatre Royal, Newcastle, October 11, 1906
   New Theatre, London, February 20, 1908 (60),
       Typescript, KL
The Road to Yesterday w/BMD (Minnie Dupree)
   Herald Square Theatre, December 31, 1906 (216)
   Dream Girl, musical version by Rida Johnson Young
   Ambassador Theatre, New York, August 20, 1924 (118) IMBD
   Filmed by Cecil B. DeMille, released November 29, 1925
   Published (New York: Samuel French, 1925)

1907

The Lilac Room, w/BMD (Amelia Bingham)
   Weber's Theatre, New York, April 3, 1907 (4)
The Arnott Will, w/BMD
   Hyperion Theatre, New Haven, CT, June 1908, Tryout
   Typescript, KL
Stigmata, story by Eva Unsell, w/BMD, tragedy, 1907
   London, February 1, 1924, toured (Phyllis Nielsen Terry)
   Typescript, KL

1908

His Own, one-act Brooklyn, April 1908
  Marlowe Players, Chicago, 1913
  Lena Ashwell Players, Century Theatre, London, February 22, 1926
The Substitute, w/BMD (Max Figman)
  American Theatre, San Francisco, December 6, 1908 + tour
  Typescript, KL

WORKS OF BEULAH MARIE DIX

[Includes date and length of initial or most significant American
and English productions, leading "star" performer, and, if not
published, where the manuscript can be located—see legend
below.]

1897

Apples of Eden, one-act
  Cambridge Social Dramatic Club, January 29–30, 1897 (2)
  Empire Theatre, December 2, 1897; Typescript, KL
Cicely's Cavalier, one-act
  Comedy Club of Medford (MA), April 13, 1897
  Cambridge Social Dramatic Club, May 8, 1897
  Published (Boston: Walter H. Baker & Company, 1896)

1898

Predestination, one-act
  Fay House, Radcliffe, April 2, 1898; typescript, KL
At the Sign of the Buff Bible, one-act
  Empire Theatre, NY, December 1, 1898; typescript, KL

1899

Ye Lustie Man of Wessaguset, one-act
  Idler Club, Radcliffe, 18 March 1899; typescript, KL

1900

To Serve for Meat and Fee (Diccon Goodnaught w/EGS)
  Fay House, Radcliffe, April 6–7, 1900; typescript, KL

1902

A Rose O' Plymouth Town, w/EGS (Minnie Dupree)
  Manhattan Theatre, September 29, 1902 (21), IBDB
  (Fortune Press, 1903) & (Chicago: Dramatic Publishing, 1908)
  As *Stolen Fruit*, a comedy in one act, adapted by Paul Moffett

1903

The Breed of the Treshams, as John Rutherford w/EGS (Martin Harvey)
  Newcastle, September 28, 1903
  Lyric Theatre, London, June 3, 1905 (48)
  London Revivals 1907, 1915, 1925
  Astra Films, London, October 1920
  Typescript, KL

1906

Boy O'Carroll (*Rapparee Trooper*), w/EGS (Martin Harvey)
  Imperial Theatre, May 19, 1906 (29); typescript, KL
  Young Fernald, w/EGS (Margaret Anglin / Henry Miller)
  May 28, 1906, Majestic Theatre, Boston
  New Theatre, London, September 28, 1910 (Evelyn Millard)
  Typescript, KL
Matt of Merrymount, w/EGS (Fred Terry, Julia Neilson)
  Theatre Royal, Newcastle, October 11, 1906
  New Theatre, London, February 20, 1908 (60)
The Road to Yesterday, w/EGS (Minnie Dupree)
  Herald Square Theatre, December 31, 1906 (216)
  Filmed by Cecil B. DeMille, released November 29, 1925
  Published (New York: Samuel French, 1925)
  Dream Girl musical, Rida Johnson Young/Victor Herbert, 1921

1907

The Lilac Room, w/EGS (Amelia Bingham)
  Weber's Theatre, April 3, 1907 (4); typescript, KL
The Arnott Will, w/EGS
  Hyperion Theatre, New Haven, CT, June 1908 (tryout)
  Typescript, KL
Stigmata, tragedy, story by Eva Unsell, w/EGS 1907
  London, February 1, 1924, toured (Phyllis Nielsen Terry)
  Typescript, KL

1908

The Substitute, w/EGS (Max Figman)
   American Theatre, San Francisco, December 6, 1908 (toured)

1910

Alison's Lad and Other Martial Interludes, Being Six One-Act Dramas
   (New York: Henry Holt & Company, 1910)
   Includes: *Alison's Lad, The Hundredth Trick, The Weakest Link,
   The Snare and the Fowler, The Captain of the Gate,* and *The Dark
   of the Dawn*

1914

Across the Border, one-act
   Princess Theatre, New York, October 17, 1914 (in repertory)
   Published (New York: Henry Holt & Company, 1915)

1915

Moloch, a play about war (Holbrook Blinn)
   New Amsterdam Theatre, September 20, 1915 (32)
   Published as Borzoi Plays II (New York: Alfred A Knopf, 1916)

1916

A Pageant for Peace, The Glorious Game, Clemency, Where the War Comes
   (Boston: American School Peace League, 1916)

1925

A Legend of Saint Nicolas and Other Plays
   (New York: Samuel French, 1925)
   Includes *A Legend of Saint Nicolas, The Weal of Wayland's Well,*
   and *The Princess Dayshine*

1927

The Girl Comes Home, one-act comedy
   (New York: Samuel French, 1927)

1934

Ragged Army w/Bertram Millhauser (Lloyd Nolan)
   Selwyn Theatre, February 26, 1934

ADDITIONAL UNDATED TITLES, TYPESCRIPTS IN KNIGHT LIBRARY, UNIVERSITY OF OREGON

An Easter Play
A Daughter of Wrath
The Day of Defeat (Nan of the Killigrews)
Diccon Goodnaught, w EGS
English-born, 1898
For the King
The Lonely Lady
The Minx w/EGS, one-act comedy
The Other Side of It, w/EGS
Phyllida w/EGS, four-act romantic comedy
The Pioneer Woman, 1927
State O' Maine (Pendleton Place), w/EGS
Supernumeraries, w/EGS
The Wise Woman of Hogsdon, adapted comedy

NOVELS, SHORT STORIES, AND ARTICLES

1898
Hugh Gwyeth, a Roundhead Cavalier, novel
   (New York: Macmillan, 1898)

1899
Soldier Rigdale, novel (New York: Macmillan, 1899, 1925)

1900
"Cavalier's sister," *St. Nicholas* v. 27 (June 1900): 702–9
"Damnabilissimus juvenis," *Lippincott's Monthly Magazine* 66
   (July 1900): 109–18

1901
The Making of Christopher Ferringham, novel
   (New York: Macmillan, 1901)

1902

The Beau's Comedy, novel w/ Carrie A. Harper
   (New York: Harper, 1902)
A Little Captive Lad, novel (New York: Macmillan, 1902)
   "Daughter of the Puritans," *Harper's Monthly Magazine* 104
      (May 1902): 907–13
   "Love of Denys de Vaudrencoeur," *Lippincott's Monthly
      Magazine* 70 (July 1902): 66–73
   "Into action," *Harper's Monthly Magazine* 105 (October 1902):
      684–90

1903

The Life, Treason, and Death of James Blount of Breckenhow, novel
   (New York: Macmillan, 1903)
"Scythe in the oak-tree," *Lippincott's Monthly Magazine* 71
   (February 1903): 211–19
"Return," *Lippincott's Monthly Magazine* 72 (October 1903): 450–57

1905

The Fair Maid of Graystones, novel
   (New York: Macmillan, 1905)

1906

Merrylips, novel (New York: Macmillan, 1906)
   "Edge o' the world," *Lippincott's Monthly Magazine* 77
      (June 1906): 721–30

1907

"Way of a will," *Lippincott's Monthly Magazine* 79
   (January 1907), 63–72

1911

Friends in the End, novel (New York: Holt, 1911)
   "Throw-back," *Harper's Weekly* 55 (June 10, 1911): 16–17
   "Girls at Whipple farm," *Woman's Home Companion* 38
   (July 1911): 23

1912

The Fighting Blade, novel (New York: Holt, 1912)
The Gate of Horn, novel (New York: Duffield & Company, 1912)
Betty Bide-at-Home, novel (New York: Holt, 1912)
   "Drusilla," *Woman's Home Companion* 39 (August 1912): 5–6

1913

Mother's Son (New York: Holt, 1913)
Glory of Youth (New York: Duffield, 1913)

1914

The Little God Ebisu (New York: Duffield & Company, 1914)
Maid Melicent (New York: Hearst's International Library, 1914)
Little Faithful (New York: Mills & Boon, 1914)
   "Hey for one-and-twenty!" *Good Housekeeping* 58 (June 1914): 728–38

1915

"Across the Border," *Good Housekeeping* 60 (Feb. 1915): 116–24
"How the Adventures Began" (Loves of the Eight E's), *Good Housekeeping* 61 (Oct. 1915): 410–20

1916

The Battle Months of George Daurella (New York: Duffield & Company, 1916)

1917

Blithe McBride (New York: Macmillan, 1917)
Kay Danforth's Camp (New York: Duffield, 1917)

1919

Hands Off! (Macmillan, 1919)

1922

The Turned-About Girls (New York: Macmillan, 1922)

1929

Their Own Desire, as Sarita Fuller (pseud.), (New York: Doubleday, 1929)

1932
Pity of God (New York: Viking, 1932)

1933
The Life of Jimmy Dolan, w/Bertram Millhauser (New York: Macaulay, 1933)
Hot Leather, paperback version (New York: Bantam, 1948)

1941
The Wedding Eve Murder (Robert M. McBride, 1941)
Robber Kitten, n.d. (Susie Sunshine Series, McLoughlin)

FILMOGRAPHY

Beulah Marie Dix worked in the movie industry as a writer from 1916 into the early 1940s. She wrote screenplays, scenarios, and adaptations, often adapting her own novels and plays and those written with Evelyn Greenleaf Sutherland. There are over 50 films attributed to her as writer. See the online Internet Movie Database (IMBD) and Wikipedia. Dix is included in *Reel Women: Pioneers of the Cinema 1896 to the Present* by Ally Acker (New York: The Continuum Publishing Company, 1991). Her daughter, Evelyn Flebbe Scott's book, *Hollywood When Silents Were Golden* (New York: McGraw-Hill, 1972) discusses her mother's years in Hollywood as a writer.

LEGEND

BMD	Beulah Marie Dix
EGS	Evelyn Greenleaf Sutherland
BR	Billy Rose Theatre Collection, New York Public Library, Lincoln Center
IBDB	Internet Broadway Database
IMDB	Internet Movie Database
KL	Knight Library, University of Oregon, Eugene, OR (Beulah Marie Dix archives)

Additional undated titles, typescripts in Dix's archives at the Knight Library, University of Oregon, Eugene, OR:

An Easter Play
A Daughter of Wrath
Diccon Goodnaught (To Serve for Meat and Fee) w/BMD,
Typescript KL
English born, 1898
The Minx w/BMD, one-act comedy
The Other Side of It w/BMD
Phyllida w/BMD, 4-act romantic comedy
State O' Maine (Pendleton Place) w/BMD
Supernumeraries w /BMD

RIDA JOHNSON YOUNG

CHAPTER 4

DRAMATIST, SONGWRITER, AND LYRICIST: RIDA JOHNSON YOUNG, 1875-1926

> Ah, sweet mystery of life, / at last I've found thee. Ah, I know at last / The secret of it all.
>
> —*Naughty Marietta*, 1910[1]

> Every morning from 8 to 1 in the afternoon I slave at my typewriter. No matter how I feel, no matter whether I have any inspiration or not, I set about my task with absolute regularity and keep at it the allotted time.
>
> —Rida Johnson Young, 1917[2]

RIDA JOHNSON YOUNG CREATED well over thirty plays and musicals, along with numerous popular songs during the first two decades of the twentieth century. Her prodigious output was the result of maintaining a practical writing schedule. "Regularity in work," explained Young, "is one of the biggest helps to success."[3] Young, who often played down her own accomplishments in interviews, related that another key factor to her success was "never undertaking anything really big" and writing plays that were popular and within her ability.[4] But Young also excelled at finding venues for her talents as playwright, lyricist, and songwriter, creating popular dramatic works and songs that brought her both celebrity and wealth. What is more, managing her own business affairs, she usually served as her own agent, took an active role in the casting and rehearsing of productions, and formed professional alliances with the likes of Daniel Frohman, Lee and J. J. Shubert, and Isidore Witmark of Witmark Music Company. When she died in 1926, the dramatist left behind a remarkable body of work, along with a number of unproduced plays.

Rida Louise Johnson was born in Baltimore, Maryland, February 28, 1875, to William A. Johnson and Emma Stuart Johnson, the fifth of six children.[5] Her father owned a lighterage/coal business and provided a respectable, middle-class living for his family.[6] The Johnson home, located at 104 Jackson Place in East Baltimore, was a few blocks south of John Hopkins Hospital and north of Fell's Point, an area which was "prominent" at the time but not especially wealthy.[7] The same location is mentioned in the 1900 census, with Emma given as head of household, revealing that apparently only four of the Johnson children still lived at that time.[8] Rida's father likely died sometime in the late 1890s.[9]

At the age of fifteen, in the fall of 1890, Rida enrolled at Wilson College for Young Women, Chambersburg, Pennsylvania, in the School of Music as a special student in piano for one year. There is no evidence to support that she attended elsewhere, although she must have received formal instruction in earlier years.[10] This is demonstrated by the fact that Rida took up writing early, her "poems, articles and stories appearing in small magazines and local newspapers."[11] When she was eighteen, she completed an ambitious play about Omar Khayyam that "contained almost one hundred characters" as Young described, and would have taken "about eight or ten hours" to perform. Convincing her reluctant parents to let her go to New York, she determined that if the play did not succeed, she would become an actress. Upon arriving in New York sometime in 1893, she first secured a $4-a-week job marketing furniture polish out of a Harlem apartment and found a room to rent at two dollars a week.[12]

When making the rounds to theatres to show her play to managers, she caught the attention of E. H. Sothern, a well-known actor-manager of the day. While Sothern did not take the Omar Khayyam piece, he must have spotted some nascent ability in Rida's first efforts, since he outlined another play for himself and asked her to write it. "I could not spare the time from my work," Young explained, "and in the end secured a place in his company for the express purpose of learning more of the stage and the technique of the drama."[13] Her first role as a lady-in-waiting in Daniel Frohman's production of *The Three Musketeers* paid $25 a week and allowed her to quit selling furniture polish.[14] Despite the theatrical training gained from playing in stock theatre and wanting to be "great," Rida considered herself "rotten" as an actress and stayed at it for less than two years, before turning to songwriting.[15]

Introduced through a mutual friend to Isidore Witmark, head of Witmark Music Publisher, Rida became "a member of the staff, assisting Witmark in the press department at twenty-five dollars a week."[16] It was not long, however, before she began creating songs to help fill the demand of a burgeoning music industry.[17] Young described the publishing house as a factory, "turning out songs at a rate that was bewildering":

> When someone singing in vaudeville made a hit, and
> an order came in for an encore verse, or two or three,
> or half a dozen, I sat down and wrote them. When a
> song was needed to fit a particular play or concern, or
> actor, someone wrote down the music, and I fitted
> words to them; or I wrote the words and someone
> fitted the music.[18]

Although sometimes pushed to write a song a day or more, Young counted her time at Witmark as valuable experience, but she quit after two years to return to the stage when offered a role in James Young's company.[19]

Rida Louise Johnson met James Young, Jr., (1872–1978) when he was on the staff of a daily Baltimore newspaper.[20] While still a teenager, James, whose father was a journalist and then a Maryland state senator, began acting minor roles on the New York stage before touring on his own and "starring" in classical works. Small-town newspapers carried the photo of the handsome actor, who was variously described in press releases as a "romantic young actor," a "new star" and "tragedian."[21] In 1896 Rida Louise, noted as quite a beauty herself, joined Young's company as "featured" actress. A Middletown, New York, newspaper advertises James Young's upcoming appearance at the Casino Theatre as being "assisted by Miss Rida Louise Johnson and a company of sixteen competent and well-chosen players."[22] Young's company toured throughout the East Coast and Midwest for about two seasons, usually booking two nights per location, one for *Hamlet*, the other for *David Garrick* with *Katharine and Petruceo*. In the process, Rida Louise must have honed her acting skills, since a Warren, Pennsylvania, reviewer described her as "delightful in her role of the young girl in love with Garrick"; she also must have been an asset to Young's company in public relations, as well, since the reviewer added, "Miss Johnson, the authoress, is well known to quite a number of Warren people and renewed many acquaintances."[23] Rida later claimed that although she liked acting better than writing, she didn't care for the "business side" of the profession, "the getting of engagements and all that."[24] The tour ended sometime in 1898 when James Young accepted an offer to join Augustin Daly's company; his experience with Daly's company, however, proved unsatisfactory even before the manager's death in June of 1899.[25]

LORD BYRON

In the meantime, Rida researched and wrote a play specifically for James Young, based upon incidences in the life of the poet Byron.[26] James Young spared no expense for his 1900 touring production of *Lord Byron*, including "four entire sets, all new and all painted by Hoyt of New York, one of the foremost scenic artists in this country." He also had furniture custom-made to match early nineteenth-century furnishings.[27] The staging of *Lord Byron* clearly impressed small-town audiences, since one of the reporters invited to the Norfolk dress rehearsal described the production as "one of the most complete and elaborate ever seen here . . . a continual feast to the eye and ear."[28] James Young earned praise for his portrayal of the moody, romantic

Byron, while the seventeen supporting cast members, including Rida Louise as Countess Varjoll, were "strong in their respective parts."[29] Above all, it must have been encouraging for the twenty-five-year-old dramatist to read that her play was "of decided literary merit." *Lord Byron*, stated the critic, "is a natural result of an ideal theme in the hands of a skillful and enthusiastic authoress, who can not only put her ideas into pleasing phraseology, but who is also a clever actress."[30] The tour continued for about eight weeks through the South, where it was highly praised, and into the Midwest, where reception turned lukewarm. Unfortunately, during the *Lord Byron* tour a New York critic panned a sketch of the play (apparently without actually seeing it), calling it "a rather commonplace piece of work" and "bad history," citing omissions or inaccuracies in the play's events. Thus, it does not appear the play was actually performed in New York City.[31] James Young had planned to take the play out again the following season, but he accepted an enticing offer from Sir Henry Irving to be one of the "leading men" of the London Lyceum company. One account tells that "Mr. Young's friends felt that it was the opportunity of a lifetime, and so the 'Byron' tour was abandoned."[32]

Rida, however, remained far from idle after *Lord Bryon* ended. Over the next few years, she wrote *Glorious Betsy*, which provided a fitting role for rising star, Mary Mannering, and *Brown of Harvard* as another vehicle for James Young, whom she married in 1904.[33] With J. Hartley Manners she wrote *The Lancers*, a translation of a German comedy, to which they added "songs and showgirls"; although the 1907 production was a flop, it began Rida's professional relationship with the powerful Shubert brothers who would produce ten of her plays and musicals over the next sixteen years.[34] Riding on the success of *Brown of Harvard*, Charles Frohman sent Rida to Oxford University in England to research another college play, but as she later explained, she had difficulty relating to English people and life at Oxford, so the play apparently never materialized.[35] In 1906 she published four short dramatic pieces and monologues through Witmark and with a co-author, Gilbert P. Coleman, wrote a novelized version of *Brown of Harvard*.[36] In addition to writing *The Boys of Company B*, she completed *Sweet Sixteen*, a musical set in a girl's school, which was never produced, although a good portion of it turned up later in her 1910 musical, *Just One of the Boys*.[37]

CATERING TO THE MATINEE GIRL:
GLORIOUS BETSY, BROWN OF HARVARD, AND BOYS OF COMPANY B

Rida Johnson Young counted *Glorious Betsy* as her "first practical play, written not for my own gratification, but for people to act and to see."[38] She used the true story of Baltimore socialite, Elizabeth Patterson, who fell in love with and married Jerome Bonaparte, brother to Napoleon. After their two-year marriage, Napoleon ordered his brother to annul the union with Betsy and marry a German princess. While the true life story did not end happily for the lovers, Young, in order to please the vast number of girls and women in the audience, exercised artistic license by having them reunite at play's end.

Glorious Betsy, initially called *Lady Betty*, then *Mistress Betty*, was taken by Mary Mannering and her manager-husband, James K. Hackett early in 1906, and began touring outside of New York in the fall. By the time it reached New York in September 1908, Young had already enjoyed success with *Brown of Harvard* and *Boys of Company*— both featuring plenty of brawny young men. As a result, Young endured carping from critics who accused her of catering to the matinee girls in the audience. A prominent example was Charles Darnton of the *Evening World* who said:

> The matinee girl will be glad. That marshmallow dramatist, Mrs. Rida Johnson Young has again opened up shop. Sweets for the sweet! Do have a chocolate. Keep a penny for the water boy! Did you get a programme? There goes the curtain! S-s-s-h-h![39]

Indeed, many critics commented on the pretty stage picture made by tall, willowy Mary Mannering in her early nineteenth-century gowns. In one "sensational" moment she appeared onstage barefoot and proceeded to put on stockings with her back to the audience, risqué indeed for 1908. Some reviewers dubbed the play flimsy and shook their heads that Mannering did not have "a better vehicle for her fine talents."[40] But Mary Mannering herself defended *Glorious Betsy* as "a great big strong love story and nothing else—that makes it appeal to women."[41] Although the play ran only three weeks in New York, Mary Mannering's touring portrayal of "Betsy" Patterson remained a favorite with audiences for five years.[42]

In order to research *Brown of Harvard*, Rida Johnson Young spent six weeks in Cambridge, Massachusetts, to observe students and college life.[43] Although it was announced in December 1905 that James Young would play the lead in *Brown of Harvard*, the title role went to Henry Woodruff, a rising, boyish-looking actor and Harvard graduate.[44] Rida may have had her differences with director Henry Miller, but she credited him for helping her shape the play [see her comments in the Introduction], and from that first Broadway production, she adapted the guiding motto: "Never be quite sure that you are right."[45] Miller's staging created an authentic collegiate atmosphere, especially in the third act boat race, which included not only a large number of cheering, flag-waving students but John Levett, known as "John the Orangeman," a familiar campus character brought in from Harvard for the production. As reported by *Town and Country*:

> He [Levette] appears but a few moments in the second act to give "local color" to the campus scene, and his appearance is the "one touch of nature" which gives reality to the picture and awakens the keenest interest and sympathy in the audience. It is the same smiling, kindly figure whom three generations of Harvard men have known in the collage yard.[46]

However, the *New York Times* critic felt differently, stating that Miller's use of "local color" by the appearance of the elderly John Levett "provided an occasion for prolonged enthusiasm, but this attempt at realism [would] hardly create satisfaction in the case of anyone with a sense of pathos."[47]

Brown of Harvard centers on Tom Brown, a likeable fellow from a well-to-do family who loves Evelyn Kenyon and privately loans money to her brother. But Kenyon, displays a constitutional weakness by making bets with Colton, an unscrupulous student, and stealing checks from Tom's checkbook. When a classmate from the Lend-a-Hand-Club asks Tom to help support Gerald Thorne, a poor southern student tutor, he responds with a generous monthly donation, insisting on remaining anonymous. Kenyon has "compromised" Marian Thorne, a Radcliffe girl and Thorne's sister; she shows up at Tom's door, looking for Kenyon as a group of Tom's friends approach, prompting Tom to hide Marian in his room at the last moment. A pivotal point follows when Marian is "discovered" by Tom's friends in the presence of Evelyn Kenyon and her mother, causing a major misunderstanding between Tom and Evelyn.

Gerald Thorne, an excellent rower, is invited to join the Harvard rowing team for an important race against the best amateur English team. But when his sister disappears prior to the race—a rouse by Colton who has bet against the Harvard team—he quits the race and rushes off to find her. Brown, as team substitute, takes his place and helps win the race. As Brown is borne aloft by his teammates in a rousing victory, Thorne rushes in to publicly accuse him of being the cause of his sister's downfall. To prevent his fiancée from learning of her brother's disgrace, Brown temporarily shoulders the blame in front of everyone. It then takes a series of revelations to ultimately vindicate Brown and reunite him with Evelyn.

When *Brown of Harvard* premiered in February 1906, it followed on the heels of two other popular collegiate plays. Young stated that she wrote the play before either of the other plays was produced, but could not "get a hearing for it."[48] As a result, *Brown of Harvard* came up against inevitable comparison with George Ade's *The College Widow* (1904) and William C. de Mille's *Strongheart* (1905). Critics were generally positive about its "conventionality," although the *Herald* felt the play was "seriously marred" by the "incident with Marion Thorne," calling it "an objectionable and unnecessary feature in its plot."

> This, the betrayal of a Radcliffe College girl by a
> Harvard student, and the prominence given to the
> affair as the play developed clearly displeased a large
> proportion of the audience and qualified what might
> have been an emphatic success for the piece.[49]

Expressing late Victorian sensibilities, the reviewer, took offence
with Marion Thorne's being "involved with" Gerald Thorne and
then "discovered" in Tom Brown's bedroom. "The unnecessary
intrigue marred it all," he stated, "turning a bright 'skit' into an
unripe problem play."[50] However, the *New York Times* critic argued
a few days later that there would not be much plot left if the Marion
Thorne "episode" were omitted: "when a suggestion involves the
elimination of the one incident upon which a whole play structure is
founded there is reasonable justification for difference of
opinion."[51]

As a novice playwright, Rida surely enjoyed this attention,
especially James Metcalfe's review in *Life* magazine, ranking *Brown of
Harvard* as "the best in the recent American invasion of the
American stage.   It shows a really stronger grasp of dramatic
possibilities than the work of the better-known literary men."[52] Her
initial Broadway run of 101 performances, while not as long as long
as Ade's play (278), did surpass de Mille's (66). *Brown of Harvard*
established Rida Johnson Young's dramatic career and toured long
after the Broadway run ended. By October 1907, the *Washington Post*
reported the play had "the unique distinction of having been
presented for seventy-three consecutive weeks"; after thirty weeks
at the Princess Theatre in New York, the production had a summer
run at the Garrick Theatre in Chicago and a road tour that lasted
through the next July. Members of the touring company, including
Henry Woodruff, then took a six-week break before starting a
second tour.[53] Following Woodruff's two seasons with *Brown of
Harvard*, James Young finally played the role originally written for
him and mounted his own touring production. Young took the play
out in the fall of 1908, still playing college man, Tom Brown, in his
late thirties, through about 1910— the year he secretly married
actress, Clara Kimball.[54]

The Boys of Company B, following fourteen months after *Brown of Harvard*, concerned a militia organization similar to the National Guard. Since the cast consisted of only four females and fourteen males, along with over ten "privates" at the camp, the play included considerable slang, jesting, boxing, blanket tossing, and various other types of horseplay similar to that of *Brown of Harvard*. Interestingly, only the *Sun* made an issue of the fact that Young was writing again on a "masculine" topic: "No masculine mystery is too deep for the keen vision of this lady dramatist, no sentiment of the manly bosom too sacred."[55] The *Theatre*, however, panned the comedy as "more of the same":

> As a substitute for playwriting proper a method has recently come into vogue of exhibiting the more or less intimate life of college cubs, football players, National Guard soldiers in camp, students at their orgies, and the like. If an audience is thus entertained, even by an intermittent current of comedy, the purpose is served.[56]

Regardless of negative commentary, audiences supported the production well into June, mostly because of its two dashing leading men.

Arnold Daly opened in the central role of Tony Allen who loves Eileen MacLane, the daughter of his commanding officer; and while Major MacLane likes Tony, Mrs. MacLane does all she can to separate the young lovers, determined that her daughter marry a wealthy man. In the opening scene in MacLane's gymnasium on the upper floor of the house, Tony outwits the vigilant mother by proposing to Eileen through a speaking tube. Of course, complications to the relationship ensue, including a moment at camp in the second act when Eileen catches Tony kissing the flirtatious Madge; when a friend asks why he did it, he explains that he wanted "to know what it was like to kiss a girl with a lisp."[57] There are, in fact, two characters in the play who lisp, Madge and Chick, her counterpart, who serve as a source of amusement throughout the play. Another comic twist occurs when Tony convinces his miserly uncle to perform his military duty by joining the unit, whereby Tony takes every opportunity to work the older man beyond endurance; in the end his uncle begs out of the military, promising Tony the $50,000 he needs to marry. John Barrymore took over the role of Tony in late May, giving publicity to the play and sparking renewed interest from matinee girls. *The Boys of Company B* toured for a few years, after which Young turned it into a musical titled, *When Love is Young*, around 1912—however, it does not appear the musical was actually produced.[58]

BIG SUCCESSES, BIG FAILURES: *THE LOTTERY MAN, NEXT!, THE RED PETTICOAT,* AND *THE GIRL AND THE PENNANT*

By 1909 Young had achieved moderate Broadway successes for three years running, but her next play, *The Lottery Man*, ultimately became her most enduring comedy. Opening at the Bijou Theatre in December 1909 and running 200 performances, the show became so popular as a touring production, the Shuberts sent out four road companies in its second and third years.[59] Unlike most Progressive Era plays, tailored to fit one particular actor/comedian and thus difficult to translate to the modern stage, *The Lottery Man* stands as a stronger comedy of the period. Indeed, there is a somewhat modern feel to the script, revealing a tightly woven plot, well-delineated characters—four of which are women—snappy dialogue, and a charming period setting.[60]

Central to the plot is Jack Wright, a young newspaperman down on his luck, who lives with and supports his mother. Jack borrows money from his friend and newspaper chief, Foxey Peyton, for a speculative scheme that fails, so he proposes a plan to Foxey that will not only sell newspapers, but will provide income for himself. Jack intends to offer himself as a prize for a marriage lottery. The paper would include a lottery ticket in each newspaper and advertise the contest; subsequent issues would feature stories of Jack's exploits as a journalist. Jack's identity and picture would be disclosed incrementally each week, but not fully revealed until the final day of the contest. The woman who has the winning number in the drawing will either "win" Jack and marry him or split the proceeds with him. Convinced that it's a sensational idea, Foxey rushes off to get the contest announcement in the morning edition.

A short time later while Jack and his mother are turning in for the night, a car crashes outside their Greenwich basement apartment. The shaken chauffer shows up at their door and asks to use the telephone; he is followed by his passengers, Mrs. Payton (Foxey's mother), her niece, Helen, and assistant, Lizzie. Almost instantly, Jack becomes enchanted with Helen; they are acquainted only briefly, but it's long enough for Jack to have a change of heart about the lottery. Once help arrives and the Payton party departs, Jack calls the newspaper to withdraw the ad, but the morning edition has already gone to press. Ultimately, the lottery exceeds everyone's expectations. Several weeks later in Act II, in Foxey's upstairs den, the lottery has just closed with 300,000 tickets sold (at $1 per ticket). Jack's identity has been revealed and the drawing will soon take place. A discussion between Mrs. Wright and Mrs. Peyton reveals that not only have the two mothers been secretly purchasing newspapers for lottery tickets to help Helen win, it appears Jack has also been "writing special articles" in order to buy newspaper, as well. At home, Jack appears through a back door, shaken, his clothes ripped by the "hundreds of women" outside. The mob turns shrill and violent, and Jack is forced to placate the women from the balcony. The winning number, however, when announced, belongs to Lizzie, Mrs. Peyton's spinsterish assistant. At first Lizzie takes every advantage of the situation, but eventually it is revealed that she actually stole the winning lottery ticket from the cupboard where the cook had stashed it. Jack mollifies Lizzie, promising her a house of her own, and makes amends with Helen, the girl he really wants to marry.

Audiences and most critics enjoyed this farce, not only for the humorous predicament, but for the likeable characters. And Young pokes fun at fads of the day, some which are still timely, such as Mrs. Payton's obsession with weight and dieting; in order to maintain her figure Mrs. Payton insists that the skinny Lizzie keep to the same diet and exercise program. Lizzie, played effectively by Helen

Lowell, sneaks food and nips liquor when no one is looking. Jack's mother, Mrs. Wright, contrasts with Mrs. Payton and is described as a "wholesome, sweet looking woman of 45," a "very motherly type" who has a "curious way of using slang."

Most all reviewers, including the *New York Times*, commented favorably, if not glowingly, on *The Lottery Man*. But, as he did with *The Boys of Company B*, the *Sun*'s reviewer berated Young's subject for her comedy because of her gender: "Mrs. Young is relentless in her pursuit of man as the inspiration of her plays. She holds him up to the inspection of her audiences with the same scientific indifference to her sufferings that the naturalist shows when he pinions the butterfly." He referred to the "masculine" domains of the college dorm and the National Guard as seen in her previous plays, remarking:

> Her latest play leads her straight to a newspaper publisher who has never before been accounted an aid to romance. Mrs. Young's cycle, however, is not destined to end until she has revealed mere man in all his infinite capacities. It looks now as if only a few uptown chop houses would escape her vigilant pen.[61]

Whatever her reaction to such commentary, Rida Johnson Young was very likely too busy counting royalty checks to worry about it.

Several years after its initial run, adverse publicity for *The Lottery Man* took the form of a lawsuit by Edith Ellis Furness, the director of the New York production at the Bijou Theatre. In 1912, Furness, a playwright and previous in-house playdoctor for the Shuberts, filed a suit against Rida Johnson Young and the Shuberts, claiming 33 1/3 percent of the royalties for rewriting *The Lottery Man*—this amounted to $10,000 plus $30,000 in damages to her reputation.[62] Furness contended that as director she had not only changed lines and made improvements, but that she had expanded the play from a one-hour running time to two and a half hours. The defense called various theatre people as witnesses, including William Brady, manager, Henry Miller, producer/actor, and Robert MacKay who played Foxey in the play. As reported in the *New York Times*, MacKay "testified that he had introduced lines that had caused thirty-nine laughs from the audience, and yet he was not considered a playwright."[63] Witnesses concurred that making changes to plays during rehearsals was a common occurrence and that helping to change lines here and there did not make one a collaborator with the playwright. The Supreme Court dismissed the charges against the Shuberts, and the following day a jury of twelve men returned a verdict in favor of Rida Johnson Young, who personally shook hands with each juror. "The suit put me in a terrible position," she said. "Mrs. Furniss [sic] and I were friends, but in bringing this action she attacked my ability as an author. I am delighted that these twelve good men found that I can write plays without the aid of anyone else."[64]

Considering the tightness of the script, it is conceivable that Furness and others contributed to shaping and improving the script of *The Lottery Man*. The outcome of the trial, however, validated Young's claim to her creative property. Young, in fact, believed so strongly in the ownership of her *idea* of *The Lottery Man* that she reacted to a news story about a young woman in Tacoma, Washington who "offered herself as a matrimonial prize in a lottery conducted by a newspaper." Young rushed off an evening telegram to J. J. Shubert, stating that this young woman was "using exactly the same idea as my play" and demanded that he "institute legal proceedings to stop this young woman from carrying out her proposed plan."[65] It is unlikely the Shuberts actually followed through on Young's demands.

Young wrote *Next!* specifically for actor-comedienne, Helen Lowell, telling Lee Shubert in October 1910 that it promised "to be the funniest one I have done yet."[66] Helen Lowell was familiar to New York audiences as a character actress who usually filled secondary roles such as the pessimistic Miss Hazy in *Mrs. Wiggs of the Cabbage Patch* and the scrawny Lizzie in *The Lottery Man*. Of Lowell's performance in *The Red Petticoat*, the musical version of *Next!*, the *New York Tribune* reviewer stated that "her rendering of a low comedy role tempts the spectator who laughs at her humor to take her acting seriously."

> It must be discouraging to be a "character" actress in this country. There are not even as many leading roles written for them as there are for contraltos in grant opera. It is hard to know why this should be. The public seems to enjoy a funny woman, though few audiences have a chance to see them outside of vaudeville. Most women farceurs are driven to the "two a day" for a hearing.[67]

With this in mind, Rida Johnson Young must have enjoyed the challenge of creating the character of Sophie Brush, woman barber, for Lowell's particular talents. *Next!*, which closed after only 18 performances at Daly's Theatre in September 1911, might as well have been the trial run to the musical version with book and lyrics by Young with Paul West, music by composer Jerome Kern. *Next!* became *Look Who's Here* in out of town tryouts and *The Red Petticoat* when it opened a year later at the same theatre.[68] Other than Lowell's part, the show was completely recast with dancers and singers.

The action takes place in a mining camp in Nevada and the curtain opens on burley, bearded, unkempt miners named Bad Jake, Sam Small, Swat Rogers and Barney Barnes. It is Otto Schmaltz's new "tonsilorium emporium," furnished with a barber chair for the new barber who is due to arrive shortly on the next stagecoach. Across the street lies Regan's Palace Opera House where "Sage Brush" Kate and her girls work. When Sophie Brush first appears, she wears a plaid traveling coat and "a small straw hat on top of her twisted knot of hair"; she carries a parrot in a cage, along with so much luggage that she can hardly stand. Otto is flabbergasted that this is the S. Brush he's been expecting. Sophie replies: "Why not, I took a correspondence course in everything from manicuring to facial massage and I reckon I'm able to tackle anything around here." Otto insists, "But I wasn't expecting a woman." And Sophie snaps back, "Well, you need one judging by the looks of things."[69]

Sophie calls for her assistants and eight young women enter, joining her in "The Correspondence School," song to explain how they learned their manicuring trade. This sets up a running joke throughout the musical, when, at every situation, Sophie declares she learned something in correspondence school. For example, when the hero, Jack, hides from the law in the cellar, she says: "I took a correspondence course in shooting once and I am just dying to try it, come out of there murderer!" and when Bad Jake is wounded, she asserts: "Oh, let me get at him, I took a correspondence course in nursing once, and I am dying to try it." Sophie's feisty personality and common sense take over and soon the whole camp is transformed, with the men becoming clean-shaven, well-groomed, and manicured. Sophie continues to hide the wrongly accused Jack in the cellar where he digs a tunnel and ends up discovering a gold vein. All is resolved through the *deus ex machina*, Sophie's parrot, who reveals the real culprit who stole the miners' gold by shouting: "Jake did it. Jake did it."

Critics found the musical unusual in a refreshing way. Alan Dale, for example, declared:

> At last a novelty—real, unadulterated and a bit audacious—and right in the realm of that much-explored, over-registered region of musical comedy . . . and instead of it turning out to be the usual mess of disguised princesses and sickly courtiers and desiccated kings it proved to be a Western melodrama set to music![70]

"Mrs. Rida Johnson Young," stated Dale, "has written a *real* story with blithe comedy and genuine situations." He goes on to praise Paul West's lyrics and declare that Jerome Kern's music was "perhaps prettier than anything in town" and "good enough to waft Kern on the crest wave of popularity."[71] During Kern's "Since the Days of Grandmama," a favorite with theatregoers, Sophie, with the aid of the younger women, sheds her "added years with her comic spinster makeup and appears a most attractive young woman."[72] Some critics expressed surprised over Helen Lowell's ability to shift to musical farce, but Lowell explained that she got her start in Gilbert and Sullivan productions.[73] While the success of much of the humor in *The Red Petticoat* comes from Sophie's character, Lowell had strong support, including "manly tenor," Joseph Phillips, dancer, Grace Field, and young dancer-singer, Donald MacDonald.

It was inevitable that as prolific as she was, Young would eventually experience a real flop. In later years, she openly admitted that her baseball comedy *The Girl and the Pennant* proved a failure.[74] For this play she drafted the assistance of Christy Mathewson, a well-known pitcher for the New York Giants, accompanying him and the team to the south during the winter.[75] Young shared credit for the play, but she most likely did all the writing while Mathewson helped to "pepper up the baseball lingo and provide her with . . . names like 'Cy Dobb,' 'Hans Hagner,' and 'Fred Terkle.'"[76] In short, the story concerns two brothers, Copley and Punch Reeves, players for the Eagles' Baseball Team of Sligo, Texas, and their lovely new owner, Mona Fitzgerald. Along with various other ballplayers and trainers, there are two unscrupulous types, Bohannan, their manager, and Welland, the owner of the rival team, the Hornets, who scheme to trick Fitzgerald into selling her franchise for far less than its worth. Copley Reeves, "custodian of the family inheritance," has been instructed by the terms of his father's will not to turn over his younger brother's share until Punch has refrained from drink for six months.[77] However, Punch gets tricked into going to a party and "off the wagon" by their manager to ensure the loss of the game and the pennant. Copley (as does Brown in *Brown of Harvard*) steps up to the plate as a pinch hitter and wins the game. He saves his brother's money by exiting one door as Punch is brought in another, thus, able to swear that he never saw his brother intoxicated during the probation period. Ultimately, he also wins the girl and helps her save the team.

Advanced publicity and Mathewson's celebrity brought out the press for opening night of *The Girl and the Pennant* at the Lyric Theatre, October 21, 1913. Both of the authors must have been disappointed in out of town tryouts, since neither of them appeared before the audience when called for at the final curtain.[78] Reviews of the New York production prove more diverting than the play itself. Acton Davies remarked that despite the valiant attempt of the actors and Edgar Selwyn, the producer/director, the play "from start to finish, never had one human moment," and "was composed of the old cut-and-dried situations which have done duty in melodrama for the last forty years."[79] However, *Theatre* considered *The Girl and the Pennant* "ingenuous entertainment" for its convincing staging of a baseball game:

> Like the horse race in "In Old Kentucky," the deciding baseball game for the pennant takes place off the stage, but is described with great verisimilitude by an imposing scoreboard and the descriptive powers of a number of the players who have been banished from the diamond because they would unduly sass that much berated individual, the umpire. This makes for an admirable theatrical scene in which the elements of the game are graphically presented and the true spirit of illusion and suspense well maintained.[80]

The ball game notwithstanding, a number of reviewers agreed with Charles Darnton that an afternoon tea party given for the ball players by Mona and her friends seemed not only incongruous to the milieu of baseball, but even erroneous.[81] The *World* suggested that "ignorance of the sport might be an advantage" to enjoying the play "because the play is apt to shatter the idols of many fans."[82] The *Sun* cruelly panned the play with condemning titles: "Baseball Didn't Make a Hit," "The National Game Caricatured at the Lyric Theatre Last Night," "Sadly Bores Audience," and "A Woman's Grotesque View of the Politics of the Diamond." As usual, the reviewer took offense over Young's audacity in tackling such a "masculine" milieu. In previous efforts she dealt with "the amateur"— "an undergraduate or a tin soldier." But, declared the outraged critic, baseball is a serious sport."[83] New York theatregoers must have agreed that baseball and theatre did not mix, as the run lasted only three weeks. *The Girl and the Pennant* served as Christy Mathewson's one and only foray into theatre.

VICTOR HERBERT COLLABORATIONS:
NAUGHTY MARIETTA AND *THE DREAM GIRL*

In May 1910 Oscar Hammerstein commissioned Rida Johnson Young and Victor Herbert to write a comic opera in which he could feature stars from his troubled opera company.[84] Young, by now a popular new playwright and lyricist, and Herbert, a talented composer with twenty-four musical productions to his credit, commenced to create memorable roles for the diminutive Italian soprano, Emma Trentini, and the three opera-trained voices who supported her: tenor Orville Harrold, contralto Marie Duchene and baritone Edward Martindel. From his former opera troupe, Hammerstein also provided Gaetano Merola as conductor, an orchestra of thirty, and over half of the company's one-hundred-voice chorus. "Not only had Hammerstein given Herbert the best group of singers ever assembled for a Broadway show," stated Frederick S. Roffman in a 1975 retrospective on *Naughty Marietta*, "but he provided a sumptuous physical production, as well," spending over $75,000 to mount the operetta.[85]

Indeed, as Gerald Bordman asserts, "the show was blessed from the start," and by the time the show opened, "its success was beyond doubt."[86] On October 24, 1910, just six months after Young and Herbert began their collaboration, *Naughty Marietta* had its first public performance in Syracuse under the direction of Oscar Hammerstein's son, Arthur. Two weeks later, the operetta reached the New York Theatre in Manhattan, which, coincidentally, Hammerstein had erected in 1895 as The Olympia but had lost within three years due to insurmountable financial woes. Now, for the first time since, Hammerstein returned to the theatre to experience the "brilliant success" of *Naughty Marietta's* opening night where virtually every number was encored" and critics issued "unstinting" praise of Herbert's melodies and "masterful orchestration."[87]

Representative of operettas of the period, Rida Johnson Young's libretto contributes significantly to the overall charm and atmosphere of *Naughty Marietta*. Set in a public square of "rough-

and-tumble" 1750 New Orleans, the opening number ("Naughty Marietta") introduces a high-spirited young maid, Marietta, the Italian Contessa D'Altena who has escaped strict parents and come from France on a *casquette* boat. Marietta hides as the morning brings out shopkeepers and flower girls. The son of the Lieutenant Governor, Etienne Grandet—who is actually the notorious pirate, Bras Pique—enters, flirts with the flower girls and rebuffs his former lover, the courtesan Adah. Captain Richard Warrington and his band of singing frontiersmen ("Tramp! Tramp! Tramp!") march in with a warrant for the arrest of Bras Pique. Etienne tells Captain Dick that while the Governor is away his father is in charge in New Orleans, when, in fact, Bras Pique holds the Governor hostage on the Isle of Pines and plans to take over Louisiana for himself. Captain Dick's men have also come to find wives from the boatload of "Casquette Maids" sent over by the King of France.[88] Lizette, a *casquette* girl, becomes enamored with Simon, one of Captain Dick's men who becomes enamored with the gold in her *casquette*.[89]

When Captain Dick encounters Marietta, she immediately is taken with him, telling him of a song that haunts her dreams and that she seeks the man who can finish her melody. Believing her to be a runaway *casquette* girl, he agrees to help her hide and gets Rudolfo, owner of a local marionette troupe, to pass Marietta off as his son. Later, Etienne sees through Marietta's disguise and guesses that she is the missing Contessa. After various invitations and rebuffs, everyone attends a masked ball. Marietta and Dick confront each other, but even when they seem to reconcile differences and reveal their feelings through song ("I'm Falling in Love With Someone"), he is still unwilling to admit his love. Angry, Marietta reveals to everyone that she is, indeed, the Contessa and accepts Etienne's proposal only to spite Dick. Adah, however, intervenes to Captain Dick, revealing Etienne's true pirate identity; this is verified by Sir Harry Blake, a member of Dick's band, who arrives to announce the rescue of the Governor. Lieutenant Governor Grandet must then arrest his own son. When Captain Dick arrives where Marietta awaits, he finishes her haunting song, "Ah, Sweet Mystery of Life," (sung in its entirety) and wins the girl.

Victor Herbert's score and the principals, notably Emma Trentini and Orville Harold, received nothing but standing ovations from audiences and generous praise from the critics. As Bordman posits, "[w]riting for such fine, thoroughly trained voices, Victor Herbert allowed himself a rare depth and range. His vocal lines were among his most operatic, his orchestrations far and away his most symphonic." Melodically, the score was probably Herbert's "most inventive and enthralling, with at least four of the songs taking their place among his finest, most popular classics."[90]

Unfortunately for Young, critics reserved almost all negative remarks for the book and libretto. Criticism leveled at *Naughty Marietta* concerned predominately comic bits inserted between songs, along with more light-hearted dialogue which reviewers found inappropriate, and they virtually lambasted the two actors playing the comic roles. Channing Pollock in *The Green Book Album*, however, blamed the "surprising bad taste of Impresario Oscar Hammerstein," for using "two clownish – vaudevillains – named Harry Cooper and Kate Elinore," and chalked it up to "the common or roof garden side of Mr. Hammerstein's nature."[91]

In writing the book for *Naughty Marietta*, Rida Johnson Young faced "almost insurmountable obstacles." Neither of the female leads, Trentini and Duchene, spoke fluent English.[92] As Pollock surmised, Hammerstein insisted on including vaudeville comedians for the comic roles in order to amuse the gallery. And "the costume designer had changed the period from 1750 to 1775 after Louisiana had reverted to Spain, a time when Captain Dick and his 'Virginians and Kaintucks' would have been up North fighting in the American Revolutionary War!"[93] Of the musical's book the *Theatre* reviewer stated: "the less said... the better... It is simply stupid and will interrupt no one's drowsing."[94] In a similar vein, the *New York Dramatic Mirror* offered: "The music contributes more to the success of *Naughty Marietta* than the libretto does," calling the book "only a necessary evil."[95] Even the *Tribune's* complimentary nod to Young held reservations:

The story chosen by Mrs. Young was a charming one, one in which there was abundant opportunity for poetic treatment. Unfortunately, the atmosphere of the dreamy creole New Orleans of two hundred years ago was only too often rudely torn apart to make room for the broadest of vaudeville stunts.[96]

The test of time, however, has shown the more enduring quality of Young's efforts in *Naughty Marietta*. In revivals over the years, musical directors, while keeping Herbert's score, have not only tampered with the original book and lyrics, but rearranged scenes or completely changed the period. Thus, problems arise concerning the validity of the whole premise of the *casquette* girls, who could not have been sent to America much after 1750 as originally written. One director stated when returning to the original, "The relation of the parts to one another makes much more sense."[97] Similarly, Jack Eddleman, who directed a New York City Opera production of *Naughty Marietta* in August 1979, explained that after attempting a previously rewritten version, they decided to return to Young's 1910 book and the original order of the musical numbers. As he described.

You can't avoid the operetta style. Yes, here and there I've changed an archaic phrase if it made the performer uncomfortable or dropped a joke that was just too corny. But I've left others in that go with the character, and where the cast can get their tongues around a swashbuckling line, the period dialogue sounds right. I've tried to keep the swashbuckling tone along with a sense of honesty. As a matter of fact, I find the romantic stuff quite moving and beautiful. There is warmth and humanity in the work.[98]

When *Naughty Marietta* opened in New York in November 1910, it was the fifteenth of the season's thirty-four musicals. Although it could have run longer, states Bordman, the show ran only 136 performances because of contractual arrangements; the show was "far from being the runaway smash of the year, [but] it was the finest show of the season. In fact, it was the American masterwork of the era."[99] In March 1935, MGM released the film version of *Naughty Marietta*, uniting for the first time the vocal talent of Jeanette MacDonald and Nelson Eddy.

Lyrics from *Naughty Marietta* resonate with wit, charm and originality. The song, "I'm Falling in Love With Someone," is still used in movies and musicals, as in *Thoroughly Modern Millie*, for example, since it so aptly describes the sensation of falling in love:

> I've a very strange feeling / I've ne'er felt before.
> 'Tis a kind of grind of depression.
> My heart's acting strangely, / It feels rather sore,
> At least it gives me that impression.
> My pulses leap madly / Without any cause.
> Believe me, I'm telling you truly,
> I'm gay without pause, / Then sad without cause.
> My spirits are truly unruly.[100]

Today, *Naughty Marietta* continues to be regularly revived by light opera companies throughout the country and, without a doubt, represents Young's most revived work.

The Dream Girl, a musical adaptation of *The Road to Yesterday* by Beulah Marie Dix and Evelyn Greenleaf Sutherland [see discussion of play in Chapter 3] produced fourteen years after *Naughty Marietta*, served as Herbert and Young's second collaboration and as the final Broadway musical for both. Although a *New York Times* announcement stated that it would be presented October 1920, *The Dream Girl's* opening was delayed four years because of contractual negotiations.[101] A five-day tryout production by the Shuberts eventually took place in New Haven, Connecticut, in April 1924, but a month later in May, Victor Herbert died suddenly of heart failure.[102] The *New York Times* critic began his review of the August

20, 1924, opening of *The Dream Girl* by saying that "Victor Herbert left this life on a high note."[103] The production marked the return of Fay Bainter to the stage, playing the role of Elspeth with "unforced charm" and "unrehearsed wistfulness."[104] Although Fay Bainter displayed considerable stage presence, her co-star Walter Woolf, a "knightly" baritone in the role of Jack Warren, possessed the stronger voice, particularly in the title song, "My Dream Girl," and a "thrilling" march with the male chorus, "A Broad Highway."[105]

The book of *The Dream Girl* follows the same story as *A Road to Yesterday*, with a young romantic American girl, Elspeth, who visits England and wishes on Midsummer Night's Eve she could go back to an earlier time. The characters resemble those from the original play and "reincarnate" as people in a previous life five hundred years earlier in the second act and return to the present in the third.[106] However, the musical version loses some of the charm of the original play, due largely to the use of 1920s contemporary language and humor; had Young's intention been to spoof the original—sometimes hinted at—she might have taken it farther and exploited the original even more. Echoing the complaints toward the comedians in *Naughty Marietta*, critics now shot salvos at Billy B. Van, who played the comic character Jimmie Van Dyke. One critic put some of the blame on the writer, Harold Atteridge, however, who was brought in by the Shuberts to assist Young with the book, very likely to add in humor.[107] The musical, stated the critic, was "harnessed somewhat unwillingly to jokes by Mr. Harold Atteridge and clowning by Mr. Billy B. Van. Neither artist, one fears, was at his best." [108]

As seen from earlier criticism directed at *Naughty Marietta*'s book, Young certainly faced challenges in creating musical books. Shortly before his death, Victor Herbert pointed out the difficulty of writing plot for a musical comedy. "The musical numbers are constantly interfering with the action. Every time a song is introduced the plot is thrown down on the floor and the interest is interrupted."[109] Thus, the challenge of the librettist lies in counteracting this "interference" by creating a book that flows from one song to the next. In the book of *The Dream Girl*, superfluous one-liners and jokes serve little purpose other than to bog down the action of the plot. Somehow, Jimmie, who is attached to his radio in 1924, manages to have it with him in 1424 when his speech often reverts inexplicably to modern banter and slang. An example of some of the humor can be seen early in the first act, when Addison and Jimmie show Elspeth's nearsighted Aunt Harriet some paintings:

> ADDISON: Now this is the work of that great master Raphael. You see his name in the corner there, Raphael.

> HARRIET: (looks at picture) Why this says Rachel.

> JIMMIE: Rachel—where? Yes, it does say Rachel. But I can explain that. You see Raphael went into bankruptcy, and put everything in his wife's name.

> ADDISON: Now Miss Harriet the title of this painting is London Bridge in a Fog.

> HARRIET: London Bridge in a Fog—I can't see the bridge.

> JIMMIE: You can't see the bridge. Why certainly not. That was painted on a very foggy day. How do you expect to see the bridge on a foggy day like that. The fog predominates. It's an Irish subject, called Fog a bolla.

But Jimmie reaches an outrageous peak at:

> JIMMIE: This is a Rembrandt. One you shouldn't miss. It's called "Omar Khayam [sic] on his Yacht . . ."

> HARRIET: What is Omar Khayam doing on a Red Boat.

> JIMMIE: What Red Boat. That's not red, that's ruby. That is the Ruby Yacht of Omar Khyam."[110]

Lighter touches of contemporary humor… seem more effective when coming from the central characters, as seen in the second act when Jack, evading capture from Lord Strangevon's men, turns back to reassure Elspeth, "There! Am I not the hero?" And Elspeth replies, "You are my hero—my Douglas Fairbanks!"[111] Burns Mantle maintained that the dream sequence between "Lady Elspeth" and "Reformado Jack" caught "something of the story's finer appeal."[112] New York audiences enjoyed *The Dream Girl* for five weeks before the show toured extensively with most of the original cast.[113]

FIVE PLAYS AND "MOTHER MACHREE" FOR IRISH TENOR, CHAUNCEY OLCOTT

It is plausible that Rida Johnson Young became acquainted with Chauncey Olcott during her two-year stint at Witmark Music Publishing, with whom he was associated. Her first venture for him was *Ragged Robin*, an Irish fairy play, in which she helped Rita Olcott, his wife, shape her ideas into a play.[114] This was followed by *Ragged Robin*, 1910; *Barry of Ballymore*, 1911; *Macushla*, 1912; *The Isle o'Dreams*, 1913; and *Shameen Dhu*, 1914.

Chauncey Olcott (1858–1932) was born to an Irish mother and American father in Buffalo, New York, and began performing while very young. By 1910 Olcott had been performing for a number of years in stock and more recently in touring productions written to suit his performing and singing abilities. Since the late 1890s Augustus Pitou had served as his agent, producer, and playwright, creating the books for romantic musical dramas which he mounted and toured.[115] Over the years with his rich tenor voice, sentimental ballads and romantic Irish themes, Olcott had built up quite a following with the Irish population, who formed enthusiastic audiences. Of a performance in Galveston, Texas, in 1910, for instance, Olcott's songs were "encored over and over again" and he had to oblige his "admirers at the end of the third act by making a speech."[116] New York audiences also fell under his spell, as noted when *Isle o' Dreams* opened in 1913:

The huge theatre was packed and the audience very soon became a prominent feature of the performance, insisting on manifesting its pleasure after every line, as is the joyful custom with Mr. Olcott's regular clientele, and fairly going mad each time he sang a song. As a result it was within one or two minutes of 11 o'clock when the curtain went up on the fourth and last act.[117]

While Rida Johnson Young was not Irish, her understanding of musical theatre and her ability to "write to order" enabled her to create for Chauncey Olcott suitable, if not ideal vehicles. In *Ragged Robin*, a light romance interwoven with Irish folklore and minstrel melodies, Olcott played "a gay-hearted beloved vagabond minstrel," who was a disinherited son of an Irish nobleman, known and welcomed by everyone for his gift of song. With the help of the fairies, the minstrel is not only restored to his rightful title, but united with his lady love.[118] *Ragged Robin* opened in Olcott's hometown of Saratoga, New York, in August 1908, toured for two years, and returned to New York where his fans packed the Academy of Music during the two-week run.[119] All in all, Young's first play for Olcott, with the story of Irish folklore provided by Rita Olcott, resulted in one of his most profitable plays.

Barry of Ballymore offered Olcott a completely different role in Tom Barry, the son of a gatekeeper in Ballymore, county Galway, who acquired wealth and prominence as an artist in Paris. Set in the eighteenth century, the drama focuses on Barry's efforts to restore his mother's half-sister, Nanette, to her rightful place as the daughter of a wealthy lord; in the process, he falls in love with the lord's other daughter, Lady Mary Bannon, for whom he must fight a duel.[120] As in all Olcott vehicles, Irish dances and songs remained an important component, but one of Young's songs in *Barry of Ballymore* ultimately became her most famous, "Mother Machree," with music by Olcott and Ernest Ball. Stated the *Sun*: "As Thomas Barry, the artist, Chauncey Olcott had an excellent chance to interpret the character of a lovable young Irishman, and several tuneful 'Olcott'songs were cleverly woven into the play. Perhaps the best of these was 'Mother Machree,' which he sings to his white-haired mother on the eve of the duel."[121] While today hardly anyone recalls the play from which it came, "Mother Machree" has evolved into one of the most popular Irish songs of all times.

Over the next three years, Young churned out three more touring vehicles for the popular singer-actor, dubbed "the Irish playboy of the theatre world."[122] With a February 1912 opening, *Macushla* ("pulse of my heart") is the name of a horse, a famous jumper owned by Sir Brian Fitzgerald (Olcott), an unwilling heir of a debt-ridden estate; Macushla wins a race and makes it possible for the hero to pay his creditors and win the lodge keeper's daughter. *The Isle o' Dreams*, opening at the end of January 1913, takes place in 1790 Ireland, where England serves as the "villain"; a young man raised as a foundling by a fishwife on the Isle o' Dreams learns that he is a nobleman, thus, enabling him to marry the princess he loves. Olcott again used "Mother Machree" in this play and also introduced his own ultimate classic, "When Irish Eyes are Smiling," lyrics by Olcott and George Graff and composed by Ernest Ball. An enthusiastic and vociferous audience of *Shameen Dhu*'s opening night in February 1914 "interrupted the performance in many places."[123] Set in Ireland in 1779, Olcott played Dare O'Donnell, a poet known as Shameen Dhu, a writer of treasonable tracts during the revolution to free Ireland. Farcical elements lie in misunderstandings with three different women while the hero evades the British hangman. Henry Miller directed all three plays which appeared at the Grand Opera House.

COLLABORATING WITH NEPHEW, WILLIAM SCHROEDER

William Schroeder was only twenty-one when he wrote his first score for the Shuberts in 1909, *Just One of the Boys*, a revamping of Young's earlier unproduced, *Sweet Sixteen*.[124] Evidently the Shuberts thought they had a potential Victor Herbert in the emerging composer, but while Schroeder never lived up to that expectation, he did achieve some success as a minor composer and arranger.[125] As mentioned previously, Schroeder contributed to the musical adaptation of *The Boys of Company B*, which appears not to have been produced. However, four of Young and Schroeder's works were produced: *Just One of the Boys*, 1910, *Lady Luxury*, 1914, *His Little Widows*, 1917 and *A Wise Child*, 1921.

By 1909, Young had created several successful plays, and although *Brown of Harvard* contained a few musical numbers, she had yet to produce a full musical. *Just One of the Boys*, a "musical play in two acts," was a significant move toward creating a full-fledged musical.[126] Unfortunately, during the tour of the musical throughout cities in upstate New York, along with Washington, DC, Chicago, Detroit, Cleveland, and Pittsburgh, critics described both the libretto and musical score as "mediocre."

Lula Glaser played Cherry Winston, a young woman who is the sole owner and manager of a lumber camp in the backwoods of Michigan. An orphan, Cherry has been raised by three uncouth, rugged woodsmen— Irish, Scottish, and American—with the result that she takes on the mannerisms of each.[127] Into their camp wanders "a proprietor of a New York boarding school, his girl pupils, and some young fellows, one of which falls head over heels in love with the sylvan beauty."[128] When Cherry's tomboyish ways contrast unfavorably with the more "feminine" behavior and attire of the other girls, she realizes she needs "finishing," and heads for New York. The second act follows Cherry's transformation, which is complicated by jealousy from other girls, the persistent attention the ardent young man, and the arrival of her three "guardsmen." Despite negative critical commentary about the musical, audiences liked Lula Glaser, so the star kept the show going. She "oxygenated it with herself," as one admirer put it. "She is as merry and champagney as ever, as deliciously awkward, and gurgles and chirps in her familiar and diverting way."[129] Although audiences paid to see the star, evidently her "effervescence" was not enough to bring the show to New York.

Lady Luxury, the next Young–Schroeder collaboration, did make it to Broadway, opening at the Casino Theatre on Christmas Day 1914, but critics were at odds about it. The plot centers on

Eloise Van Curler, an orphan who is about to celebrate her twenty-first birthday and inherit a family house and fortune. She has been brought up strictly by an old-fashioned uncle, living in a fusty old house, but Eloise has different ideas and at five o'clock, the minute she comes of age, her plan takes effect. Suddenly, the house "becomes a mansion and is filled with up-to-the-minute guests, dancers, chaperones, singing teachers, and other necessities of modern musical comedies."[130] Eloise's uncle decides to teach her a lesson and disappears into a secret room over the fireplace. Most of the fun occurs when Sam Warren, a Texas youth who likes Eloise, tries to carry food and drink to the man in hiding, but comes under suspicion of committing various acts, including making Van Cuyler disappear. Eventually the old gentleman comes out of hiding, and Eloise changes from her sumptuous gown to her initial conservative dress and agrees to go with Warren to his ranch in Texas. The *New York Times* called the idea of the story "novel" and the *New York Review* dubbed the book "a genuine surprise in its cleverness and sustained interest"; but the *Sun* maintained that "Mrs. Young's text departs at no point from the most familiar material of the libretto writer."[131] Schroeder's musical score was, according to critics, a "modification" of old favorites and relatively conventional.[132]

Ina Claire, a well-known musical theatre actress, played Eloise, but despite pleasing looks and manner, her "tiny" voice was not up to Schroeder's more ambitious pieces. Following thirty-five performances in New York, the show went on tour with new principals, bolstered by the addition of a trained singer in the lead role. For the first touring company, Young drafted Florence Webber, who had played the lead in the touring production of *Naughty Marietta*, while Yra Jeane, a "dainty little Prima Donna played Eloise in the second tour."[133] Apropos of what 1916 theatre-goers sought in their entertainment, a newspaper ad for *Lady Luxury* touted: "Notable Cast of Singing Principals and Beauty Chorus—GIRLS, GOWNS, SCENERY, MUSIC, SINGING AND DANCING."[134]

His Little Widows, according to Heywood Broun in the *Tribune*, was the only musical comedy of the 1918–17 season in which the chief interest was the story. "The book is not brilliant," he stated, "but it is built around a coherent and ingenious idea which helps not a little in making a theatrical evening pleasant." Indeed, *His Little Widows* remains one of Young's more interesting musicals, marking her second collaboration in writing lyrics with William Carey Duncan and the most commercially successful one with Schroeder.[135] Other critics, as well, thought her plot about polygamy to be quite engaging in its different spin on a clichéd situation—"the story of the thing is its best ingredient," stated *Theatre*, and complained that people were always interrupting the plot to "sing."[136]

The musical tells of Pete Lloyd and his partners at Lloyd, Grayson and Hale, three young brokers who "have been taking a flyer in copper" and now find themselves bankrupt—the news brought to them in the midst of a posh party at a fashionable restaurant. While they try to determine how they are going to pay for the night's festivities, upon the scene enters Abijah Smith, a Morman elder who informs Pete his uncle has died and left him three million dollars; the terms of the will, however, stipulate he must marry all eleven of his uncle's wives. How this "brash" New Yorker deals with this situation, with his friends accompanying him to Salt Lake City and falling in love with two of the wives as Pete falls for the prettiest, comprises the plot. Pete goes through with the polygamous marriage, counting on a judge to show up shortly thereafter to annul it, but the judge doesn't appear, having left town. By the close of the final curtain, however, Pete manages to wind up with only one wife of his choosing.

The musical score of *His Little Widows* was considered pleasing enough—"the music tinkles, though without distinction"—but more critical attention went to several song-and-dance performances.[137] Four Haley sisters, for instance, "one of them with a baritone voice—were genuinely amusing in an old-fashioned ragtime song that brought roars of laughter."[138] Overall, the musical provided amusing entertainment at the Astor Theatre for their first summer show.

Production of Young and Schroeder's collaborative work ended on a weak note in a Boston tryout of *A Wise Child* in August 1921. The show was announced as Vivienne Segal's first major acting role, serving as a departure from previous musical roles. She played Yonnie Leslie, a young, lively vaudevillian who is approached by a lawyer to impersonate the long-lost daughter of a wealthy dying man; the lawyer convinces her that in doing so, she will give happiness to the old man in his final days. John Dent, the elderly father, however, becomes so overjoyed to finally locate his daughter that he is rejuvenated. And when he cannot persuade Yonnie to quit the stage, he sets up his "daughter" and her partner/fiancé, Tim, with the Palais Rose, a dance restaurant, in which to perform. But Tim then leaves over a misunderstanding. In another twist of fate, John Dent learns that he is bankrupt and has a physical set back, throwing Yonnie into a difficult situation. But she rises to the challenge, and, confessing the truth to everyone in the household, she stays to take care of the old man who loves her. In an "avalanche of sentiment," Tim, now a "moving picture star," returns to purchase the Palais Rose and reunites with Yonnie.[139] One of the few reviews of the play ended with "It is reasonably good sentimental entertainment, but tiresome toward the end."[140] Although apparently Schroeder provided strong tunes for Segal and opportunities for her to display her singing and dancing abilities, *A Wise Child* contained a melodramatic plot with several reversal of fortunes that did not impress critics. It appears not to have gotten much further than the Boston tryout.

It must have been a disappointing year for Young, since she experienced another flop earlier in 1921 with a straight play, *The Front Seat*. Presented by Arthur Hammerstein at Poli's theatre in Washington, DC, the play revolves around Constance, a woman who "glories in her pseudo-freedom" and tries to regain the love of a man whom she had thrown into the arms of her sister. Taking place over thirty-five years, the play attempts, a bit too evidently—according to a write-up on the opening—"to trace the bachelor maid of unconventional views and gold-digging tendency to the lair of her declining years. She succeeds in proving that marriage is a reasonably successful institution."[141] Apparently, Young was trying for a more contemporary theme in *The Front Seat*, showing the struggles of young flappers, artists, and philosophers in Greenwich Village, but the play did not fare well in the trial showing. Conceivably, given more time to work on this theme, Young may have turned it into a successful musical.

WARTIME ENTERTAINMENT: *CAPTAIN KIDD, JR.,*
HER SOLDIER BOY, MAYTIME, SOMETIME, LITTLE SIMPLICITY

Upon reading Young's *Captain Kidd, Jr.*, it becomes puzzling as to why the title changed, since in earlier showings it was called more appropriately *Buried Treasure*—evidently producers Cohan and Harris thought the title too revealing and renamed it.[142] The story opens in MacTavish & Company, a bookshop owned and operated by Andrew MacTavish and his granddaughter, Mary; they are assisted by Jim Anderson, an aspiring young writer who is like a son to MacTavish and a bantering beau to Mary, with whom she constantly argues. The action begins with the delivery of a box of books that Jim has purchased from an estate auction, much to Mary's chagrin; when he opens the box, he discovers old cookbooks, along with a book containing a treasure map telling the location of buried treasure in Cape Cod. Several people come by the bookshop looking for the book, but it is William Carlton, grandson and heir of the owner of the map, who strikes up a deal with the threesome to team up and look for the treasure. All sorts of whimsical situations occur in the small Cape Cod town as they dig for the treasure, posing as geologists under the curious eye of landlady Luella Bush (played by Zelda Sears) and a wary constable who suspects they have robbed the local bank. When others come snooping around and arguments ensue, Mary purchases the farm with her entire savings of two thousand dollars to ensure their having the treasure. But when the "treasure box" is finally discovered, all that it contains is a letter to Carlton from his grandfather, extolling "good health, fresh air," and "honest work," the very things they have all just experienced in the process of digging up the box. Everyone is deflated. At the top of the third act "MacTavish and Company" mull over the bleak future of the bookstore, not to mention the expenditures of their two-week treasure hunt and Mary's extravagant purchase of a farm. First, Carlton drops in to insist on paying rent on the farm where he needs to go to soak up fresh air for a year before his inheritance comes due, but then the constable shows up to offer Mary $2,500 for the farm she now owns. But soon thereafter comes Mr. Greyson, a man they thought was a surveyor, but who now admits to owning a fish cannery five miles west of Mary's farm and who wants to purchase her property to build an access road. After some haggling, he writes Mary a check for $25,000, and everyone is relived that the treasure hunt paid off, after all. Other things get resolved, as well, as when Jim and Mary stop fighting, when Carlton declares his love for his secretary and when Jim discovers a returned manuscript from a publisher to be not a rejection, after all, but an acceptance with a check.

Theatre felt that not only was it a poor title, but a "poor play"—"a somewhat baffling mixture of farce, comedy, and inevitable bathos."[143] "Bathos" as used by the critic and defined by *Webster's Dictionary* refers to "a ludicrous decent from the exalted or lofty to the commonplace; anti-climax."[144] Indeed, the interest generated in the first act over the possibility of treasure becomes heightened not only by Jim's excitement over the information he finds, but the three characters' increasing enthusiasm over the map. Once they team up with Carlton and the adventure begins, the playwright has achieved a strong sense of expectation.

The second act generates more humor with the introduction of new "local" characters, as the four treasure hunters—Mary, her grandfather, Jim and Carlton—go about digging holes under the guise of being geologists. When the farmer, Lem, comes to check on them, for instance, Jim orders, "Geologize!" and they each pick up handfuls of dirt to study. Asked if they'd found any "val'able specimens," Jim replies: "Well, we've found a little cosmoditious and few uniform perciflages, but otherwise we haven't made much progress here. We are thinking of pursuing our investigations in the next amphibious section." "My, my!" states Lem, "Funny how a feller kin live in a place all his life and not know what he's a steppin' on."[145] But there's not a large payoff to all their secrecy and hard labor; even getting a nice, large settlement for Mary's two thousand dollar investment in the third act seems only compensatory. The characters were well delineated as portrayed by the strong cast, although most critics felt that Zelda Sears was wasted on her small role of the country landlady. Even so, Young found a fan in the *Tribune* critic:

> The amount of real humor which Mrs. Young manages to inject into this story is astonishing. It is true that she is greatly aided by the work of a generally excellent cast, but one departs with the feeling that Mrs. Young should be severely spoken to for wasting so much time in the writing of average musical comedies.[146]

The title of *Captain Kid, Jr.*, changed yet again to *Lot 79* in London where it played a couple of weeks in April 1918.

When *Her Soldier Boy* opened in December 1916, the United States was on the verge of officially entering World War I, and, naturally, this occupied the thoughts of most Americans. Some, as did one critic, felt that war plays were "in singularly bad taste." However, as *Puck* described, the "musical play" had no "mission to perform" and constituted the "best vehicle for any theatrical entertainment with 'war' in it. Until 'Her Soldier Boy' came to town, we had not savored the pleasure of this possibility."[147] Indeed, *Her Soldier Boy* represented the first musical to deal with the war head-on, albeit through a romantic theme livened with comedy.[148] Initially, the Shuberts opened the musical in the Astor Theatre, later moved it to the Lyric, and then housed it in the Shubert Theatre between December 1916 and summer 1917. War-ravaged Londoners welcomed the musical even more heartily when it opened in June 1918 toward the end of the war and played twice as long as the successful New York run.

The creation of *Her Soldier Boy* began sometime at the end of summer 1915 when J. J. Shubert asked Young's opinion of a two-act German play, *Gold Gave I For Iron (Gold gab ich Fuer Eisen)*, by Victor Leon.[149] Leon's work centers on the relationship between two army comrades, Franz and Alvin; on the battlefield, Franz recalls the home he has not seen in fifteen years and "begs Alvin, if he falls, to take his love to his mother and sister. Alvin has heard so much of the old castle, the gentle mother and the pretty sister, that he feels acquainted with them all, and tells Franz laughingly that he would like to marry Marline, although he only knows her by her picture."[150] Later, Alvin arrives at the castle of Gubendorf in lower Austria where peasants bring all their gold ornaments to the lady of the castle to be used to raise funds for the war effort; in return, each is given an iron ring with the inscription "Gold Gave I for Iron"—an old Austrian custom.[151] Sorrowfully, Alvin stands before the door, ready to deliver the sad news of Franz's death to his mother and sister, when Vitus, an old peasant farmer learns what he is about to do; Vitus declares that the shock will kill Franz's mother and begs Alvin to instead, impersonate Franz, as they have not seen him in so many years. The Baroness remains a little doubtful toward Alvin, and Marline gradually realizes that his love for her is not that of a brother. But the truth becomes fully revealed when Franz turns up alive, returning home to high honors for bravery, thus allowing Alvin to marry Marline, after all.[152]

Young responded to J. J. Shubert in September, telling him that *Gold Gave I for Iron* "could be made into a very charming and unique play."[153] They conferred about the play, he sent her a $300 advance, and by the end of October with only one act written, Shubert went about casting the musical, *Her Soldier Boy*.[154] The "starring" role of Teddy McLane, one of several characters added by Young, went to the talented Clifton Crawford, while his counterpart, Amy, an American Red Cross volunteer, was played by Adele Rowland.

In Young's version, the musical opens with a Prologue "somewhere in Belgium" behind enemy lines with Alfred Appledorf leading a small crowd of soldiers in song. Alain and Frantz, two comrades-in-arms, come on talking, and what is revealed follows the original play, except that bombs actually explode and

Frantz is hit and dragged off by Alain. The first act shows the crumbling old castle of Ghistelle, Frantz's home, and introduces Elsje, a Dutch servant, Marlene, Frantz's sister, Teddy McLane, an American war correspondent and his traveling companion, Monty Mainwaring, an English correspondent. Teddy flirts with village girls and becomes involved with affairs of the villagers, especially Baron Van Artveldt, the precinct captain, and Vitus Appledorp, a rich farmer, both of whom want to marry their sons to Marlene. Teddy instigates much of the action, such as persuading Monty with the promise of fifty pounds to let Teddy arrest him as a spy in order to impress the American girl, Amy. However, his scheme to impress Amy backfires when she gets Monty released from the filthy cellar where he is incarcerated and then pampers him back to health, much to Teddy's jealous displeasure. When Alain arrives to tell Frantz's mother and Marlene about Frantz's death on the battlefield, it is Teddy who convinces him that, since the mother is blind and Frantz has been gone for 15 years, he should impersonate his comrade until the regiment marches to spare the mother's grief. Alain gets swept along with the deception when family and friends assume he is Frantz. In the second act Alain and Marlene begin to fall in love while the two village fathers haggle over which son will marry her, even though one son, Alfred, wants to marry Desiree, a village girl. And despite confusion over who is betrothed to whom, it all resolves when Alain confesses his quite unbrotherly love for Marlene and her real brother arrives home alive and well.

All elements—book, lyrics, music, staging and acting—came together for *Her Soldier Boy* to create an excellent show for New York audiences. Critics remained unanimous in their praise and found nothing to complain about. The *New York Times* enthused that *Her Soldier Boy* was "full of good things": "Indeed, this new wartime piece which came gaily and victoriously to the Astor last evening is so full of things to applaud and things to hum, and, above all, things to laugh at, that it proves to be one of the most enjoyable musical plays to pass this way in the last five sea- sons."[155] First to praise came the music of Emmerich Kalman; "his 'Kiss Waltz,' for example," stated the *Dramatic Mirror*, "is an exquisite bit of romance tinged with awakening emotion—and supplementing the music, or rather accompanying it in many instances, is crisp, bright comedy, all as clean as a snowflake."[156] John Charles Thomas as Alain "carried off the vocal honors of the night" in his love duets with Beth Lydy as Marlene. Clifton Crawford provided the bulk of the humor with his "easy, graceful way of winning your good opinions," stated Charles Darnton in the *World*.[157] And while several lasting songs came out of this musical, the international hit was "Smile, Smile, Smile," as belted out by Adele Rowland—the words, "Pack up your troubles in your old kit bag and smile, smile, smile," used as both American and British marching songs.[158] While Young was aided by the strength of Leon's original story, she received much praise for her book, as well as lyrics, with critics expressing relief over a musical with a "real plot."

Even though 1917 marked America's official entry into "the Great War," professionally speaking, the year proved to be an outstanding one for Rida Johnson Young. *His Little Widows* opened in New York at the end of April while *Her Soldier Boy* was still running; and shortly after the closing of those two productions, the Shuberts opened *Maytime* at the Shubert Theatre in August, beginning the longest run Young would ever enjoy with any her musicals.

J. J. Shubert gave another German work to Young called *'Twas Once in May* "with instructions to remove the last trace of Teutonic flavor." She went about doing so "effectively, centering the entire action around the Washington Square section of Manhattan."[159] *Maytime*, called a play with music, follows several generations in four acts taking place in 1840, 1855, the 1880s and in the present, 1917; three acts take place in the Van Zandt home in Washington Square while the second act occurs in Madam Delphine's, "a celebrated gambling house and dancing salon."[160] The action opens in a garden at the rear of the Van Zandt home near the cooper shop where young Richard Wayne and his father make casks and barrels.[161] Ottilie, the spirited Van Zandt daughter, and Richard have grown up together, a romantic affection developing between them. For her sixteenth birthday he gives her an apple tree, but before they plant it in the garden, they put her jewel casket under it with a ring, a lock of her hair and a piece of paper with their song, "Will You Remember" on it, each taking a key for the casket. But Ottilie's father, Col. Van Zandt, and other family members view Richard as "inferior" and insist that Ottilie marry a cousin who is on equal social standing. Dick defies Van Zandt and when ordered to leave, he vows to Ottilie that he will come back her equal or "not return at all" and secures her promise that she will wait for him.[162] Fifteen years later, Richard returns a wealthy man, ready to fulfill his promise, but Ottilie has married her scoundrel cousin Claude Van Zandt, who gambles nightly at Madame Delphine's popular establishment. When Ottilie and her friend Alice arrive at Madame Delphine's to "observe" Claude, it is Alice who first sees Richard and she tells him that Ottilie married her cousin when pressured by her dying father. Ottilie's and Richard's reunion upsets them both, knowing what might have been; when Claude sees them together he flies into a jealous rage, causing a scene and making threats to Ottilie about their child. So, to protect Ottilie, Richard turns to her friend Alice and proposes, citing this as the reason for his return.

In Act Three of *Maytime*, thirty years later and the apple tree is in full bloom, but all furnishings in the Van Zandt house are being sold at auction. Ottilie is an impoverished widow in her late fifties. Richard, now married to Alice, appears with an assistant who has orders to buy everything in the house. In a bittersweet moment, he and Ottilie stand at the window, watching their grandchildren play around the apple tree. When Richard leaves, his assistant gives Ottilie the deed to her property; Richard has purchased all of her possessions for her, keeping only her portrait. The story comes full circle in Act Four with their namesakes, Ottilie's granddaughter and Richard's grandson. She is a successful dressmaker in the old Van Zandt home and resists Dick's attention, even though he provides business for her by purchasing dresses for showgirls. When the dying apple tree is dug up and they find the casket, however, "the curtain falls upon the promise of fulfillment of the romance that was blighted three generations before."[163]

Young experienced a mega hit with *Maytime*. Bordman tells that "Its bittersweet tale and exquisite songs struck some responsive chord in troops embarking for overseas. Among departing soldiers it quickly became the ticket most requested. The demand for tickets was so great a second company had to be opened across the street from the original."[164] But Bordman also points out that more importantly to its immediate success, was that the long run of *Maytime* kept "the vogue for operetta alive during the height of the war."[165] In addition to which, Sigmund Romberg as composer came to the fore, with one of his best scores and the long-remembered "Will You Remember" ("Sweetheart, Sweetheart, Sweetheart").

Sometime, opened the following year and provided a marked contrast to *Maytime*, perhaps something Young aimed for. The score by Rudolph Friml provided a number of arias, duets and chorus numbers, notably the theme song, "Sometime," which achieved popularity even after the successful run of 283 performances. The plot of *Sometime* is nothing new, essentially a boy-loves-girl story taking place within the exploits of a troupe of actors. The action opens on a stage with Loney, the doorkeeper (Ed Wynn) and some of the chorus girls getting ready for rehearsal. Some of the humor throughout addresses current events, as when a stagehand asks Loney if he wants a sandwich, to which Loney, a vegetarian, replies: "My landlady has supplied me with a fine loaf of war cake. No milk, no eggs, no butter. (Takes a rubbery lump from pidgeon [sic] hole of letterbox.) No flour, no sugar. Just a tasty collection of baked air holes surrounded by bran and sweetened with prune juice. See, it is so light it bounces! (He bounces it on floor.) Oh, how I love the Kaiser!"[166] When the chorus girls check for mail, Loney asks Mayme (May West) about all her mail, and she admits: "I write these to myself to keep the girls from guying me. I haven't made a hit with nobody since tights went out of fashion!"[167] Loney and Mayme have known each other for years, and Loney has always had "a thing" for the wise-cracking Mayme. But Mayme's always looking for something else, as expressed in "What Do You Have to Do?":

I'm getting awful fed up on the way this world is run,
Some girls have men to throw away and some girls can't get one,
It really is discouraging when all is said and done,
To plainly see your finish start before you have begin.[168]

Enid Vaughn, the star of the show, peeks through the curtain and spots a man in uniform sitting in the front row, Richard Carter, the man she has loved and lost. She tells the chorus girls her story in several flashbacks— a technique made popular by early film and thought quite novel by critics who reviewed *Sometime*. In several scenes, it is revealed that Loney, Enid, and her father, Henry Vaughn, were poor actors who became stranded, when Loney "managed to get the lease of an old furnished house on 23rd Street and started a theatrical boarding house."[169] Here, Richard offers Enid a leading ingénue role in his current play and includes her protective father in the offer. Mayme appears at the door, a hungry out-of-work actress. In subsequent flashbacks, the story evolves and Enid's star status rises, ultimately causing tension and then division between her and Richard. While Mayme finally realizes in the last scene just what a good man Loney really is, Enid's father convinces her to follow her heart and go after the man she loves—the last image on stage showing Enid and Richard slowly embracing.

Sometime was "one of the biggest hits of the season." Bordman shares that the "great 1918 flu epidemic was raging, and one critic praised the show as 'catchy as the grip and likely to last longer.'"[170] The use of flashbacks contributed to the novelty of the musical, but the comic abilities of Wynn and West undoubtedly helped to boost ticket sales. Bordman suggests that Ed Wynn wrote some of the lyrics and "won laughs with his lisping delivery of lines such as, 'What is a man to do in wartime when he can't make both ends meat?—Make one end vegetables!'"[171] Prior to taking the role of the tough chorus girl, Mayme, May West had been on the road with vaudeville acts "where she observed blacks dancing the Shimmy." It was in *Sometime* where "she introduced her version of the shimmy dance," very likely in the number "Any Kind of Man," which one critic thought was "marred by vulgarity."[172] Indeed, the song seems written for Mae West:

I was born a scamp/Meant to be a Vamp
If I'd had the chance I could have did/Theda Bara tricks,
Paralyze the hicks!
Nothing could have stopped me but the lid!
But somehow my style has got a cramp,
I can't find a single soul to "Vamp."
Refrain: All I want is just a little loving,
Just a little spooning and a squeeze,
I was really made for turtle-doving
Lead me to it,/Let me do it—please
Send an S.O.S. and get me someone
Try to get a live one if you can./Please!
I'd be satisfied with just a dumb one,
If the book can walk,/He don't have to talk!
Send me any kind of man!

One wonders whether West had a hand in these lyrics, since sexual innuendo represents quite a departure from Young's usual style. Despite being a huge success in New York, *Sometime* did not fare nearly as well in London without the comic abilities of Ed Wynn and May West.

For Young's next musical, *Little Simplicity*, the music provided by Augustus Barratt likely served as the most enduring aspect. It played for 112 performances at the end of the war in 1918. In brief, the plot of *Little Simplicity* concerns a young, innocent girl, Veronique, who sells flowers and sings in a French café in Tunis. Veronique meets Alan, an American art student, traveling with friends and an eccentric professor, Duckworth. When a lecherous "sheik" makes untoward demands on Veronique, Lulu, a French cabaret singer, protects her. The owner of the café, Lulu's uncle, orders them to leave, prompting the students to urge the women to join them in the Latin Quarter in Paris; there Veronique and Alan proceed to fall in love, while Lulu and Duckworth form their own oddly romantic attachment. But Veronique learns of Alan's engagement to an American woman when his father shows up, worried about his involvement with the flower girl. Lulu takes Veronique and disappears; over five years later outside of Paris at a

YMCA hut for troops, Alan, who has enlisted in the army, and his friends are all involved with the war effort. Duckworth has secured Victoria Del Mar, a grand opera singer to entertain the soldiers, and discovers that the woman he thought was Victoria's mother, is actually Lulu in disguise. When Veronique appears, Alan immediately recognizes her, despite her acquired sophistication, telling her that he has searched the world for her. As he is about to leave for the front, she reappears in a Red Cross uniform, giving up "her career to nurse the soldiers" and informs him she is joining him at the front.[173]

Correspondence between Young and the Shuberts, November 1917 through August 1918, indicates the musical was originally called *Miss I Don't Know*, taken from a line in the play when Alan and Veronique first meet. He asks her why she says "I don't know" all the time. She tells him: "Because Lulu told me to. She says that I don't know are the three greatest words in the world to put a damper on conversation."[174] Young sent the Shuberts a number of suggestions for titles and casting.[175] In fact, Young disagreed with the Shuberts' casting of Carolyn Thomson in the role of Veronique, feeling Thomson was "too unattractive to carry a new play;" she stated "I do not believe that you could get a new play over with Miss Thomson, because people do not like her personality."[176] Critics seem to back up Young's opinion about Thomson's ability, the *New York Times* calling her voice "a trifle immature" and the *Herald* stating that she was "pretty" in the role of Veronique, but "left much to be desired when it came to acting opportunities"; this became most evident when on stage with Marjorie Gateson, who played Lulu with "verve and charm and intelligence."[177] Overall, the plot of *Little Simplicity* did not wow audiences and critics, who found it "far from inspired." While the background of war provided a romantic aid to the story, it was a "bit dull on occasion," the fault lying in "the extreme tenuousness of the story." On the lack of humor in the piece, the review remarked tongue-in-cheek that there was "no humor of a sufficiently robust nature to cause Dr. Copeland to caution the audience to use its handkerchiefs while laughing."[178]

BEAUTY, WEALTH AND PLENTY OF HARD WORK

Journal and newspaper articles from the 1910s and 20s portray Rida Johnson Young as a distinctly beautiful woman. Isidore Witmark referred to her as one of the "most beautiful women ever to come from Baltimore," while a journalist—very likely male—raved she was "the most beautiful playwright in captivity."[179] But women, too, admired Young's striking appearance. Elizabeth Lonergan described her as "one of the most attractive and charming of the women playwrights."[180] Shirley Burns provided readers a thorough description of thirty-five-year-old Young: "Mrs. Young is a beautiful woman, radiant with youth, tall and graceful, with liquid brown eyes and raven black hair always artistically coiffured. Hers is the languid, good-natured kind of beauty. She wears filmy draperies and big picture hats, and looks as if she had nothing to do but smile as the world goes by."[181] Accented by large hats in many photographs of the period, Young's dark features contributed to her allure. What is more, according to Burns she was well-liked by those who knew her. Mary E. Mullett in 1917 described her as "unspoiled by her successes" and that "even a disgruntled rival would lose his grouch if he could see her and talk with her. Uncommonly "easy to look at," stated Mullet, "she wears her beautiful clothes so well that one cannot envy her the riotous royalties which enabled her to buy them."[182] Although Young attended social events, she did not relish speaking in public, preferring to putter in her garden when she was not writing or attending plays and rehearsals.

A number of articles emphasized her earning power and portrayed a materialistic impression of the playwright, far more so than other woman dramatists with similar earning power. But this notion may have become embellished by a series of robberies in which Young's jewelry and other possessions were stolen. An early report appeared in the *Dramatic Mirror*, for example, stating that she was "awfully sore because some of her jewels had been purloined":

Now when a hard-working girl puts all her royalties into jewelry, it is more than a shame to have them stolen. It is a downright outrage. Mrs. Young caused the arrest of a colored maid at the Webster apartment for disposing of a $450 brooch, which represents practically a week's royalty on the *Boys of Company B* or *Brown of Harvard*.[183]

Almost a year later, a reporter said that Young had again been "victimized by burglars" for the third time in a year, her summer home in Greenwich "despoiled of a small fortune in silver, rare books and rugs." Young, apparently taking things in stride, said "with manifest good cheer" that after three times, she could now "leave her valuables around unguarded in perfect security," having been "burglarized up to the point of perpetual immunity." Concluded the article: "And to show her confidence in that respect the handsomest of feminine playwrights carelessly swung upon the tip of her forefinger a gold mesh purse through whose gleaming links a big yellow roll of royalties was plainly visible."[184] But three years later, while the playwright was in Texas researching her baseball play, her Greenwich home was again robbed of "thousands of dollars' worth of wearing apparel, house linen, and silverware." By this time, Young had procured burglary insurance.[185]

Young's five-acre Italian villa in the "millionaire suburb, Belle Haven," apparently served as a magnet for thieves. Not only was it set back from the road and "screened by many splendid oak trees," it was often closed and unoccupied in the winter. Prior to Belle Haven, while writing her first three plays, Young resided for about four years in a cottage in Greenwich, Connecticut, located on Steamboat Road, near the Indian Harbor Yacht Club.[186] She moved into the spacious Belle Haven home in 1906 when still married to James Young. An article in the *Ogden Standard* in 1910 described a twenty-five-mile stretch of Connecticut along the north shore of Long Island Sound as being "the Great American Playwright Belt"; over twenty-five playwrights with impressive country homes lived along this stretch of land, including Augustus Thomas, Clyde Fitch,

Edward Milton Royle, George Hobart, Leo Ditrichstein, Charles Rann Kennedy, Henry Miller, Ivy Ashton Root, Charles Klein, and Rida Johnson Young. Very likely discouraged by all the break-ins, Young sold her villa in 1913, later purchasing at least two other homes, located in Long Island, New York, and Stamford, Connecticut.

Young, however, was not one to laze about luxurious homes and gardens. Dividing part of the year into a New York residency, in the city she attended theatre, business meetings and social events, met with producers and directors, and attended rehearsals both in the city and out of town.[187] Of course, in order to complete all the dramatic work that she did, she kept a steady pace at writing, working four to five hours every morning at her desk. Young attributed her training at Witmark Music Publishing to keeping regular hours: "I learned to be on the job at 9 in the morning, and I have never unlearned it. It has been worth a good deal to me, too."[188] Even on vacation, she took work with her. "She doesn't write in a spurt of energy and then loaf for weeks and months," stated Mullett. "She is everlastingly at it." Said Young: "I've had eighteen productions in ten years. As I tear up half of what I write, you can figure out that I must have worked pretty steadily."[189]

But in various interviews, Young insisted she did not relish the actual process of writing. An article in the *Syracuse Herald* revealed Young's feelings toward her "daily labor" and the alternate life she would have preferred.

> The truth is I hate work and playwriting is a business with me, not a labor of love. If I had my own way, I would not write at all. I should divide myself to my home and the entertainment of my friends. If I had a dozen children I should have been happy, but fate has made me a playwright and I must be content.[190]

Young expressed that "playwriting is a field in which there are no handicaps for a woman." She did not think it necessary for a woman to "unsex herself to compete with a man. A woman may be a dramatist and still be a woman." Young did not believe in "those strenuous occupations for women which call for almost every masculine attribute," stating that while some women got "along nicely in the professions as lawyers and doctors... that kind of work doesn't appeal to me. I would rather go out in my garden and hoe cabbage than argue a case before the court of appeals."[191] Indeed, a number of articles stress Young's passion for gardening. In May 1917, Young declared:

> This summer I'm going to get a vacation if it's my last act! I've bought a new country place at Southfield Point near Stamford, Conn. And I'm going to dig and hoe and scratch in the ground to my heart's content. . . . I'd rather be outdoors working in a garden than doing anything else. I'm going to plant everything I can get my hand on, flowers and trees and vegetables. And I'm going to earn a niche in the Hall of Fame by giving away the potatoes I raise.[192]

Young actually donated spinach instead of potatoes for the Stage Women's War Relief, according to an article that revealed how theatre women raised crops for the war effort.[193] In addition to gardening, Young enjoyed access to the beach at the edge of her lawn for her daily swim and also kept trim by playing tennis. In her Stamford home, Young maintained a household staff of three families, including a chauffeur.[194]

LITTLE OLD NEW YORK

Little Old New York, opening September 1920, carried through an idea begun in *Maytime*, when Young included the real-life character, P. T. Barnum. But *Little Old New York*, set in 1810, features several historical characters, including John Jacob Astor, Cornelius Vanderbilt, Washington Irving, and Henry Brevoort. The play, in fact, was a return to the "costume play" so popular at the turn of the century, and New Yorkers enjoyed glimpsing their own history of some hundred years ago. The "keen relish for our own past is something new," stated *Bookman*. "It is a most recently acquired taste in the theatre."

> There was a curiously piquant pleasure for New York
> audiences in seeing Peter Delmonico peddling
> sandwiches from a basket; in hearing Cornelius
> Vanderbilt, a young ferryman, insist that steamboats
> were practicable and that sometime they would be
> running regularly between New York and Albany.[195]

Although some critics felt they dominated the play, these historical characters support the story as friends and acquaintances of the central character, Larry Delevan.

At the heart of the story is Patricia O'Day, a seventeen-year-old Irish girl; Patricia's father convinces her to impersonate her dead brother in order to inherit the fortune left to him by a New York kinsman. If the money is not claimed, it will go to Delevan, her step-cousin. Dressed as a boy, "Pat" arrives in New York with her father, much to Delevan's disappointment. Nevertheless, the terms of the will appoint Delevan as guardian to Pat, and he sets about making the most of the situation, particularly after Pat's father soon dies. Over time, Pat grows fond of Delevan, despite his taunting her over her girlish mannerisms. But she begins to feel guilty over the deception, particularly when he needs money to invest in steamboats with Vanderbilt. When she causes a riot at a boxing match by setting the fire alarm, Pat confesses that she is a girl in disguise, impersonating her brother, and risks going to prison. But when Larry Delevan sees her in a proper dress, he realizes his feelings for her were there all along, and Patricia confesses her love for him. Astor helps Patricia avoid prosecution by getting them on one of his ships where they will marry and go to Ireland until they can safely return to New York.

During the play's healthy run, audiences particularly enjoyed the fresh performance and "engaging personality" of Genevieve Tobin as Patricia.[196] Marion Davies appeared as Pat in the first film version of *Little Old New York* in 1923, and Alice Faye and Fred MacMurray starred in the 1940 version, which varied somewhat from the original.

WORKING WITH THE SHUBERTS

Correspondence in Rida Young Johnson's file in the Shubert archives lends insight into Young's experience as a playwright and her attention to detail in handling the business affairs of her career. A few examples discussed here provide a glimpse into these aspects, along with what it might have been like to work with the Shuberts. Well into Young's career and after the sensation of *Her Soldier Boy*, the Shuberts valued Young's expertise enough to ask her opinion about plays and potential properties for musicals. For a time, roughly 1917–18, she evaluated works, giving her thoughts in letters.[197] In September 1917, for example, Young wrote to one of the Shuberts, J. J. or Lee, of a script, *Who's Looney Now*. "I think it would be a mistake to try to make a musical play of this. Even a farce needs some foundation in probability, and that insanity germ idea is too far-fetched. Besides it is such a [sic] old-fashioned idea to try to get fun out of supposed insanity. Then too it would be hard to get any sentiment into it an [sic] I work best with material that offers some sentimental interest." Young closed with "If you have any more books, will you kindly send them to me to read."[198] In November, she wrote regarding *The Texas Steer* and *We Should Worry*, seeing no chance of "making an attractive musical play out of them. The comedy is old fashioned and there is no romance or chance for dainty attractive atmosphere."[199] In March of 1918, she wrote Shubert about a play he apparently sent her to see at the Yorkville Theatre the night before: "and while I think it is very funny, I feel that it is not the kind of play I could do well, so had rather not attempt it."[200]

In her dealings with the Shuberts, Young at times had to struggle for better contractual terms. Because of this, she and the Shuberts had a bit of a falling out in 1919. Correspondence with Jack Morris, the Shuberts' lawyer, shows that Young had agreed to write a musical book of *The Dancing Fool*, a story for which the Shuberts purchased the musical and dramatic rights. "Did you receive a copy of the agreement? Mr. Shubert is anxious to have you start work on "THE DANCING FOOL," wrote Morris in June.[201] But on October 21, Young replied: "I am very sorry that I cannot accept the contract as altered by Mr. [William] Klein [Shubert attorney]. I told Mr. Shubert that I would sign this same contract with him that I have signed with other managers.[202] Morris immediately wrote Young a note, asking her to call, "as I feel sure that we can fix the contract up satisfactorily."[203] It is not clear what transpired over the next few weeks, but Young wrote to Lee Shubert a handwritten letter on November 14th: "I am so sorry about the 'The Dancing Fool.' I supposed that you were not willing to sign my contract, so I took other work which will prevent my doing that play for this year at least."[204] Lee Shubert shot back on November 17: "It must give you quite a bit of satisfaction to feel as independent as you do, but do not forget that we had a lot to do towards making you so. However, I will not bother you anymore about writing any plays for us."

Wishing to maintain a positive relationship with the Shuberts, Young immediately placated Lee Shubert:

> I am sorry when I received your letter this morning to feel that I had seemed to act as though I felt independent of you. I don't feel that way at all. I heartily wish that you had the plays which are under contract now and for which the managers cannot get theatres. You always have theatres and you always stick to plays loyally and I am more than grateful for the success I have had under your management. You must not blame me if I want to get a more satisfactory contract than I have had before. I think that is only natural when one has served his apprenticeship in any profession.
>
> The reason I cannot do "The Dancing Fool" now is because I am working on two plays—not musical—which I have promised to have ready for tryouts in the Spring. Also doing some re-writing on a play which Sam Harris is going to do in the Spring. [Little Old New York].
>
> I should be sorry to feel that you think me ungrateful and I hope you will let me prove that I am not, by letting me do something for you later on.
>
> With all good wishes
> Most truly, Rida Johnson Young[205]

In addition to contractual issues, Young had so many productions of her plays touring at once, some in other countries, such as England and Australia, that it must have been a chore to constantly read trade papers and keep track of royalties—all of which she apparently did without a manager. She often wrote the Shubert office, inquiring after certain shows. Some of her letters indicate that she at times struggled financially. For instance, in February 1920 (possibly after she had been diagnosed with cancer), Young wrote to Lee Shubert from Florida concerning royalties of one of the touring companies of *Maytime*: "I am down here in Florida with my mother who is ill, and I have had so much sickness and expense in my family this winter, that I am most anxious to get all of the money due me as quickly as possible.[206] Shubert responded with a check for $1424.96, covering royalties on the No. 3 *Maytime* Company, asking if she would care to sell all her rights in *Maytime*, "including the picture and future royalties? . . . If you will put a price on this which will be satisfactory, I may be able to close with you at once."[207] While Young appreciated the check, she stated:

> I would not care to dispose of my rights in "Maytime," either picture rights or future royalty as I feel, with a good company, this play could go on indefinitely. I understand that the Famous Players offered fifty thousand and a percentage for the picture rights and that you refused it, so I imagine we will get a very good price for this, and I'd rather take a gamble on it than sell now.

Shubert replied that he made her the offer because "when you were here last time you told me you needed money." As for *Maytime*, he stated he "never had any offer for pictures as I informed everyone that it was not in the market."[208] Fortunately, sometime later she did receive royalties for two different film versions of *Maytime*.

LAST PLAY AND FINAL DAYS

Cock o' the Roost, Young's last Broadway play in her lifetime, was the second production of the newly formed and short-lived Dramatists' Theatre.[209] *Cock o' the Roost* opened in a tryout production as *The Rabbit's Foot* in April 1924 at the Stamford Theatre in Connecticut and continued on to Boston. Enthusiastic residents turned out to support Young, thoroughly enjoying the "light," "frothy" comedy. A local critic wrote that the play "hit the bull's eye of popular approval with deadly accuracy."[210] Another claimed: "The literary skill, ingenius [sic] constructive talent and delicious humor that are exhibited in other compositions of Mrs. Young are again shown in 'The Rabbit's Foot.' Some critics might go so far as to assert that this is the best work done by her so far." The writer went on to say that Young differed from well-known playwrights who failed to maintain standards set in early works. Added the critic: "It is an American play of today, and yet, from curtain to curtain, there is no hint of war or whiskey—a welcome and refreshing innovation in current comedy."[211] Despite the skimpy plot in *Cock o' the Roost*, most all of the reviews, even those of the New York opening, were highly favorable because of the characters, the lines, and the outstanding cast.

Briefly, the play touts the power of positive thinking through the main character, Jerry Hayward, who, as the *Boston Globe* described, is essentially a "she-Pollyana." Jerry loves Phyllis Dawn, daughter of Pierce Dawn, a frustrated novelist who is forced to write "trivial but profitable mystery stories" to keep up a home and life style that are beyond his means, when he would rather be writing more serious literary work.[212] Falling in love has turned Jerry's life around; previously he accomplished very little with his life, but now is filled with optimism and purpose. When Phyllis and her mother leave town for the summer, Jerry convinces the father to lease their extravagant home and rent a "model tenement" on the East Side. Consequently, Mr. Dawn becomes transformed, now free of money worries and able to write what he truly wants to write. In the meantime, Jerry invests his money and begins building his own wealth. Although Phyllis loves Jerry, however, she is also captivated by a wealthy, but socially inept oil speculator, who has impressed Mrs. Dawn, a selfish woman obsessed with looking even younger than her daughter. When Phyllis expresses a dread for poverty and tenements, it appears that things go against Jerry, but in the end his good luck holds and he manages to bring "one and all into a saner and cleaner atmosphere."[213]

Critics generally favored the directing of James Forbes and the acting of a cast which included Donald Foster as Jerry, Harry Davenport as Mr. Dawn, Katherine Wilson as Phyllis, and Elizabeth Risdon, who in her portrayal of the self-focused Mrs. Dawn was often cited for an outstanding performance. But some reviewers felt the comedy held too much similarity with George Kelly's *The Show Off*, a huge success playing six blocks away, and others expressed that Young's "lesson" about optimism came across as "sanctimonious."[214] Broadway audiences enjoyed the quippy dialogue and fun of *Cock o' the Roost* for about a month. The comedy ran for two weeks in London during the summer of 1926, but, unfortunately, Rida Johnson Young did not live to see it.[215]

Perhaps it was not a coincidence that Young, a Christian Science practitioner, chose positive thinking as the theme for her last play. She had been battling breast cancer for some time. The *New York Times* reported in December 1925 that she was critically ill and had been "taking Christian Science treatments" for a number of years. Her illness had been kept secret, and although she apparently rallied for a time, she died on May 9, 1926, at the age of fifty-one.[216] Quite a number of theatre people attended her funeral which was held at her Stamford home. According to a published account, Young left an estate worth $90,411.[217] She left $15,000 to her mother and $5,000 to her only surviving sibling, Samuel Johnson. She gave $1,000 each to two employees and the rest of her property, including control over her dramatic work, went to her nephew, William A. Schroeder, the executor of her estate.[218]

Although she is not widely known today and much of her dramatic work would not translate well to the modern stage, over an eighteen-year period Young contributed significantly to American theatre by providing plays and musicals for thousands of theatregoers. A columnist in the *New York Sun* stated retrospectively in 1936 that Rida Johnson Young was "for years Broadway's leading woman dramatist."[219] Early in her career, a *New York Times* reviewer commented on Young's writing in *The Boys of Company B*: "Mrs. Young has the faculty of writing pleasing little plays about the sort of people in whom one is never too old to be interested. One does not expect much ingenuity of plot in a play of this sort, and one does not get it. Mrs. Young is more successful in lines than in plot, and she translates the vernacular of up-to-date juvenile smartness to her plays with excellent effect."[220] Indeed, when discussing her method for plotting plays, Young stated: "I never make out a complete scenario. I just get a lot of characters together and throw them all overboard. Sometimes they survive, and sometimes they don't."[221] Calling herself a "manufacturer of entertainment," she explained that because of her work with Witmark as a "lyricist, librettist, and press writer," she had "fallen into the habit of looking at everything from the standpoint of getting 'a laugh.'"[222] And, indeed, this approach showed in her early plays and musicals. Several years later, Lucy France Pierce stated that Young's calling herself an "entertainer" was in self-defense "in the face of caviling criticism."[223] Indeed, some critics do appear to show resentment towards Young's success. In an overview of women playwrights on Broadway in 1917, for instance, Anna Steese Richardson commented in *McClure's*: "Rida Johnson Young has an admirable sense for selecting plays worth translating and adapting, themes worth re-clothing, lines worth re-writing. Her plays are as neat as the figures turned out by a Fifth Avenue corsetiere."[224] Like many plays and comedies of the era, some of Young's works *were* adaptations of foreign work, but in later musicals her craftsmanship demonstrated her ability to shape a book, bringing dialogue and song together in a seamless and ultimately pleasing way.

Young defended herself by claiming no desire to "write the great American play," always maintaining that she wrote for the money and enjoyed what royalties could buy. And yet, despite public modesty in describing her work as "little plays that have no mission, except to be clean and amusing," she succeeded, for the most, at providing enjoyable entertainment for audiences, strong vehicles for leading actors and singers of the day, and commercially viable works for managers. She demonstrated to aspiring writers that one could be a graceful public figure and still maintain a daily writing schedule that produced an impressive body of work.[225] She not only honed her craft as a writer, but she also met the demands of producers and the theatre going public and served as her own business manager. Indeed, as both playwright and lyricist, Rida Johnson Young stands out as exceptional for any period in theatre history.

WORKS OF RIDA JOHNSON YOUNG

[Includes date and length of most significant American and English productions, source material, collaborators, leading "star" performer (s), publisher, and, if not published, where the typescript may be located. If no location is noted, the work is likely not extant. See legend at the end.]

1898
*Lord Byron** (James Young)
  Academy of Music, Norfolk, VA, January 19, 1900

1906
Brown of Harvard (Henry Woodruff)
  Princess Theatre, February 26, 1906 (101)
  Majestic Theatre, December 24, 1906 (46) + tours, IBDB
  Published script (New York: Samuel French, 1909)
  Novel w/ Gilbert P. Coleman (New York: G. P. Putnam's Sons 1907)
  Filmed 1911, 1918, 1926—IMDB
Rida Johnson Young's One Act Plays, Dramatic Scenes and Monologs
  (New York: M. Witmark & Sons, 1906)
  Includes *Barbara's Dilemma, Chatterton, The Last of the Cargills*, and *John Clayton, Actor*
Sweet Sixteen, girls' college play typescript, SA

1907

The Boys of Company B (Arnold Daly/John Barrymore)
    Lyceum Theatre, April 8, 1907 (96)
    Musical, *When Love is Young,* c1912
    Book & Lyrics by R. J. Young / William Cary Duncan; Music,
    William Schroeder
    Typescript BR, TW, SA; IBDB
The Lancers, entertainment w/music, w/ J. Hartley Manners
    Adapt from German of von Moser and von Schontham
    Daly's Theatre, December 3, 1907 (12) IBDB

1908

Glorious Betsy (Mary Mannering)
    Lyric Theatre, September 7, 1908 (24)
    Novelized by Arline De Haas (New York: Grosset & Dunlap, 1928)
    Filmed 1928, 1936—as *Hearts Divided*—IMDb

1909

The Lottery Man (Cyril Scott)
    Bijou Theatre, December 6, 1909 (200) + 4 touring productions IBDB
    Published (New York, Samuel French, 1909)
    Films 1916, 1919 – IMDB

1910

Ragged Robin w/Rita Olcott (Chauncy Olcott)
    Academy of Music, January 24, 1910 (16)
Just One of the Boys, musical, adapted from *Sweet Sixteen* (Lulu Glaser)
    Book, R. J. Young; music, William A. Schroeder
    Van Curler Opera House, Schenectady, NY, January 28, 1910
    Filmed as *The Little Boss,* 1919, IMDB
Naughty Marietta, opera (Emma Trentini / Orville Harrold)
    Book & Lyrics, R. J. Young; composer, Victor Herbert
    New York Theatre, November 7, 1910 (136) IBDB
    Jolson's 59th Street Theatre, October 2, 1929 (16)
    Erlanger's Theatre, November 16, 1931 (24)
    Filmed, 1935 w/Jeanette MacDonald & Nelson Eddie
    Television adaptation 1955 – IMDB
The Candidate, unproduced play, ca. 1910

1911

Barry of Ballymore, drama w/music (Chauncy Olcott)
  Book & Lyrics, R. J. Young; composers C.Olcott and Ernest Ball;
  Featured song, "Mother Machree"
  Academy of Music, January 30, 1911 (24)
  Grand Opera House, February 20, 1911 (24)
Next! (Helen Lowell)
  Daly's Theatre, September 28, 1911 (18)
  Typescript BR, HTC; IBDB
Yellow Streak,*three-act play, unproduced

1912

Macushla (Chauncy Olcott)
  Grand Opera House, February 5, 1912 (16)
  Typescript BR, SA; IBDB
The Red Petticoat, musical based on *Next!* (Helen Lowell)
  Book, R. J. Young; lyrics, Paul West; music Jerome Kern
  Daly's Theatre, November 13, 1912 (61)
  Typescript, SA

1913

The Isle o' Dreams (Chauncy Olcott)
  Grand Opera House, January 27, 1913 (32)
The Girl and the Pennant w/Christy Mathewson
  Lyric Theatre, October 23, 1913 (20)
  Published (New York: Samuel French, 1917)

1914

Shameen Dhu (Chauncy Olcott)
  Grand Opera House, February 2, 1914 (32)
Lady Luxury, musical (Ina Claire)
  Book & Lyrics, R. J. Young; music, William A. Schroeder
  Casino Theatre, December 25, 1914 (35)
  Typescript, TW; IBDB

1916

Captain Kid, Jr. (also *Buried Treasure*) (Edith Taliaferro)
  Cohan and Harris Theatre, November 13, 1916 (128)
  As Lot 79, Queen's Theatre, London, April 20, 1918 (17)
  Film, 1919 w/ Mary Pickford, IMDB
  Published (New York: Samuel French, 1920)

Her Soldier Boy, musical (based on German play by Victor Leon)
    Book & Lyrics, R. J. Young; music, Emmerich Kalman
        w/ additional numbers by Sigmund Romberg
    Astor Theatre, December 6, 1916 (198) IBDB
    Apollo Theater, London, June 26, 1918 (374)
    Typescript, SA
The Marriage Bond (Nat C Goodwin) Film
    Film based on R. J. Young's play, IMDB

1917
His Little Widows, musical
    Book & Lyrics, R. J. Young/William Carey Duncan;
    Composer, William A. Schroeder
    Astor Theatre, April 30, 1917 (72) IBDB
    Wyndham's Theatre, London, June 16, 1919 (172)
    Published (London: Keith, Prowse, 1919)
    Scores/promptbooks, TW; University of California, Berkeley
Maytime, play with music
    Book & Lyrics, R. J. Young; music Sigmund Romberg
    Stamford Theatre, Stamford, CT August 7, 1917
    Shubert Theatre, August 16, 1917 (492) + 4 other theatres & 2 casts
    Published (New York: G Schirmer, 1917)
    Filmed 1923, 1937 w/Jeanette MacDonald & Nelson Eddy, IMDB
    Typescript, SA; IBDB

1918
Sometime, musical (Mae West / Ed Wynn)
    Book & Lyrics, R. J. Young; music, Rudolf Friml
    Shubert Theatre, October 4, 1918 (283) IBDB
    Vaudeville Theatre, London, February 5, 1923 (28)
    Published (New York: Schirmer, 1946); typescript, SA;
Little Simplicity (Miss I Don't Know)
    Book & Lyrics, R. J. Young; music, Augustus Barratt
    Astor Theatre, November 4, 1918 (112) IBDB
    Typescript, SA

1920

Little Old New York, comedy
    Plymouth Theatre, September 8, 1920 (308) IBDB
    Published (New York: Samuel French, 1928)
    Filmed 1923, 1940 – Alice Faye and Fred MacMurray IMDB
    Novel (New York: Grosset & Dunlap, 1923)

1921

The Front Seat, play
    Poli's Theatre, Washington, DC, May 21, 1921
    Typescript, BR
A Wise Child, comedy w/music
    Book & Lyrics, R. J. Young; music, William A. Schroeder
    Colonial Theatre, Boston, August 15, 1921
    Typescript, BR

1924

The Story of Mother Machree (New York: Grossett & Dunlap, 1924)
    Filmed 1928, Fox Film Corp, John Ford, director IMDB
    Based on Young's "Mother Machree," (short story)
        Munsey's Magazine, February 19, 1924
The Dream Girl, musical (based on *The Road to Yesterday* by Beulah
    Marie Dix and Evelyn Greenleaf Sutherland)
    Book & Lyrics, R. J. Young / Harold Atteridge; music Victor Herbert
    Ambassador Theatre, August 20, 1924 (118)
    Typescript BR, SA, TW
Cock o'the Roost (The Rabbit's Foot) (Donald Foster)
    Stamford Theatre, CT, tryout production
    Liberty Theatre, October 13, 1924 (24)
    Garrick Theatre, London, July 2, 1926 (18)
    Typescript, BL; IBDB

1925

Out of the Night, novel (New York: Grosset & Dunlap, 1925)
    Film version, *Hell Harbor,* 1930, IMDB

1927

Red Owl, novel (New York: Curtiss, 1927) LC
The Woman Who Did Not Care, film from Young's story, IMDB
A Play Without a Name
    Rialto Theatre, Syracuse, April 4, 1927, The Temple Players

Productions where Rida Johnson Young was credited for "additional lyrics":

The *Voice of McConnell*, play with music (Chauncy Olcott)
    Manhattan Opera House, December 25, 1918, (30)
The Midnight Rounders of 1921, musical revue
    Century Promenade, February 7, 1921 (49)
Gypsy Blond, musical featuring songs/lyrics by Rida Johnson Young
    Lyric Theatre, June 25, 1934 (24)
Thoroughly Modern Millie, musical
    Marquis Theatre *(Apr 18, 2002 - Jun 20, 2004)*

There are over 65 credits for Rida Johnson Young's music listed on IMDB on movie soundtracks. The songs most used are:

"I'm Falling in Love With Someone," "Ah, Sweet Mystery of Life," and "Italian Streetsong" from *Naughty Marietta, 1910;* "Mother Machree," from *Barry of Ballymore, 1911;* "Do You Remember" from *Maytime, 1917*

LEGEND

* Copyrighted title listed in *Dramatic Compositions Copyrighted in the United States, 1870 to 1916*, 2 Vols. (Washington, DC: Government Printing Office, 1918)

BL	British Library, Lord Chamberlain's Collection
BR	Billy Rose Theatre Collection, New York Public Library
HRL	Humanities Research Library, New York Public Library
HTC	Harvard Theatre Collection
IBDB	Internet Broadway Data Base
IMDB	Internet Movie Database, http://usimdb.com
LC	Library of Congress, Washington, DC
SA	Shubert Archives, New York, NY
TW	Tams-Witmark Wisconsin Collection

NOTES

INTRODUCTION

1. Ali Baba, "Mirror Interview: XXI—Martha Morton," *Dramatic Mirror*, November 7, 1891, p. 8.
2. Helen Ten Broeck, "Rida Young—Dramatist and Garden Expert," *Theatre* (April 1917): 202.
3. See Progressive Era at http://www.wikipedia.com.
4. Rachel Crothers (1878–1958), considered America's first modern feminist playwright for her social comedies and woman-centered themes, is the only woman usually included within the "canon" of playwrights during the Progressive Era. Her production in 1906 of *The Three of Us* marked the beginning of a thirty-year career as a professional playwright and director in American theater. Her plays were well-constructed and dealt with pertinent issues of the time, such as the unfairness of the double standard and women's conflicts between career and motherhood; her plays are still revived today. Unlike the other women in this study who are essentially "unknown," Crothers has been extensively written about in dissertations and journals and, therefore, is not included in this study. For a recent article on Crothers, see Brenda Murphy, "Feminism and the Marketplace: The Career of Rachel Crothers," in *The Cambridge Companion to American Women Playwrights*, ed. Brenda Murphy (New York: Cambridge University Press, 1999), 82–97.
5. About fifty-one women dramatists achieved two or more productions in New York between 1890 and 1920. Portions of this chapter are from Sherry Engle, "An 'Irruption of Women Dramatists': The Rise of America's Woman Playwright, 1890–1920," *New England Theatre Journal* 12 (2001): 27–50.
6. A prime example is Morton's *The Movers* (1907), which despite being a box office failure, was defended by several prominent critics.

7. Rosemary Gipson, "Martha Morton: America's First Professional Woman Playwright," *Theatre Survey* 23 (November 1982): 213–22, is the only in-depth article on Morton to appear since Morton's death in 1925. See also Sherry Engle, "New Women Dramatists in America, 1890–1920: Martha Morton and Madeleine Lucette Ryley" (PhD diss., University of Texas 1996), chapter 4. Louisa Medina (1813–38) is often cited as America's *first* professional woman playwright. As house playwright for the Bowery Theatre, she wrote several popular melodramas but did not live long enough to establish a lengthy career.

8. Of thirty-seven known titles for Morton, about twelve are not extant, but the titles themselves reflect the volume of her work, particularly during early years.

9. The honorary title for Morton, "Dean of Women Dramatists," may have originated with Ada Patterson's article, "A Chat with the Dean of America's Women Playwrights," *Theatre* (October 1909): 127–30. Bronson Howard, who founded the American Dramatists' Club, is still referred to as the Dean of American Playwrights; since "American Playwrights" originally referred to men only, Morton's honorary title acknowledged her valuable leadership among the women dramatists.

10. Engle, "New Women Dramatists," chapter 5.

11. See the interview with Ryley from *The Vote* March 26, 1910, included at the end of Chapter Two.

12. Gerald Bordman, *American Theatre: A Chronicle of Comedy and Drama, 1869–1914* (New York: Oxford University Press, 1994), 601.

13. ASCAP (American Society of Composers, Authors and Publishers) lists sixty-three songs by Rida Johnson Young (http://www.ascap.com). Numerous biographical entries on Young are published in musical theater and theater anthologies, but the only recent examinations of Young's life and career are Yvonne Shafer's chapter in *American Women Playwrights, 1900–1950* (New York: Peter Lang, 1995), 203–15, and a chapter in Candice Marie Coleman, *Gender Issues as Reflected in the Lives and Plays of Three Women Playwrights, 1900–1930* (PhD diss., Kent State University, 1993).

14. Young was produced primarily by the Shuberts, in part because of their preference for musicals. See Gerald Bordman, *Oxford Companion to American Theatre*, 2nd ed. (New York: Oxford University Press, 1992), 623.

15. In recent years in feminist literary history, two generations of the "New Woman" have been delineated: The first living and writing in the 1880s and 1890s, the second in the 1920s and 1930s. See Sally Ledger, *The New Woman* (Manchester: Manchester University Press, 1997), 1–2. The term is applied to the five subjects in this book because they entered a "male profession" and gained financial independence.

16. The only exception is possibly Sutherland who may have inherited some wealth from her merchant father who died when she was three.

17. Lucy France Pierce, "Women Who Write Plays," *World Today* (July 1908): 725–31.

18. Karen J. Blair, *The Torchbearers* (Bloomington: Indiana University Press, 1994), 31.

19. *New York Federation of Women's Clubs Handbook*, 1913, New York Historical Society.

20. "Dramatist Scores 'Movies,'" *Brooklyn Eagle*, December 24, 1913, clipping, Billy Rose Collection, New York Public Library, Lincoln Center.

21. Dorothy and Carl J. Schneider, *American Women in the Progressive Era, 1900–1920* (New York: Doubleday, 1993), 49.

22. Lower salaries offered to women teachers were justified by three assumptions: "women, unlike men, did not have to support a family; women were only working temporarily until they married; and the free workings of the economic marketplace determined cheaper salaries for women." Kathryn Kish Sklar, "Catharine Beecher: Transforming the Teaching Profession," in *Women's America: Refocusing the Past*, ed. Linda K. Kerber and Jane DeHart-Mathews, 2nd ed. (New York: Oxford University Press, 1987), 164–65.

23. Frances Elizabeth Willard, *Occupations for Women: A Book of Practical Suggestions for the Material Advancement, the Mental and*

Physical Development, and the Moral and Spiritual Uplift of Women (Cooper Union, NY: Success Company, 1897), 305–9; University of Wisconsin History Collection, http://digital.library.wisc.edu/1711.dl/History.

24. David Belasco, "The Great Opportunity of the Woman Dramatist," *Good Housekeeping* 53 (1911): 632.

25. "Mrs. Shakespeares," *Every Week*, February 26, 1917, p. 11.

26. Helen Christine Bennett, "Mother Machree," *American Magazine*, December 1920, p. 34.

27. "Big Earnings of Big Plays," *Theatre* 18 (1913): 153.

28. See Engle, "An 'Irruption' of Women Dramatists," 31–24

29. Shirley Burns, "Women Dramatists," *Green Book Album*, September 1910, p. 634.

30. Rida Johnson Young, "Mother Machree," *Munsey's Magazine*, February 19, 1924; *The Story of Mother Machree*, New York: Grossett & Dunlap, 1924. Internet Movie Database, http://us.imdb.com. An earlier film called *Mother Machree* was released in 1922, but Young is not listed as the source.

31. Garff B. Wilson, *Three Hundred Years of American Drama and Theatre*, 2nd ed. (Englewood Cliffs, NJ: Prentice-Hall, 1982), 182.

32. *Boston Journal*, February 12, 1908, n.p.

33. "Living on $100 a Month," *New York Times*, November 17, 1912, sec. 7, p. 11.

34. According to Garff B. Wilson, "more than five hundred theatrical companies were on the road" in 1900 (p. 160)

35. *Chicago Tribune*, October 2, 1898, sec. 5, p. 42.

36. Burns Mantle and Garrison P. Sherwood, eds., *The Best Plays of 1899–1909* (New York: Dodd, 1947), 346–67; Burns Mantle, ed., *The Best Plays of 1919–1920* (Boston: Small, 1920), 335–37.

37. Arthur Hobson Quinn, *A History of the American Drama from the Civil War to the Present Day* (New York: Appleton-Century-Crofts, 1936), 50.

38. Oscar G. Brockett, *History of the Theatre*, 6th ed. (Boston: Allyn, 1991), 425.

39. Howard Taubman, *The Making of the American Theatre* (New York: McCann), 965, 118.

40. Virginia Frame, "Women Who Have Written Successful Plays," *Theatre* 6, no. 68 (1906): 265.

41. "Talk with a Woman Playwright," *Dramatic Mirror*, April 4, 1896, n.p.

42. Ibid.

43. Walter Prichard Eaton, "Women as Theatre-Goers," *Woman's Home Companion*, October 1910, p. 13.

44. Bennett, "Mother Machree," 178.

45. Walter Prichard Eaton, "Mrs. DeMille Demands Book of 'Double Life,'" *New York Times*, December 28, 1906, p. 9.

46. Bennett, "Mother Machree," 185.

47. Frame, "Women Who Have Written Successful Plays," 265–66.

48. "Women Playwrights," *Fort Wayne News* (Indiana), June 14, 1900, p. 8; "Famous Women Playwrights as the Camera Catches Them," *Mansfield News* (OH), April 18, 1903, n.p.

CHAPTER 1-Martha Morton

1. Ali Baba, "Martha Morton," *Dramatic Mirror*, November 7, 1891, p. 8.

2. "An American Woman Who Writes Plays," *Dramatic Mirror*, May 30, 1896, p. 2.

3. "Playwrights Dine By the Sea," *New York Times*, August 10, 1892, p. 5.

4. "A New Society of American Dramatic Authors," *Theatre* 8 (March 1907): 84. Ironically, the one male member of the newly formed Society of Dramatic Authors was Charles Klein, the guest of honor at that evening's event.

5. "A Triumph of Pluck and Patience," *Illustrated American*, June 27, 1891, p. 281.

6. Lucy France Pierce, "Women Who Write Plays," *The World Today* 15 (July 1908): 725.

7. Shirley Burns, "Women Dramatists, *Green Book Album* (September 1910): 633.

8. From the 1880 New York census, cemetery information at Mt. Hope Cemetery (Hastings-on-Hudson, NY) and other sources, the birth and death dates of the Morton family ascertained are Joseph, 1819–95; Amelia, ca. 1829–99; Joseph Halfield, ca. 1850–?; Esther, ca. 1851–1907; Phoebe, ca. 1853–1919; Amelia,

ca. 1855–?; Michael, 1864–1931 (died in London); Martha, 1865–1925; Henry, ca. 1867–1919; and Victoria (Morton Favary) 1870–1935.

9. Ada Patterson, "A Chat with the Dean of America's Women Playwrights," *Theatre* 10 (October 1909): 130.

10. John Maddison Morton, obituary, *New York Times*, December 22, 1891, p.2. According to Phyllis Hartnoll, ed., *The Concise Oxford Companion to the Theatre* (London: Oxford University Press, 1972), 366, Thomas Morton is best remembered for creating Mrs. Grundy, symbol for conventional British propriety; Mrs. Grundy was a character who is discussed but who never appears in the comedy, *Speed the Plough* (1800). His best-known work was most likely *The School of Reform* (1805).

11. Patterson, "A Chat with the Dean," 130. Morton also mentioned that Alfred Sutro, dramatist and translator, was a member of her family, although she did not tell exactly how he was related.

12. "Mr. Michael Morton," *London Times*, January 13, 1931, p. 14

13. Frances E. Willard and Mary A. Livermore, eds., *A Woman of the Century* (New York: 1893), 525.

14. Patterson, "A Chat with the Dean," 130.

15. "An American Woman Who Writes Plays."

16. Ibid.

17. "Mr. Michael Morton."

18. The charity was for the Monteviore Home for Chronic Invalids. See: "The Travesty on 'May Blossom,'" *New York Times*, May 2, 1885, p. 8. "Burlesquing 'May Blossom,'" *New York Times*, May 4, 1885, p. 5. George C. D. Odell, *Annals of the New York Stage* (New York: Columbia University Press, 1949), 13:496. The Academy of Music was located on 14th Street, two blocks east of Union Square. Mary C. Henderson notes in *The City and the Theatre* (New York: Back Stage Books, 2004), 100: "Until the late 1860s, the Academy marked the northern end of the theatrical zone."

19. "The *Theatre*'s Prize Play Competition," *Theatre Advertiser*, January 1904, n.p.

20. *New York Times*, May 1, 1888, p. 4.

21. *New York Tribune*, May 1, 1888, p. 4.

22. *New York Times*, October 30, 1889, p. 4.

23. "Big Earnings of Big Plays," *Theatre* 18 (November 1913): 153. The first showing of *Hélène* was at Daly's 5th Avenue Theatre, located "uptown" on 30th Street and Broadway; Union Square Theatre, where it ran a year later, was considered "the most prestigious legitimate theatre" on Union Square and was located near the junction of Broadway and 4th Avenue—Henderson, *The City and the Theatre*, 123.

24. Martha Morton, *Hélène Buderoff; or, A Strange Duel* (New York: John W. Lovell, 1889); *A Strange Duel; or, HélènBuderoff* (New York: Lovell, Coryell & Company, 1895).

25. Mary Penfield, "Women Play-Makers of To-Day" (1895), 961, Billy Rose Theatre Collection, New York Public Library clipping. (Hereafter cited as BR.) A theatrical note in the *New York Times*, November 10, 1890, p. 8, gives November 24 as the opening date of *The Refugee's Daughter* in Newark, New Jersey, starting Tanner's tour.

26. "An American Woman Who Writes Plays."

27. "A Triumph."

28. "Miss Martha Morton," *Critic* (January 30, 1897): 80.

29. Penfield, "Women Play-Makers of To-Day," 961.

30. Ibid., 961–62.

31. "Martha Morton," *Dramatic Mirror* 7, November 1891, clipping, BR.

32. Odell, *Annals of the New York Stage*, 14: 273–74.

33. Ibid., 274.

34. "An American Woman Who Writes Plays."

35. *The Merchant* must have been one of the last plays produced under management of Albert M. Palmer, whose tenure at the Madison Square Theatre ended that year; this theater, located on Broadway at 28th Street, became renowned both here and abroad in the late 1870s when Steel MacKaye took it over and completely renovated with new inventions, including a "primitive but effective means of air conditioning." See Henderson, *The City and the Theatre*, 128–29.

36. *New York Times*, May 5, 1891, p. 5.

37. *New York Times*, May 10, 1891, p. 13.

38. *New York Tribune*, May 5, 1891, p. 7.

39. *New York Times*, May 10, 1891, p. 13.
40. "Theatrical Gossip," *New York Times*, June 1, 1891, p. 8.
41. "A Triumph."
42. Ali Baba.
43. "Pleased with Her Trip," *Dramatic Mirror*, October 31, 1891, clipping, BR.
44. *New York Times*, April 1, 1892, p. 4.
45. "A Triumph."
46. "Pleased with Her Trip."
47. Ali Baba.
48. Odell mentions *Miss Prue* in 15:239. Penfield cites *The Little Blacksmith*, 961, as does Shirley Burns, "Women Dramatists," *Green Book Album* (September 1910): 633. Very little can be found on *Prue* and *The Little Blacksmith*, which were toured by Lizzie Evans. A review in *The Republican*, Hamilton (OH), September 9, 1892, n.p., may be an indication as to why one of them did not make it to New York:

> The Little Blacksmith is an interesting and instructive drama. It contains sufficient comedy to keep an audience in a good humor, and the plot, if such it may be called, keeps the spectator at all times looking eagerly ahead for developments. The only weak point in the play may be said to be the lack of any remarkable dramatic situations, but with this single exception, the drama far excels a number of the road shows of today.

49. *New York Times*, March 21, 1893, p. 4.
50. Gerald Bordman, *The Oxford Companion to American Theatre*, 2nd ed. (New York: Oxford University Press, 1992), 173.
51. Odell, *Annals of the New York Stage*, 15:302.
52. *New York Times*, March 12, 1893, p.13. Originally Wallack's Theatre, then 13th Street Theatre, the Star Theatre on Bowery and 13th Street, became "a combination" house, leased out for particular productions. See Henderson, 101.
53. *New York Tribune*, March 21, 1893, p. 7.

54. Martha Morton, *Brother John*, typescript, hereinafter cited as ts, BR, Act I, p. 11.

55. Ibid., Act II, p 4.

56. *New York Times*, February 25, 1894, p. 15.

57. Morton, *His Wife's Father*, ts, BR, I:8.

58. *New York Times*, February 26, 1895, p. 3.

59. *New York Times*, March 3, 1895, p. 14.

60. *New York Times*, February 26, 1895, p. 3.

61. *New York Times*, March 3, 1895, p. 14.

62. *Boston Evening Traveler*, August 9, 1898, n.p.

63. "Women as Playwrights," *New York Tribune*, December 13, 1896, sect. III, p. 3.

64. Ibid.

65. Ibid.

66. *Critic*, December 5, 1896, p. 370.

67. Ibid.

68. *New York Times*, December 2, 1896, p. 5.

69. Ibid.

70. *Critic*, December 5, 1896, p. 371.

71. Martha Morton, *A Fool of Fortune*, ts., BR, Act III, p. 19.

72. Ibid., Act III, p. 19–26.

73. *New York Times*, December 6, 1896, sect. IV, p. 8.

74. Arthur Hoeber, "A Fool of Fortune," *Illustrated American*, December 19, 1896, p. 828.

75. "Crane in 'Fool of Fortune,'" *New York Times*, January 13, 1912, p. 7.

76. "Crane Back from Europe," *New York Times*, September 22, 1912, p. 17.

77. Martha Morton, *The Senator Keeps House*, 1911, ts, BR, Act I, p.2.

78. Ibid., Act III, p.19.

79. *Everybody's* 26 (February 1912): 242.

80. *Bookman* 34 (February 1912): 650–51.

81. John Chapman and Garrison P. Sherwood, *The Best Plays of 1894–1899* (New York: Dodd, 1955), 34.

82. "An American Woman Who Writes Plays."

83. Morton's address by this time was very likely 53 E. 83rd Street, New York City, located on the Upper East Side, within two blocks of the Metropolitan Museum of Art and Central Park.

Noted in Joseph Morton's obituary, *New York Times*, August 27, 1895, p. 5.

84. "An American Woman Who Writes Plays."

85. Ibid.

86. "Women as Playwrights."

87. "Grace Sherwood Wins her Suit," *New York Times*, February 21, 1894, p. 9.

88. "An American Woman Who Writes Plays."

89. Burns, "Women Dramatists," 633.

90. "Women as Playwrights."

91. Joseph Morton's obituary states that he was survived by his wife and six children. Shirley Burns in "Women Dramatists," 633, also says: "Some idea of her [Martha's] responsibility may be had from the fact that for many years, in the early part of her career, she supported her mother and seven younger brothers and sisters."

92. Morton's will, March 1, 1908. Morton outlived Phoebe. When her husband died two years later, his estate continued her bequest by providing an annual income of $2,400 for Victoria who lived until 1935. Herman Conheim's will, July 8, 1927.

93. "An American Woman Who Writes Plays."

94. Baily Millard, "The Merriwold Dramatists," *Bookman* (August 1909): 619.

95. For example, a photo accompanying the Pierce article, "Women Who Write Real Successes," p.1061, shows Morton at her summer place, sitting on a low stone wall.

96. Morton-Conheim Marriage Certificate, Surrogate Court, City of New York; *New York Times*, August 26, 1897, p. 5; *New York Tribune*, August 26, 1897, p. 6.

97. "Hermann Conheim, Zionist, Dead at 69," *New York Times*, May 3, 1927, p. 27.

98. Burns, "Women Dramatists," 633. The photograph is one of several Morton photos in the Byron Collection at the Museum of the City of New York.

99. Ibid. Upon the death of Hermann Conheim, most of the library was sent to the Hebrew University in Palestine, "among them complete editions of classic writers in belletristic and history"

such as Votaire's works (43 vols.), a collection of famous classics (60 vols.), Hegel's works (20 vols.), Ruskin (27 vols.), Macauley (20 vols.), Victor Hugo (47 vols.), Scribe (76 vols.), Balzac (22 vols.), Daudet (20 vols.), and Hawthorne (22 vols.). Letter from Rafael Weiser, Director, Department of Manuscripts & Archives, The Jewish National & University Library, Jerusalem, June 16, 1994.

100. Patterson, "A Chat," 127. Photos from the Byron Collection.
101. Hermann Conheim obituary. According to Rafael Weiser, apparently, the scholarship no longer exists.
102. Ibid.
103. *New York Tribune*, August 26, 1897, p. 6.
104. Sol Smith Russell obituary, *New York Times*, April 29, 1902, p. 9. Russell apparently did quite well with performing, investing his earnings in real estate in Minneapolis; by the time he died, the comedian had a total value of more than $2 million.
105. Martha Morton, *A Bachelor's Romance* (New York: Samuel French, 1912), 6.
106. *New York Times*, September 21, 1897, p. 6.
107. Morton, *A Bachelor's Romance*, 4.
108. Ibid., 9–10.
109. Ibid, 65–68.
110. *Athenaeum*, September 19, 1896, p. 396.
111. *New York Times*, December 29, 1896, p. 5.
112. *Chicago Tribune*, January 10, 1897, p. 34.
113. *New York Times*, September 21, 1897, p. 6.
114. Ibid. This is clearly demonstrated in William H. Crane's opening nights.
115. Metcalfe, "Score One for Clean Art," *Life*, September 30, 1897, p. 272.
116. "Martha Morton Accused," *New York Times*, November 16, 1897, p. 2.
117. The Duchess (Mrs. Hungerford), *A Little Rebel* (Montreal: John Lovell & Son, 1891). Project Gutenberg e-book, http://www.gutenberg.org.

118. According to a report in the *Steubenville Herald* (OH), November 27, 1897, n.p., the publishers of *A Little Rebel*, George W. Munro's Sons, had "intimated that the matter would be taken up in the courts." Apparently, however, nothing came of it.

119. "The Novel and the Play," *New York Tribune*, November 16, 1897, p. 7.

120. Metcalfe, "Score One for Clean Art."

121. Edward A. Dithmar, *New York Times*, September 26, 1897, sect. III, p. 4.

122. J. T. Grein, "Mr. John Hare in 'A Bachelor's Romance'" (January 9, 1898), in *Dramatic Criticism* (London: John Long, 1899), 26; *Athenaeum*, January 15, 1898, p. 96.

123. Bernard Shaw, "The Comedy of Calf-Love," *Saturday Review*, January 15, 1898, p. 75.

124. Einar Lauritzen and Gunnar Lundquist, eds., *American Film-Index 1908–1915* (Stockholm: University of Stockholm, 1976), 31.

125. *Dramatist* (January 1915): 596.

126. *Boston Transcript*, October 25, 1898, p. 5.

127. *New York Times*, April 30, 1901, p. 5.

128. Martha Morton, *Her Lord and Master* (New York: Samuel French, 1912), 33.

129. Ibid., 42.

130. Ibid., 8.

131. Ibid., 15.

132. Ibid., 28–30.

133. *New York Times*, February 25, 1902, p. 6.

134. *New York Tribune*, February 25, 1902, p. 6.

135. *Theatre* 2 (April 1902): 7.

136. *Current Literature* (December 1907): 559; includes commentary with segments of the script.

137. *New York Times*, September 4, 1907, p. 7.

138. Martha Morton, *The Movers*, 1907, ts sides, BR, Chudley, Act I, p. 4.

139. *Current Literature* (December 1907): 559. Quite likely Morton's theme in *The Movers* theme came, in part, from her own experience with the "ups and downs" of her father's china trade.

140. Morton, *The Movers*, Marion, Act I, p. 9.

141. *Current Literature* (December 1907): 660.

142. Ibid.

143. Ibid., 663.

144. Ibid., 604.

145. *New York Times*, September 4, 1907, p. 7.

146. Walter P. Eaton, "Martha Morton on Women," *Sun*, September 4, 1907, p. 5.

147. Walter P. Eaton, "Weighty Words on Women," *Sun*, September 8, 1907, p. 5.

148. *Theatre* 7 (October 1907): xi.

149. Eaton, "Weighty Words," 5.

150. *Theatre* 7 (October 1907): xi.

151. *New York Times*, September 4, 1907, p. 7.

152. Patterson, "A Chat," 129.

153. "Martha Morton Criticises [sic] the Critics," 1902, clipping, BR.

154. *Theatre* 2 (April 1902): 8.

155. Bordman, *The Oxford Companion to American Theatre*, 156.

156. *New York Times*, March 21, 1902, p. 6.

157. Ibid.

158. "Martha Morton Criticises [sic] the Critics."

159. *Theatre* 3 (March 1903): 55.

160. "The Theatre's Play Competition," *Theatre* 3 (December 1903): 316.

161. *New York Times*, February 9, 1904, p. 7.

162. Ibid.

163. Patterson, "A Chat," 130.

164. "Unlucky 'Four Leaf Clover,'" February 8, 1903, n.p., clipping, BR; *New York Times*, August 23, 1903, p. 9.

165. *New York Times*, October 4, 1905, p. 9.

166. "Martha Morton's 'Truthtellers,'" 1903, clipping, BR.

167. *New York Times*, September 26, 1905, p. 6.

168. "Martha Morton's 'Truthtellers.'"

169. *New York Times*, September 26, 1905, p. 6.

170. Gerald Bordman, *American Theatre: A Chronicle of Comedy and Drama, 1869–1914* (New York: Oxford University Press,

1994), 562–63.

171. *Theatre* 6 (December 1906): 340. Includes a photo of Maude Fealey and her leading man, Jack Webster, from *The Illusion of Beatrice*.

172. *New York Times*, October 5, 1909, p. 9.

173. Clayton Hamilton, "Imitation and Suggestion in the Drama," *Forum* 42 (November 1909): 440.

174. *New York Tribune*, October 5, 1909, sect. VII, p. 1. Dixie Hines and Harry Prescott Hanaford, eds., *Who's Who in Music and Drama* (New York: Hanaford, 1914), 259.

175. Patterson, "A Chat," 128.

176. *New York Times*, October 10, 1909, p. SM14.

177. Patterson, "A Chat," 128.

178. Martha Morton, *The Model*, 1910, ts, BR, Act I, scene 9.

179. Bordman, *The Oxford Companion to American Theatre*, 566.

180. *Theatre* 22 (July 1915): 6.

181. *New York Tribune*, June 4, 1915, p. 9.

182. *Dramatic Mirror*, June 9, 1915, p. 8.

183. "Martha Morton, Playwright, Dies," *New York Times*, February 20, 1925, p. 17.

184. Patterson, "A Chat," 128.

185. Ibid.

186. Burns, "Woman's Dramatist," 633.

187. Ibid.

188. Ada Patterson, "The Story of a Successful Woman Playwright," *Theatre* 7 (November 1907): 302.

CHAPTER 2-Madeleine Lucette Ryley

1. Curtis Brown, "What Mrs. Ryley Thinks the Audiences Think of Dramatists," Spring 1902, clipping, Billy Rose Collection, New York Public Library (hereafter cited as "BR").

2. Max Beerbohm, *Saturday Review* 93 (February 15, 1902), 204.

3. News clippings state that Madeleine Lucette Ryley was 75 when she died in February 1934. Although the 1871 London census form gives "age in 1871," her age is listed as twelve, but she

20, 1881, p. 6.

8. *New York Times*, October 18, 1882, p. 5.

9. Frederic Archer, "The Sorcerer," *Music and Drama*, October 21, 1882, p. 7.

10. *Spirit of the Times*, October 21, 1882, clipping, BR.

11. "As They Looked a Quarter Century Ago."

12. Unmarked clipping, December 23, 1882, BR.

13. "Music and Drama," January 27, 1883, clipping, BR.

14. *New York Times*, May 1883, p. 8.

15. "Theatrical World," November 17, 1883, clipping, BR; despite scathing remarks on Ryley's singing ability, her picture accompanies the review of *Amorita* with the caption, "Pretty Madeline Lucette."

16. *New York Times*, May 8, 1888, p. 5.

17. "Mrs. Ryley Scores Several Successes," states that she was "starred by Arthur Rehan in a number of Augustin Daly's

comedy successes"—most likely in a touring company.

18. Gerald Bordman, *American Theatre: A Chronicle of Comedy and Drama, 1869–1914* (New York: Oxford University Press, 1994), 310.

19. D'Oyly Carte Opera Company Web site.

20. J. H. Ryley died on July 28, 1922, at the age of eighty-one, placing his birth year in 1841; J. P. Wearing, ed., *American and British Theatrical Biography* (Metuchen, NJ: Scarecrow, 1979); George B. Bryan, comp., *Stage Deaths*, vol. 2 (Westport, CT: Greenwood, 1991), 1095.

21. According to Ganzl, J. H. Ryley had at least two daughters, Wallace and Rosina Harriette, and a son, Samuel, who died at seven months. E-mail letter, February 17, 2005. In her court testimony, Maria Barnum mentioned only Wallace.

22. J. H. Ryley quoted in "Mrs. Ryley Alleges Collusion," *New York Times*, June 11, 1892, p. 6.

23. Curtis Brown, "Mrs. Ryley Explains How She Writes Plays," April 19, 1903, clipping, BR.

24. George C. D. Odell, *Annals of the New York Stage* (New York: Columbia University Press, 1945), 15: 32–33. *New York Times*, October 7, 1893, p. 3; December 2, 1895, p. 7.

25. Beaumont Fletcher, "*Christopher, Jr.,*" *Godey's Magazine* (January 1896): 18.

26. December 25, 1900, clipping, BR. "In Another New Field," *The Washington*, May 5, 1895, p. 11.

27. Fletcher, "*Christopher, Jr.,*" 18.

28. December 25, 1900, clipping, BR.

29. Esther Singleton, "American Women Playwrights," *Ev'ry Month*, July 1898. Ryley also copyrighted a play entitled *Junior Partner* in 1890. Bordman, *American Theatre: A Chronicle of Comedy and Drama, 1869–1914*, 320, relates that Daniel Frohman commissioned a play called *Junior Partner*—an adaptation from the French of Alexandre Bisson and Albert Carre; the author' name is not given, but it seems unlikely that the work is Ryley's because she is quoted in "Talk With a Woman Playwright," *Dramatic Mirror* (April 4, 1896), as saying that she read "French but little" and had been "too busy to study the drama of that

language."
30. "Talk with a Woman Playwright."
31. Odell, *Annals of the New York Stage*, 15:331.
32. Spelling is not certain. "In Another New Field."
33. Madeleine Lucette Ryley, *The Merchant of Pongee*, typescript, Shubert Archives, New York, hereinafter cited as SA.
34. Ibid., Act I, p.13.
35. Ibid., Act II, p. 2–3.
36. Some critics (see *Critic* October 12, 1895) assumed the play had been written specifically for John Drew, but Singleton's article discounts this.
37. Madeleine Lucette Ryley, *Christopher Junior* (New York: Samuel French, 1917), Act I, p. 15–16.
38. Ryley published a short story with this same theme: "The Double-Bedded Room," in *Frank Leslie's Popular Monthly* 37 (November 1894): 542–43. A young woman, in a crowded hotel takes a room with two beds and falls asleep; in the night, a weary young man, mistaking the room numbers, enters and gets into the other bed, assuming his roommate to be a man. When she awakens, the young woman sees the man asleep in the other bed but does not wake him; she quietly dresses and leaves. The next time she sees the young man, she is introduced to him as a friend of her brother-in-law's, thus beginning their courtship, but she keeps her secret for now.
39. Ryley, *Christopher, Junior*, Act I, p. 8.
40. Ibid., Act I, p. 31.
41. *New York Times*, September 9, 1894, p. 10.
42. Ibid., Act I, p. 12.
43. Ibid., Act I, p. 6.
44. *New York Times*, September 4, 1894, p. 5. The reference is to E. H. Sothern, popular lead actor of the Lyceum Theatre.
45. *New York Tribune*, October 8, 1895, p. 7.
46. *New York Times*, October 8, 1895, p. 5.
47. *Critic* (October 12, 1895): 237.
48. Singleton, "American Women Playwrights."
49. *London Times*, February 15, 1896, p. 12.

50. *Athenaeum* (February 22, 1896): 259.

51. "Talk with a Woman Playwright."

52. J. T. Grein, "Shaftesbury Theatre: Revival of 'Jedbury Junior,'" (June 22, 1902); *Dramatic Criticism*, vol. 4 (London: Nash, 1904), 126.

53. George Bernard Shaw, *Saturday Review* (February 22, 1896): 198.

54. Interesting to note is that at Terry's Theatre, Frederick Kerr elected to present the play in "condensed form," which proved highly successful. When he staged it the second time at the Globe, it was "substantially as originally written" and appeared to give the play yet another "lease of life." *London Times*, December 22, 1896, p. 4.

55. *Critic* (May 15, 1897): 340.

56. *New York Times*, April 20, 1897, p. 9.

57. Edward A. Dithmar, *New York Times*, April 25, 1897, sec. III, p. 8.

58. Metcalfe, *Life* (May 6, 1897): 380.

59. *Critic* (April 24, 1897): 293

60. Arthur Hoeber, *Illustrated American* (May 29, 1897): 719.

61. *London Times*, May 30, 1900, p. 8.

62. *New York Times*, September 14, 1897, p. 6.

63. Albert White Vorse, *Illustrated American* (September 25, 1897): 402.

64. Edward A. Dithmar, *New York Times*, September 19, 1897, sec. III, p. 1.

65. Metcalfe, *Life* (September 23, 1897): 252.

66. *New York Tribune*, September 14, 1897, p. 6.

67. Vorse, *Illustrated American* (September 25, 1897): 402.

68. "Mrs. Ryley's New Play Proves Very Damp and Lachrymose," December 17, 1900, clipping, BR.

69. *New York Times*, January 9, 1901, p. 8.

70. Ryley's obituary in the *London Times*, February 20, 1934, p. 16, states: "Three of her plays, *The Mysterious Mr. Bugle*, *A Coat of Many Colors*, and *An American Citizen*, were running simultaneously in New York in 1897, a record for a woman dramatist."

71. "Talk with a Woman Playwright."

72. *New York Times*, January 5, 1897, p. 7; *Chicago Tribune*, January 10, 1897, p. 34.

73. *New York Tribune*, October 20, 1897, p. 6.

74. Albert White Vorse, *Illustrated American* (November 6, 1897): 607.

75. Madeleine Lucette Ryley, *An American Citizen* (New York: Samuel French, 1906), 63.

76. Vorse, *Illustrated American*, 605–6.

77. Edward A. Dithmar, *New York Times*, October 24, 1897, sec. IV, p. 4. Although Dithmar had no real objection to it, Goodwin's "most persistent fault . . . is his habit of glancing directly at the spectators every now and then and deliberately taking them into his confidence. This glance is irresistible."

78. *London Times*, June 20, 1899, p. 10.

79. Max Beerbohm, *Saturday Review* (June 24, 1899): 781.

80. The film was released by Famous Players Film Company York on January 10, 1914. Patricia R. King Hanson, ed., *American Film Institute Catalogue of Motion Pictures Produced in the United States*, vol. F1 (Berkeley: University of California Press, 1988), A writer in *Motography* declares John Barrymore as "the most 'tangible' person seen on the screen to date... Mr. Barrymore has made so marked a success in his first picture appearance, that it is hoped and believed he will not let it be his last."

81. Bordman, *American Theatre*, 500.

82. *New York Times*, October 7, 1902, p. 9.

83. *New York Times*, October 21, 1902, p. 9.

84. Madeline Lucette Ryley, *An American Invasion*, ts, MU, Act I, p. 12.

85. Interesting to note in the typescript are two lines that have been marked out. Sophie, complaining about Lucy's exhibition with the motor bike incident, quips about the American to her husband: "He is about five feet nothing in his boots." To which her husband replies: "So was Napoleon, and several other beastly energetic chaps." This description, along with Brainard's ample supply of comedic lines, and the difference in age between him and Lucy, suggests that Ryley had Nat C. Goodwin (who was shorter and older than his wife) and Maxine Elliott in mind when she wrote the play.

86. Ryley, *An American Invasion*, Act I, p. 23.

87. Ibid., Act II, p. 39.

88. Ibid., Act III, p. 77.

89. Max Beerbohm, *Saturday Review* 95 (April 4, 1903): 421.
90. "Mrs. Ryley, Dramatist, at Home," 1903, 336–37, clipping BR.
91. Madeleine Lucette Ryley, *The Altar of Friendship*, ts, MU, Act I, p.13.
92. *New York Tribune*, December 2, 1902, p. 9.
93. Ibid.
94. *Theatre* 3 (January 1903): 6.
95. Diana Forbes-Robertson, *My Aunt Maxine: The Story of Maxine Elliott* (New York: Viking, 1964), 295. Maxine Elliott went on to become a star performer, and eventually opened her own theatre in New York.
96. Curtis Brown, "Mrs. Ryley," BR.
97. *Athenaeum* (March 28, 1903): 412.
98. Grein (24 March 1903), vol. 4 (1971), 52–54.
99. Beerbohm, "The Altar of Friendship."
100. *Chicago Tribune*, October 11, 1898, p. 8.
101. Ibid.
102. *Who Was Who in the Theatre: 1912–1976*, 2101; "Madeleine Ryley, Playwright, Dead," *New York Times*, February 22, 1934, p. 24.
103. *New York Times*, October 18, 1898, p. 6.
104. Madeleine Lucette Ryley, *Realism*, ts, p. 8; Lord Chamberlain's Collection, British Library.
105. William Archer, *The World*, October 10, 1900, p. 23. *Era*, October 6, 1900, p. 13, includes a synopsis of the play.
106. Louise Closser Hale, "Historic Englishmen on the American Stage," *Bookman* (August 1901): 535–44.
107. "Talk with a Woman Playwright."
108. *New York Times*, February 5, 1901, p. 9.
109. *New York Times*, January 2, 1901, p. 7.
110. *New York Times*, February 5, 1901, p. 9.
111. *New York Times*, February 8, 1901, p. 5.
112. Edward A. Dithmar, *New York Times*, February 10, 1901, sect. II, p. 20.
113. William Winter, *New York Tribune*, February 5, 1901, p. 7.
114. Forbes-Robertson, *My Aunt Maxine*, 139.
115. Gertrude Elliott, letter to Melville Stone, November 26, 1899, reprinted by Forbes-Robertson, *My Aunt Maxine*, 142.

116. Sir Johnston Forbes-Robertson, *A Player under Three Reigns* (Boston: Little, 1925), 220. Neither Gertrude's sister, Maxine, nor Nat C. Goodwin attended the wedding. According to Diana Forbes-Robertson, Maxine "absolutely forbade the marriage." She said that at forty-seven, Forbes-Robertson was far too old, that Gertrude at twenty-three was far too young, and "that to marry an actor promised an unstable life" (153–54). But by the time the Goodwins returned to England six months later, Maxine had accepted Forbes-Robertson and "set about making the very best of it" (158).

117. Curtis Brown, "Mrs. Ryley Explains How She Writes Plays." Brown states that Ryley "for the last two years had been making her home in London"; her London address given in *Green Room Book* in 1906 and 1907 is 38, Maida Vale, W

118. J. Forbes-Robertson, *A Player under Three Reigns*, 222.

119. *London Times*, January 28, 1902, p. 8.

120. Burns quotation is included in the Programme, reprinted in *The Play-Pictorial* 1 (April 1902): n.p.

121. Madeleine Lucette Ryley, *Mice and Men* (New York: S. French, 1909), Act I, p. 5.

122. Ibid., Act I, p. 6.

123. Ibid., Act IV, p. 66.

124. J. T. Grein, "Lyric Theatre: 'Mice and Men'" (February 2, 1902), *Dramatic Criticism*, vol. 4 (London: Nash, 1904), 19–20.

125. Max Beerbohm, *Saturday Review* 93 (February 5, 1902): 204.

126. *London Times*, January 28, 1902, p. 8.

127. Grein, "Lyric Theatre," 20.

128. *Athenaeum* (February 1, 1902): 156.

129. Grein, "Lyric Theatre," 20.

130. Dithmar, *New York Times*, p. 5.

131. Brown, "What Mrs. Ryley Thinks," BR.

132. *New York Times*, December 30, 1902, p. 9.

133. Clipping, c. 1915, BR.

134. *New York Times*, January 20, 1903, p. 9.

135. *New York Tribune*, March 1, 1904, p. 9.

136. John Parker, ed., *Who's Who in the Theatre* (London: Pitman, 1926), 319.

137. "Mice and Men," *Motography* 15 (January 22, 1916), 197; *American Film Institute Catalogue*.

138. M.O.K., "Mrs. Madeleine Lucette Ryley," *The Vote*, March 26, 1910, pp. 256–57. In this interview, Ryley is quoted as saying: "being a thrifty woman I invest a portion of my earnings." See article included at the end of this chapter.

139. Brown, "What Mrs. Ryley Thinks."

140. *Theatre* 3 (February 1903): 30.

141. Brown, "What Mrs. Ryley Thinks."

142. *London Times*, June 5, 1902, p. 15.

143. Ibid.

144. Grein (June 8, 1902), vol. 4 (1904), 112–14.

145. Madeleine Lucette Ryley, *Mrs. Grundy* (London: "The Stage" Play Publishing Bureau, 1924), I, 5. See also Marguerite Merington, "The Obsolescent Mrs. Grundy," *New York Times Magazine*, July 20, 1924, p. 2. Mrs. Grundy was an invention of Thomas Morton (Martha Morton's ancestor) in his play, *Speed the Plough*, first performed at Covent Garden in 1800. Mrs. Grundy is a character never seen in Morton's play, but often referred to. Thus, "What will Mrs. Grundy say?" came into popular usage to denote the fear of what the neighbors think.

146. *London Times*, November 17, 1905, p. 6.

147. Max Beerbohm, "A Play Adrift," *Saturday Review* (November 25, 1905), 678–79. Beerbohm states the child in the production was six, whereas the script calls for a ten-year-old.

148. *Athenaeum* (November 25, 1905): 733–34.

149. *London Times*, November 17, 1905, p. 6.

150. *Athenaeum* (November 25, 1905): 733–34.

151. "The Ryley's Are Here," November 9, 1906, clipping, BR.

152. "Stage Less Frivolous," November 9, 1906, clipping, BR.

153. Curtis Brown, "Frohman's Plans Surprise London, *Chicago Daily Tribune*, July 22, 1906, p. H2.

154. *London Times*, March 5, 1907, p. 5.

155. *Athenaeum* (March 9, 1907): 299–300.

156. Madeleine Lucette Ryley, *The Sugar Bowl*, 1904, ts, BR.

157. *Athenaeum* (October 12, 1907): 455.

158. Ryley, *The Sugar Bowl*, I, 19.

159. Ibid., I, 27.

160. Ibid., II, 3.

161. Ibid.

162. *New Idea*, November 1909, clipping, BR.

163. *London Times*, July 20, 1904, p. 10

164. Viv Gardner, ed., *Sketches from the Actresses' Franchise League* (Nottingham: Nottingham Drama Texts, 1985), 41.

165. *London Times*, November 13, 1909, p. 12.

166. Listings in *The Stage Year Book* (London: Stage Offices, 1911–18) give Ryley as one of several vice presidents of the Actresses' Franchise League.

167. Actress Franchise League Secretary's Report, 1909/1910.

168. *Era*, December 19, 1908, p. 23.

169. *London Times*, December 13, 1908, p. 4; December 20, 1908, p. 4; *Era*, December 12, 1908, p. 18; December 19, 1908, p. 23; February 13, 1909, p. 16.

170. "Come Out of the Kitchen," *London Times*, March 17, 1920, p. 14.

171. Madeleine Lucette Ryley, "Watching the Crowd," *English Review* 36 (June 1923): 525; "Destiny," *English Review* 37 (December 1923): 744; "Anticipation," *English Review* 39 (September 1924), 400.

172. Kurt Ganzl, *Encyclopedia of the Musical Theatre*, vol. 3 (New York: Shirmer Books, 2001), 1773.

173. George B. Bryan, comp., *Stage Deaths* (Westport, CT: Greenwood, 1991), 2:1095; *London Times*, July 29, 1922, p. 1.

174. Ryley obituary, *New York Times*, February 22, 1934, p. 24.

175. When Comfort died in 1979 at the age of eighty-one, she had the distinction of being London's oldest understudy for *The Mouse Trap*, Agatha Christie's long-running play. Sometime after 1979, the John Ryland Library, Manchester University, purchased fifteen typescript leather-bound plays by Ryley which had been in Comfort's possession—see listing of Ryley's work at the end of the chapter.

176. Ryley's Will, Probate Sub-Registry, York, England.

177. Ryley obituary.

178. Interview by M.O.K. in *The Vote* (March 26, 1910): 256–

CHAPTER 3 - Dix & Sutherland

1. Evelyn Greenleaf Sutherland, "To Mademoiselle Bas-Bleau of the Harvard Annex," *The Manhattan (1883–1884)*, June 1884, p. 648.

2. Beulah Dix Flebbe, "Reminiscences [sic] of a Radcliffe Playwright," *What We Found at Radcliffe* (Boston: McGrath-Sherrill Press, c. 1920), B. M. Dix Papers, University of Oregon, Knight Library, hereafter cited as KL.

3. Franklin, "Boston's Great Array of Literary People," *Chicago Daily Tribune*, August 23, 1902, p. 15.

4. Information on Evelyn Greenleaf Sutherland's life is compiled from: *Who's Who on the Stage*, 2nd ed. (New York: W. Browne & F. A. Austin, 1908); Johnson Briscoe, *The Actors' Birthday Book* (New York: Moffat, Yard and Company, 1908), 208; Helen M. Winslow, *Literary Boston of Today* (Boston: L. C. Page & Company, 1903), n.p.; Julia Ward Howe's entry on Sutherland in Mary Elvira Elliott et al., compilers, *Sketches of Representative Women of New England* (Boston: New England Historical Publication Company, 1904), n.p.

5. Howe entry, *Sketches of Representative Women*, n.p.

6. Sylvain Cazalet, "History of Homoeopathy Biographies," http://www.homeoint.org/history/bio/s/sutherlandjp.htm.

7. Evelyn F. Scott, *Hollywood When Silents Were Golden* (New York: McGraw-Hill, 1972), 41.

8. Ibid. Allan Rowe is mentioned frequently in Dix's theatre journal as accompanying the two women to the theatre, most notably during their trip to Great Britain in 1906. Dr. Sutherland, who died on February 22, 1941, may have outlived his adopted son, as Allan Rowe is not mentioned in his will, dated November 5, 1937—Suffolk County Probate Court, Boston, Massachusetts.

9. Ibid.

10. James Herne, letter to Sutherland, February 22, 1893, Boston Public Library, hereafter cited as BPL.

11. David Belasco, letter to Sutherland addressed to Dramatic Editor, Jenks, 1893, BPL.
12. Alexander Salvini, letter to Sutherland, March 9, 1896, BPL. The same spring, Salvini produced one of Sutherland's one-acts, *Rohan the Silent*, to use in his 1896–97 season as a curtain raiser to *The Fool's Revenge*. Unfortunately, it was the last role created by Salvini, as he died in 1896 while still in his thirties.
13. William Gillette, letter to Sutherland, spring 1897, BPL.
14. Rudyard Kipling, undated letter to EGS from Naulakha, Brattleboro, Vermont.
15. Scott, *Hollywood When Silents Were Golden*, 41.
16. Howe, *Sketches of Representative Women*, n.p.
17. Charles Henry Meltzer, "An Actor's Summer Colony," *The Cosmopolitan* (September 1902): 550.
18. Howe, *Sketches of Representative Women*, n.p.
19. Mildred Buchanan Flagg, *Notable Boston Authors: Members of the Boston Authors' Club, 1900–1966* (Cambridge, MA: Dresser, Chapman & Grimes, 1965). Another playwright involved with organizing the club was Josephine Preston Peabody.
20. "Present Aspect of Woman Suffrage," A symposium, Boston, c. 1897, online, Harvard University, Collections Development Department, Widener Library.
21. The *New York Evening Post*, December 16, 1892, p. 4, lists all the guests. The Theatre of Arts and Letters, headed by Henry Burton McDowell, was an attempt of "a group of minor authors" to establish subscription audiences in New York and other major cities and present "plays of literary merit," but it lasted only one season. See Gerald Bordman, *Oxford Companion to American Theatre* (New York: Oxford University Press, 1992), 663. Sutherland may have become acquainted with Emma Sheridan Fry when the actress was with the Boston Museum Theatre in the early 1890s. Fry rejoined Richard Mansfield's company for a time in the fall of 1891 but eventually left the stage to write.
22. *New York Times*, December 16, 1892, p. 4.
23. *New York Herald*, December 16, 1892, p. 4.

24. *New York Times*, December 16, 1892, p. 4.

25. *New York Herald*, December 16, 1892, p. 4.

26. Gerald Bordman, *American Theatre* (New York: Oxford University Press, 1994), 393.

27. *Evening Post* (NY), February 18, 1896, p. 8.

28. Henry Woodruff graduated from Harvard in the spring of 1899; *Chicago Tribune*, August 12, 1898, p. 5.

29. Evelyn Greenleaf Sutherland, *Po' White Trash* in *Po' White Trash and Other One-Act Dramas* (Chicago: Herbert S. Stone and Company, 1900), 2.

30. Sutherland, *Po' White Trash and Other One-Act Dramas*, 5–8.

31. Ibid., 14.

32. Ibid., 17.

33. *New York Herald*, April 23, 1898, p. 12.

34. *New York Times*, April 23, 1898, p. 7.

35. The play, *Po' White Trash*, however, had an extended life when Alfred Hickman played Drent Dury in Daniel Fraley's Western tour during the season of 1898–99. Noted in Sutherland, *Po' White Trash and Other One-Act Dramas*, 230–32.

36. Lula Vollmer (1898-1955) is often cited as a pioneer of the American folk-play, her most well-known work being *Sun-Up*, 1923. See Bordman, *Oxford Companion to American Theatre*, 695.

37. Evelyn Greenleaf Sutherland and Emma Sheridan Frye, *In Far Bohemia*, in Sutherland, *Po' White Trash and Other One-Act Dramas*, 35–55.

38. Evelyn Greenleaf Sutherland and Percy Wallace Mackaye, *A Song at the Castle*, in Sutherland, *Po' White Trash and Other One-Act Dramas*, 127–154.

39. Susan Croft, author of *She Also Wrote Plays* (London: Faber and Faber, 2001), shares this information from unpublished research on Sutherland.

40. *Aunt Chloe's Cabin*, as performed by the Woman's Professional League in New York City, May 12, 1898, has about sixteen "negro" characters and was a part of their yearly minstrel show. While the portrayal of stereotypical negroes in numerous and comical ways would likely be found offensive today, the play

could provide insight into attitudes of the era toward race, as well as the participation of women in minstrelsy. In *In Office Hours, and Other Sketches for Vaudeville or Private Acting* (Boston: W. H. Baker & Company, 1900), 35–50. *Mars'r Van* and *His Own* are not extant.

41. James Metcalfe, "Drama," *Life* (April 9, 1908): 388.
42. Ibid.
43. Ibid.
44. *Indianapolis Sunday Star*, February 2, 1913, p. 15.
45. Program, Century Theatre, February 22, 1926, Theatre Museum, London. Lena Ashwell (1872–1957), English actress, is known for having organized companies of professional actors to entertain the allied armies in France after the commencement of the First World War. After the war, she "started the Once-a-Week Players (later known as the Lena Ashwell Players) that, extending the idea of the troop entertainers, presented plays with minimal scenery and props in village and suburban halls. After this, she managed the Century Theatre from 1924 to 1929." http://www.collectorspost.com/cgi-bin/ShopLoader.cgi?Actors/lena_ashwell.html.-
46. Howe, *Sketches of Representative Women*, n.p.
47. *Chicago Tribune*, September 8, 1897, p. 8.
48. *New York Times*, March 30, 1897, p. 7.
49. *Chicago Tribune*, August 26, 1897, p. 10.
50. Ibid.
51. Ibid.
52. Ibid.; *Chicago Daily*, August 31, 1897, p. 12.
53. Ibid.
54. *Chicago Tribune*, September 12, 1897, p. 42.
55. *Chicago Tribune*, September 8, 1897, p. 8.
56. *Monsieur Beaucaire* (New York: Grosset & Dunlap, 1900) was Booth Tarkington's second novel; he went on to enjoy a successful career as a novelist and dramatized twenty comedies for the stage. See *Chicago Daily Tribune*, May 22, 1946, p. 18.
57. Adolf Klauber, "As to Dramatized Novels," *New York Times*, December 8, 1901, p. SM3.
58. *New York Times*, December 3, 1901, p. 9.

59. Dix, *Theatre Record*, Vol. II, Colonial Theatre, Boston, October 21, 1901.

60. James Metcalfe, *Life*, December 12, 1901, p. 518.

61. William Archer, *World*, October 20, 1902, p. 692.

62. Ibid.

63. *New York Times*, March 12, 1912, p. 8.

64. *Portsmouth Herald* (NH), November 6, 1901, n.p. *Joan o' the Shoals* does not appear to be extant.

65. *New York Times*, February 2, 1902, p. 11.

66. Bordman, *American Theatre*, 492.

67. *New York Sun*, February 4, 1902, p. 7.

68. Evelyn Greenleaf Sutherland defended herself and her play in a letter to the editor, *New York Dramatic Mirror*, February 22, 1902, n.p., Billy Rose Collection, hereinafter cited as BR.

69. *New York Times*, February 4, 1902, p. 6.

70. Ibid.

71. *New York Sun*, February 4, 1902, p. 7.

72. Ibid.

73. Sutherland, *New York Dramatic Mirror*, n.p., BR.

74. Ibid.

75. Eileen McCann, "Beaulah [sic] Dix Flebbe, Noted Novelist, Vividly Recalls Her Childhood in Chelsea," *Chelsea Evening Record*, c. 1932, clipping, n.p., Dix Papers, KL. Portions on Dix were taken from a paper at the American Literature Association Conference, May 2003.

76. Scott, *Hollywood When Silents Were Golden*, 16–17.

77. McCann, "Beaulah [sic] Dix Flebbe," n.p.

78. Ibid.

79. Scott, *Hollywood When Silents Were Golden*, 17.

80. McCann, "Beaulah [sic] Dix Flebbe," n.p.

81. For short story publications, see "Works of Beulah Marie Dix" at the end of the chapter.

82. McCann, "Beaulah [sic] Dix Flebbe," n.p.

83. "Beulah Dix Flebbe, Reminiscences of a Radcliffe Playwright," in *What We Found at Radcliffe* (Boston: McGrath-Sherrill Press, 1920), 21–22. Dix wrote approximately ten plays for The Idlers

at Radcliffe.

84. Ibid. *Cicely's Cavalier* was likely a version of Dix's first Idler production, *The Wooing of Mistress Widdrington*—Cicely's last name is Widdrington. The play concerns a young impetuous woman, a royalist sympathizer, who lives unwillingly with her half-brother, a major for Parliament. Her brother brings home a prisoner, Captain Richard Carewe, a royalist cavalier, who has been carrying an incriminating letter written by Cicely and given to her cousin, which begs safe passage to her mother's family. Cicely's brother tells Carewe he must marry his sister within the hour or be shot, and despite resistance and misunderstandings, this leads to the romantic union of Cicely with her cavalier. An interesting note about this short play is that when it was produced at Radcliffe, George Pierce Baker played the role of Carewe, while his wife took the role of Cicely. Additionally, this same plot device—i.e., the forced marriage because of a letter written by the heroine—turns up later in Dix and Sutherland's *Boy O'Carroll*.

85. George Pierce Baker, who taught playwriting at Radcliffe and then Harvard, is known today as "the father of American playwriting." Dix says that because he had given courses on the drama and had acted, along with his wife, in the Cambridge Dramatic Club, she sought him out for advice on *Cicely's Cavalier*. Flebbe, "Reminiscenses [sic] of a Radcliffe Playwright," 22.

86. Ibid., 23.

87. Amos K. Fiske, "Miss Dix, Author of 'Hugh Gwyeth,'" *New York Times Saturday Review*, reprinted in *Book News*, Philadelphia, September 1899, n.p.

88. *New York Times*, April 13, 1901, p. 259.

89. McCann, "Beaulah [sic] Dix Flebbe," n.p.

90. Scott, *Hollywood When Silents Were Golden*, 41–42.

91. Dix's theatre journals are with her archives in Special Collections at the University of Oregon's Knight Library.

92. Dix, *Theatre Record*, Vol. I, *Monte Cristo*, Boston, May 28, 1892; *The King's Musketeers*, Hollis Street Theatre, Boston, April 27, 1899; *The Song of the Sword*, Hollis Street Theatre, December 13, 1899.

93. Dix, *Theatre Record*, Vol. II, *L'Aiglon*, Boston Theatre, April 17, 1901.

94. Dix, *Theatre Record*, Vol. III, *The Music Master*, Bijou Theatre, NY, May 10, 1905; *Hedda Gabler*, Tremont Theatre, Boston, January 12, 1906; *Peter Pan*, January 1906.

95. "Week's Film Programme Offers Many Big Stars," *New York Tribune*, September 26, 1915, sect. III, p. 4.

96. Bordman, *Oxford Companion to American Theatre*, 559.

97. Hector Turnbull, "Four New Plays at the Princess," *New York Tribune*, November 25, 1914.

98. *New York Times*, November 25, 1914, p. 11.

99. Beulah Marie Dix, *Across the Border* (London: Methuen, 1915), 1; "The Crier," playbill, Toy Theatre, Boston, MA, December 30, 1914, to January 6, 1915.

100. Ibid., 18.

101. Ibid., 32.

102. Ibid., 44.

103. Hector Turnbull, "Four New Plays at the Princess," *New York Tribune*, November 25, 1914; *New York Times*, November 25, 1914, p. 11.

104. *New York Times*, November 25, 1914, p. 11; Burns Mantle, "New York Sees the First War Play," *Chicago Daily Tribune*, November 29, 1914, p. E1.

105. *New York Herald*, November 26, 1914, p. 6.

106. Beulah Marie Dix, *Moloch* (New York: Knopf, 1916).

107. Ibid., 94.

108. George C. Tyler, *Whatever Goes Up* (Indianapolis: Bobb-Merrill, 1934), Tyler recounts that when Holbrook Blinn first gave him *Moloch*, he immediately felt it was theatrically gripping, but not being a pacifist himself, he worried that it might be too propagandistic. He sent the play to Colonel Theodore Roosevelt for his opinion, but in the meantime was urged by fellow producers to begin production. When Roosevelt finally replied in October during the run of the New York production, he shared his thoughts on the play. The first act he felt showed "real strength," demonstrating an "Aeschylean horror and dignity of the portrayal of the blind working of fate which brings evil on evil." But he wrote that the "lesson" of the play

as a whole was "both very foolish and very wicked" in that the play does not discriminate between "wanton or iniquitous war," or a war of "righteousness." His letter is reprinted in its entirety in Tyler's memoir (pp. 265–67).

109. Ibid.
110. "High Comedy in America," *Bookman* (November 1915), 269.
111. "A Line o' Type or Two," *Chicago Daily Tribune,* July 6, 1940, p. 8.
112. *Boston Transcript,* undated clipping, in letter to Dix from Frances Sprague, KL.
113. For further discussion on *Across the Border* and *Moloch,* see Maria Christine Beach, "Women Staging War: Female Dramatists and the Discourses of War and Peace in the United States of America, 1913–1947" (PhD diss., University of Texas at Austin, 2004).
114. Beulah Marie Dix, letter to Evelyn Greenleaf Sutherland, April 13, 1901, Boston Public Library. Although Dix suggested the title of *Kit the Kestrel,* the early four-act romantic drama might be extant under a different title.
115. Flebbe, "Reminiscences of a Radcliffe Playwright," 22.
116. *New York Evening Post,* September 30, 1902, p. 12.
117. Beulah Marie Dix and Evelyn Greenleaf Sutherland, *A Rose o' Plymouth- Town* (Chicago: Dramatic Publishing, 1908), 11.
118. *New York Evening Post,* September 30, 1902, p. 12.
119. Minnie Dupree had previously acted in about six of Sutherland's one-acts.
120. *New York Sun,* September 30, 1902, p. 7.
121. *New York Times,* September 30, 1902, p. 9.
122. Dix and Sutherland, *A Rose o' Plymouth-Town,* pp. 12–13.
123. *Boston Transcript,* May 5, 1902, n.p., clipping, KL.
124. "Miss Dupree's Play Crude and Insipid," *New York Herald,* September 30, 1902, p. 8.
125. John Corbin, *New York Times,* October 5, 1902, sect. II, p. 14.
126. *Massillon Independent* (OH), October 16, 1902, n.p.
127. John Corbin, *New York Times,* August 31, 1902, p. 8.
128. Scott, *Hollywood When Silents Were Golden,* 41.
129. John Martin-Harvey, *The Autobiography of Sir John Martin-Harvey* (London: Sampson Low, Marston & Company, Ltd., 1933), 289.

The actor went by Martin Harvey earlier in his career; after being knighted in 1921, he added the hyphen to his name. See also http://www.webrarian.co.uk/martin-harvey/index1.html.

130. Ibid., 292.

131. *Stage*, June 8, 1905, p. 14.

132. Pasted into Beulah Marie Dix's theatre journal, 1903. Although the cable is undated, it was undoubtedly sent shortly after the opening at Newcastle, England, September 28, 1903. Martin-Harvey notes in his memoirs that touring could be quite lucrative; weekly receipts for the first tour of *The Breed of the Treshams* before it had been seen in London averaged £937, whereas when it played at the Lyric Theatre in London the weekly average was £512. Martin-Harvey, *The Autobiography of Sir John Martin-Harvey*, 314.

133. Dix, *Theatre Record*, Vol. III, Theatre Royal, Dublin, week of October 26, 1903.

134. Martin-Harvey, *The Autobiography of Sir John Martin-Harvey*, 292.

135. Ibid., 292–93.

136. Ibid., 293.

137. Ibid.

138. Dix, *Theatre Record*, Vol. III. *The Breed of Treshams*, Royal Lyceum, Edinboro, April 21, 1906; Theatre Royal, Newcastle, April 28, 1906.

139. Ibid.

140. *Times* (London), December 6, 1921, p. 8.

141. http://www.webrarian.co.uk/martin-harvey/breed.html.

142. Martin-Harvey, *The Autobiography of Sir John Martin-Harvey*, 343.

143. *Sketch*, May 30, 1906, p. 208.

144. *Era*, May 26, 1906, p. 15.

145. Ibid.

146. Dix, *Theatre Record*, Vol. III. *Boy O'Carrol*, Theatre Royal, Newcastle, April 27, 1906; Liverpool, May 1–3, 1906; Imperial Theatre, London, May 19, 1906.

147. *Times* (London), May 21, 1906, p. 4.

148. *Era*, May 26, 1906, p. 15.

149. Martin-Harvey, *The Autobiography of Sir John Martin-Harvey*, 343.

150. *Stage*, September 29, 1910, p. 15.

151. Beulah Marie Dix and Evelyn Greenleaf Sutherland, Young

NOTES271

Fernald, typescript KL, I, 23.

152. *Times* (London), September 29, 1910, p. 12.

153. *Era*, February 22, 1908, p. 21.

154. *Times* (London), February 21, 1908, p. 10.

155. Beulah Marie Dix and Evelyn Greenleaf Sutherland, *The Road to Yesterday* (New York: Samuel French, 1925 revised version), Act 1, 9–16.

156. Ibid., Act 1, 28–29.

157. Ibid, Act II, p. 55.

158. *Town and Country*, May 18, 1907, p. 48.

159. *New York Herald*, January 1, 1907, p. 14.

160. Alan Dale, *Chicago Examiner*, January 8, 1907, n.p., clipping, BR.

161. *New York Times*, January 6, 1907, sect. IV, p. 1.

162. Ibid.

163. Clipping, Museum of the City of New York.

164. Dix, *Theatre Record*, Vol. III, *The Lilac Room*, Academy of Music, Norfolk, VA, October 29, 1906.

165. Dix, *Theatre Record*, Vol. III, *The Lilac Room*, Webers Theatre, NY, April 3, 1907.

166. *Theatre*, May 1907, p. 117.

167. *Sun*, February 4, 1902, p. 9; *New York Times*, April 4, 1907, p. 9.

168. *Evening Post* (New York), April 4, 1907, p. 9.

169. At this time, Max Figman was an experienced performer with a number of serious roles to his credit, including that of Torvald Helmer in *A Doll's House* with Minnie Maddern Fiske; interestingly, he also directed *The Triumph of Love*, Martha Morton's prize-winning failure in 1904. The year before, Figman had toured with *Man on the Box* by Grace Livingston Furniss. Many reviewers of *The Substitute* placed him alongside prominent comedians of the day.

170. Waldemar Young, "Figman Triumphs in His New Play," *San Francisco Examiner*, December 7, 1908, n.p.; the Shubert archives have several sheets of reviews of *The Substitute* compiled from Figman's touring production.

171. Beulah Marie Dix and Evelyn Greenleaf Sutherland, *The Substitute*, Act IV, p. 7, KL.

172. Scott, *Hollywood When Silents Were Golden*, 45.

173. Beulah Marie Dix, *Theatre Journal*, December 1908, KL.

174. Jacob North, "The Death of Mrs. Sutherland," *New York*, January 1, 1909, clipping, BR.
175. *Illustrated London News*, October 8, 1910, p. 526.

CHAPTER 4-Rida Johnson Young

1. Rida Johnson Young, "Ah, Sweet Mystery," *Naughty Marietta* (New York: Witmark, 1910).
2. "Woman Playwright's Secret of Success," *Syracuse Herald* (NY), November 18, 1917, n.p.
3. Helen Christine Bennett, "Mother Machree," *American Magazine* (December 1920): 187. This is the most extensive interview with Rida Johnson Young available—the primary source for the dramatist's early years for most biographical accounts written on her in recent years.
4. Ibid.
5. While Rida's birth date differs in various biographical entries, it is substantiated here by two sources, the 1900 Census and her registration at Wilson College. From census records, the Johnson children and year of birth include George Stewart, 1866; Emma 1868; William, 1870; Marion? [not clear] 1872; Rida Louise, 1875; Samuel M., 1881. The 1900 census tells that there were seven children born, with four surviving, while the 1910 census states six children, with four surviving—possibly one child died in infancy. William's birth date is uncertain; his age is given as thirty-seven in 1870 and forty-two ten years later in 1880. Similarly, Emma, the mother's age varies in four different censuses, but a news article in 1925 states that she was observing her 83rd birthday, which puts her birth year at 1842. *New York Times*, December 20, 1925, p. 29.
6. A lighter, according to *Webster's College Dictionary* (New York: Random House, 2000), 769, is a large, open, flat-bottomed boat used for transporting goods; William Johnson was a coal dealer who conveyed coal on barges. According to the 1910 census, his son Stewart was also in the towing and lighterage coal

business.

7. Related by Marc Warren, assistant librarian, Maryland Historical Society.

8. Ten years later, the census reveals Emma living in a different part of Baltimore with her two sons, Stewart and Samuel, and Theresa, Stewart's wife.

9. William Young is not listed in the 1900 census and since Rida refers to her father in an article in 1893, he possibly died around 1900. Young's obituary in the *Stamford Advocate*, May 10, 1926, p. 6, states that she had lost her father twenty-five years before.

10. Information comes from Wanda J. Finney, Archivist, Wilson College, via e-mail, October 18, 2002. According to college records, she came from Baltimore Women's College (now Goucher College), although Goucher records do not show that she graduated from there—Kathy Fasolo, Goucher College, via e-mail, December 19, 2005. In addition, some early articles claim that she attended Radcliffe College, but Radcliffe records do not show her ever attending there.

11. Bennett, "Mother Machree," 182.

12. Bennett, "Mother Machree," 182–84. Young's telling of her early days in eking out a living in New York does not support other descriptions of her as being a "Baltimore socialite" from a wealthy family.

13. Elizabeth Lonergan, "Women Who Write Plays," *Strand Magazine* (June 1911): 594–601.

14. Bennett, "Mother Machree," 185.

15. Ibid.

16. Isidore Witmark and Isaac Goldberg, *The Story of the House of Witmark: From Ragtime to Swingtime* (New York, Lee Furman, 1939), 348.

17. James Walvin in *Leisure and Society 1830–1950* (London: Longman, 1978) tells of the turn-of-the-century passion pianos and the proliferation of sheet music at this time.

18. Bennett, "Mother Machree," 34.

19. Ibid., 34.

20. See Lonergan, "Women Who Write Plays," 597. It may have been

the *Baltimore American* where James worked; Howard Fitzalan in his column in the *Morning Telegraph*, October 24, 1910, p. 4, credits Louise Malloy ("Josh Wink"), dramatic editor of the *Baltimore America*, for "advising and counseling" Rida Johnson with her budding playwriting career. The resource for James Young's birth date comes from http://www.allmovie.com.

21. *New York Times*, March 17, 1895, p. 12; *Middletown Daily Argus* (NY), October 21, 1896, n.p.; *Syracuse Daily Standard*, November 8, 1896, p. 2; *The News*, Frederick, MD, September 14, 1897, n.p.; *Lincoln Evening News*, October 13, 1900, p. 3.

22. Middletown Daily Argus, October 21, 1896, p. 2.

23. *Evening Democrat* (Warren, PA), January 3, 1898, n.p; Candice Marie Coleman in "Gender Issues as Reflected in the Lives and Plays of Three Women Playwrights: 1900–1930" (diss., Kent State University, 1993), p. 178, mentions in a footnote that Young used "Louise Jansen as a stage name" when touring throughout the south. Yvonne Safer also mentions this in *American Women Playwrights, 1900–1950* (New York: Peter Lang, 1995), 204. However, I have not been able to confirm that Young ever used a stage name; on the contrary, articles and ads use her given name of Rida Louise Johnson.

24. Shirley Burns, "Women Dramatists," *Green Book Album* (September 1910): 634.

25. *The Lincoln Evening News* (Nebraska), October 13, 1900, p. 3, gives the account that Daly was so pleased with James Young's reading of Shylock in the *Merchant of Venice*, that he engaged him for the role; however, *Cyrano de Bergerac* was staged instead and Young played Christian for a time, but was abruptly withdrawn due to being "disliked" by Ada Rehan, Daly's lead actress. According to the *New York Times*, January 24, 1899, p. 7, and January 14, 1900, p. 16, James continued to be relegated to small parts."

26. Since no extant copy can be found, it is difficult to determine the plot of *Lord Byron*. Rida revised the script during the first few weeks' run, as mentioned in the notice in *The Constitution* (Atlanta, GA), February 1, 1900, p. 12; only a few reviews are available, but commentary focuses on staging and performance

of the play, rather than its plot.

27. *Virginia-Pilot* (Newark), January 18, 1900, n.p.

28. Ibid.

29. *Virginia-Pilot* (Newark), January 20, 1900, p. 12.

30. *Virginia-Pilot* (Newark), January 21, 1900, n.p.

31. *New York Times*, January 28, 1900, p. 16.

32. *Lincoln Evening News*, October 13, 1900, p. 3; *Fort Wayne News* (IN), October 5, 1900, p. 6. It is not known why James Young's engagement with Irving was cut short, but he was back in New York in 1902, playing Krogstad in Ibsen's *A Doll's House*; see "Mrs. Fiske as Nora," *New York Times*, May 22, 1902, p. 9.

33. Albert Nelson Marquis, ed., *Who's Who in America*, vol. 12 (Chicago: A. N. Marquis & Company, 1922), 3417.

34. Young also had some initial association with the Shuberts during *Brown of Harvard*, which they possibly co-produced with Henry Miller produced, as they were apparently involved in casting the play. Sam, Lee and J. J. Shubert went up against the Theatrical Syndicate who had a monopoly on theatres in the late 1800s; after the death of Sam in 1905 in a train wreck, Lee and J. J. continued to expand the organization to become the largest theatre owners in New York and throughout the country and throughout the country, essentially forming their own monopoly. Gerald Bordman, *American Theatre: A Chronicle of Comedy and Drama, 1869–1914* (New York: Oxford University Press, 1994), 621.

35. Bennett, "Mother Machree," 186. There are conflicting reports regarding the "Oxford play" that Young preferred not to acknowledge in Bennett's interview. However, an article in the *Morning Telegram* (NY), January 28, 1910, p. 4, stated that her "latest comedy, based on the 'undergrad' life in the various colleges of Oxford, will be given a London production by Charles Frohman presently." Young also stated earlier in Shirley Burns' 1910 article, that she wrote an Oxford play for Frohman called *The Duffer*.n

36. *Rida Johnson Young's One Act Plays, Dramatic Scenes and Monologs* (New York: M. Witmark & Sons, 1906) includes two monologues, *Barbara's Dilemma* and *Chatterton*, and two short

plays, *The Last of the Cargills* and *John Clayton, Actor*, according to Isidore Witmark, Young wrote one-act plays for the publication department at Witmark—see Witmark and Goldberg, *The Story of the House of Witmark: From Ragtime to Swingtime*, 348. Rida Johnson Young and Gilbert P. Coleman, *Brown of Harvard* (New York: G. P. Putnam's Son's, 1907).

37. *Washington Post*, August 12, 1906, p. 4. A typescript copy of *Sweet Sixteen* is in the Shubert Archives, New York.

38. Bennett, "Mother Machree," 185.

39. Charles Darnton, "Glorious Betsy Gives the Matinee Girl Sugar-coated History," *Evening World* (NY), September 9, 1908, n.p.

40. *Toledo Blade*, November 12, 1907, n.p.

41. Mary Kouncelor Brookes, "Miss Mary Mannering Talks of Love Stories," *Fort Worth Record*, February 16, 1908, n.p.

42. Bennett, "Mother Machree," 185.

43. Ibid.

44. *New York Times*, December 5, 1905, p. 9. Henry Woodruff was at an excellent stage of his acting career to take on the starring role of Tom Brown. As discussed in the previous chapter, even before graduating from Harvard, Woodruff began his acting career with a number of one-act plays by Evelyn Greenleaf Sutherland, most notably, *Po' White Trash* and *A Bit of Instruction* in 1898. He spent the next five or so years playing supporting "leading men" roles in stock companies, such as with Henrietta Crossman's.

45. Bennett, "Mother Machree," 185–86.

46. "The Theater," *Town and Country*, March 10, 1906, p. 48.

47. *New York Times*, February 27, 1906, p. 9.

48. Virginia Frame, "Women Who Have Written Successful Plays," *Theatre*, 6 (October 1906): ix. Young's play also competed with three major successes which opened the previous fall: J. M. Barrie's *Peter Pan* (brought in from England), David Belasco's *The Girl of the Golden West* and Charles Klein's *The Lion and the Mouse*.

49. *New York Herald*, February 27, 1906, p. 12.

50. Ibid.

51. *New York Times*, March 4, 1906, p. PX3.

52. James Metcalfe, *Life* (March 8, 1906): 313.

53. *Washington Post*, October 27, 1907, p. 3.

54. It is not known exactly when Rida and James Young were divorced, but, conceivably, it was before September 1910. A brief notice in the *Daily News* (Frederick, MD), June 30, 1914, p. 2, concerning an automobile accident in which James Young killed an eight-year-old boy, mentions that he married actress Clara Kimball in September 1910, but their marriage was not actually announced "until sometime in 1911."

55. *Sun* (NY), April 9, 1907, p. 9.

56. *Theatre*, May 1907, p. 115.

57. Rida Johnson Young, *Boys of Company B* (*When Love is Young*) (1907), ts, Shubert Archives, New York, NY, hereinafter cited as SA, Act II, p. 17.

58. Young and William Cary Duncan wrote the book and lyrics, while William Schroeder composed the music. Young communicated with J. J. Shubert on September 17, 1912, asking when she could read him the musical. SA.

59. Broeck, Helen Ten, "Rida Young—Dramatist and Garden Expert," *Theatre* (April 1917): 250.

60. Rida Johnson Young, *The Lottery Man* (New York: Samuel French, 1910).

61. *Sun* (NY), December 7, 1909, p. 9; although his byline is not given, the critic may well have been Lawrence Reamer, who dubbed most plays as "rotten," according to "Critics as Seen by John Held," *Theatre*, March 1917, n.p.

62. *New York Times* articles: "Writer Sues Shuberts," October 29, 1912, p. 13; "No Theft in Play," November 1, 1912, p. 8; "Mrs. Furness Loses Suit," November 2, 1912, p. 13.

63. "No Theft in Play." The October 29 account tells that in August 1909, Furness signed a six-month contract for $100 per week to "correct, rewrite and revise play manuscripts which had been submitted to the Shuberts." Furness claimed that it "was agreed" that she would receive 33 1/3 percent of the royalties for revising *The Lottery Man*, although the Shuberts denied entering into any such agreement.

64. Ibid.

65. Telegram from R. J. Young to J. J. Shubert, November 11, c. 1910, SA.

66. R. J. Young, letter to Lee Shubert, October 17, 1910, SA.
67. *New York Tribune*, November 14, 1912, p. 4. "Two a day" referred to vaudeville shows.
68. The title was first announced as *The Girl and the Miner* in the *New York Times*, August 12, 1912, p. 9.
69. Rida Johnson Young, *The Red Petticoat*, ts., 1912, SA, Act I, p. 16.
70. Alan Dale, "Red Petticoat" Is Full of Fun," November 14, 1912, clipping, Donald MacDonald scrapbook, Billy Rose Theatre Collection, New York Public Library, hereafter cited as BR.
71. Ibid.
72. *The Evening Mail*, clipping, Donald MacDonald scrapbook, BR.
73. *New York Times*, November 17, 1912, p. X9.
74. Bennett, "Mother Machree," 186.
75. "Mathewson a Playwright," *New York Times*, April 8, 1913, p. 13.
76. "Interview" with Christy Mathewson (as impersonated by Eddie Frierson) by Bob Palazzo. "The Diamond Angle," *The Eclectic Baseball Magazine* Web site, http://www.thediamondangle.com/achive/aug02/matty4. Accessed September 13, 1903.
77. *New York Dramatic Mirror*, October 29, 1913, p. 6.
78. Apparently, Mathewson was not in attendance, and Rida Johnson Young "sent word that as she was not a suffragette she couldn't make a speech." Acton Davies, "News of the Theatres," October 24, 1913, n.p., clipping, BR.
79. Ibid.
80. *Theatre* (December 1913), xii.
81. Charles Darnton, *Evening World*, October 24, 1913, clipping, BR.
82. *World*, October 24, 1913, clipping, BR.
83. "Baseball Play Didn't Make a Hit," *Sun*, October 24, 1913, p. 7.
84. Frederick S. Roffman, "Ah, It's Sweet Mystery Time," *New York Times*, May 11, 1975, pp. D1, 17.
85. Roffman, "Ah, It's Sweet Mystery Time," p. 17.
86. Gerald Bordman, *American Musical Theatre* (New York: Oxford University Press, 1978), 261.
87. Roffman"Ah, It's Sweet Mystery Time," p. 17.
88. Steven Daigle explains in the Director's Notes for the 2000 production of *Naughty Marietta*, that in the early to mid-1700s,

the King of France sent young unwed maids, mostly nurses and teachers, to establish residency with the locals of New Orleans. Each came with a wooden chest, or *casquette*, containing an "allotment of gold" and a land deed.

89. The comic character, Simon, later became "Silas Slick," as indicated in a *New York Times*, October 22, 1929, review of a revival of *Naughty Marietta* at the Jolson Theatre in New York. Subsequent revivals appear to have retained the name; for Ohio Light Opera Company's 2000 production, he was called "Silas Simoneaux from the Bayou."

90. Bordman, *American Musical Theatre*, 261.

91. Channing Pollock, "Naughty Marietta," *The Green Book Album* (January 1911): 117.

92. Trentini was a house guest at Young's Greenwich, CT, home while she studied her part for *Naughty Marietta*. "The Great American Playwright Belt," *Ogden Standard* (UT), August 20, 1910, n.p.

93. Roffman, "Ah, It's Sweet Mystery Time," 17.

94. *Theatre* (December 1910): 165.

95. *New York Dramatic Mirror*, November 16, 1910, p. 7.

96. *New York Tribune*, November 8, 1910, p. 7.

97. James Stuart, "Program Notes for Ohio Light Opera Production," Summer 2000.

98. Raymond Ericson, "City Opera Restores 'Naughty Marietta,'" *New York Times*, August 31, 1979, p. C20.

99. Bordman, *American Musical Theatre*, 261.

100. Ohio Light Opera production, Summer 2000, reprinted in CD notes, 25–26.

101. *New York Times*, August 9, 1920, p. 6. According to copies of contracts in Beulah Marie Dix's papers (Knight Library, University of Oregon), the musical comedy rights for *The Road to Yesterday* were first sold to Edgar J. MacGregor in September 1917. Despite a paragraph in the *New York Times*, June 20, 1920, p. XI, stating that "Mr. MacGregor and Mr. Erlanger are also making ready 'The Dream Girl,'" production continued to be delayed. When MacGregor's option ran out in October 1920, managers at the American Play Company began a series

of negotiations involving T. B. Harms and Company, who held the music publishing contract with Herbert and Young, as well as with George M. Cohan, who also considered producing *The Dream Girl*. Ultimately, the Shuberts produced the musical in August 1924.

102. *Bridgeport Telegram*, April 21, 1924, p. 3. "Victor Herbert Dies on Way to Physician," *New York Times*, May 27, 1924, p. 1.

103. *New York Times*, August 21, 1924, p. 12; According to Bordman, *American Musical Theatre*, 390: "With Herbert unable to supply last-minute changes, the Shuberts discreetly added uncredited Sigmund Romberg interpolations."

104. *New York Times*, August 21, 1924, p. 12.

105. *New York Herald Tribune*, August 21, 1924, p. 8.

106. Dates within the play script at the Shubert Archives vary, suggesting it is not the final version. For instance, Elspeth wishes to go back 300 years, although 500 years is mentioned in the reviews and Jimmy says that it's the "first year of our new king Jamie the Scot," (1603), confusing things even further.

107. Harold Atteridge was the Shuberts' in-house librettist beginning in 1911. Bordman, *Oxford Companion to American Theatre*, 42.

108. Ibid.

109. Cited in *New York Times*, May 27, 1924, p. 1.

110. Rida Johnson Young, *The Dream Girl*, ts, SA, Act I, p. 25–27.

111. Young, *The Dream Girl*, Act II, p. 32.

112. Burns Mantle, rev. *The Dream Girl*, *Chicago Tribune*, August 31, 1924, p. D1.

113. Although the *The Dream Girl* opened on a sad note with Victor Herbert's death, the touring production concluded sadly, as well, with the death of a cast member the following spring. As a celebration of their one-hundredth performance of the tour, Fay Bainter held a masquerade party for the cast in Toronto, at which time Carl A. Lynn died of injuries sustained in a fall down a stairway. "Fay Bainter Now Admits Booze in Fatal Party," *Chicago Tribune*, April 26, 1925, p. 27.

114. Shirley Burns, "Women Dramatists, 634.

115. Bordman, *Oxford Companion to American*, 548. Perhaps Pitou ran out of ideas as a playwright, because from 1904 on, others

provided plays for Olcott—in 1904, Mrs. Edward Nash Morgan wrote an adaptation of *Terence*, a novel by Mrs. B. M. Croker, and thereafter in 1905, 1906, and 1907, Theodore Burt Sayre wrote three plays for Olcott. Following Rida Johnson Young's plays from 1910 to 1914, Olcott performed in two Rachel Crothers' plays, *The Heart of Paddy Whack*, 1914, and *Once Upon a Time*, 1918.

116. *Galveston Daily News*, May 29, 1910, p. 30.
117. *New York Times*, January 27, 1913, p. 7.
118. *New York Times*, January 25, 1910, p. 9.
119. *Galveston Daily News*, August 9, 1908, p. 20; May 29, 1910, p. 30.
120. *New York Times*, January 31, 1911, p. 10.
121. *Sun*, January 31, 1911, p. 7.
122. *New York Tribune*, February 6, 1912, p. 7.
123. *New York Herald*, February 3, 1914, p. 10.
124. Presumably, William A. Schroeder, born in Brooklyn, was the son of Young's only sister, Emma. Schroeder had residences in both Brooklyn and in the Stamford, CT, area, and remained close to Young up to her death. His obituary can be found in the *Wilton Bulletin* (CT), April 27, 1960, p. 13A.
125. *Nebraska State Journal*, December 12, 1909, n.p.
126. Playbill, Belasco Theater, Washington, DC, March 1910, Museum of the City of New York, hereinafter cited as MCNY.
127. Ibid.
128. *Washington Post*, March 8, 1910, n.p.
129. *Cleveland Leader*, April 19, 1910, n.p.
130. *New York Times*, December 26, 1914, p. 7.
131. Ibid.; *New York Review*, December 26, 1914, n.p.; *Sun*, December 26, 1914, p. 7.
132. *New York Telegram*, December 26, 1914; *Sun*, December 26, 1914, p. 7.
133. *Atlanta Constitution*, March 27, 1915, n.p.; *Warren Evening Times* (OH), October 25, 1916, p. 5.
134. *Olean Evening Herald* (NY), October 30, 1916, p. 4.
135. William Carey Duncan (1874–1945) went on to write book and lyrics for numerous musicals, including *The Royal Vagabond*, which chalked up 348 performances in 1919.

136. *Theatre* 30 (June 1917): 343. Even though *Polygamy*, a play by Harvey O'Higgins and Harriet Ford, ran for 159 performances (opening December 1, 1914), reviews of *His Little Widows* suggest that Young's musical was a better treatment of the subject.

137. Ibid.

138. Charles Darnton, *World*, May 1, 1917, clipping, MCNY.

139. W. A. MacDonald, *Boston Evening Transcript*, August 16, 1921, p. 6.

140. Ibid.

141. *New York Times*, May 22, 1921, p. 70.

142. *New York Times*, November 12, 1916, p. 6.

143. *Theatre* 24 (December 1916): 394.

144. *Webster's College Dictionary* (New York: Random House, 2000), 114.

145. Rida Johnson Young, *Captain Kid, Jr.* (New York: Samuel French, 1920), Act I, p. 42.

146. *New York Tribune*, November 14, 1916, p. 7; *New York Times*, November 12, 1916, p. 6.

147. *Puck*, December 30, 1916, p. 23.

148. Bordman, *American Musical Theatre*, 318.

149. A letter to R. J. Young from J. J. Shubert dated October 8, 1915, uses the original title, *Gold gab ich Fuer Eisen*.

150. Synopsis from a reader, June 15, 1915, *Gold Gave I for Iron*, SA.

151. One wonders why this was not included in Young's play, as it is a patriotic and touching tradition; perhaps it would have been too reminiscent of the original play.

152. Ibid.

153. Letter from R. J. Young to J. J. Shubert, September 6, 1915, SA.

154. Letters from J. J. Shubert to R. J. Young, September 7, 1915, September 18, 1915, October 4, 1915, October 8, 1915, SA.

155. *New York Times*, December 7, 1916, p. 11.

156. *New York Dramatic Mirror*, December 16, 1916, p. 7.

157. Charles Darnton, *The Evening World*, December 7, 1916, n.p., clipping, MCNY.

158. The *New York Times* tells that this hit song was put into the production at the last minute to "plug a hole in the entertainment."; the song is sometimes attributed to Romberg and Young, but it was actually written by George Asaf and Felix Powell. *New York Times*, July 15, 1917, p. 66.

159. *Munsey's Magazine* (September 1917): 305.

160. Rida Johnson Young, *Maytime*, ms., SA, Act II, p. 1.

161. Webster's College Dictionary (New York: Random House, 2000), p. 294.

162. Ibid., Act I, p. 31.

163. *New York Dramatic Mirror*, August 25, 1917, p. 8.

164. Bordman, *American Musical Theatre*, 324.

165. Ibid.

166. Rida Johnson Young, *Sometime*, ts, SA, Act I, p. 1.

167. Ibid, Act I, p. 6.

168. Ibid.

169. Ibid., Act I, p.12.

170. Bordman, *American Musical Theatre*, 334.

171. Ibid., 335. Ed Wynn is credited in IBDB for additional lyrics.

172. Fran Hassencahl, "Mae West," Alice M. Robinson et al., eds, *Notable Women in the American Theatre* (New York: Greenwood, 1989), 915.

173. Rida Johnson Young, *Little Simplicity*, ts, SA, Act III, p. 24.

174. Ibid., Act I, p. 23.

175. R. J. Young letters to Shubert, October 18, 1918, and another undated.

176. R. J. Young letters to Shubert, undated and June 28, 1918.

177. *New York Times*, November 5, 1918, p. 11; *New York Herald*, November 5, 1918, II, p. 7.

178. *New York Times*, November 5, 1918, p. 11. Dr. Royal S. Copeland, President of the New York Board of Health, "gained much positive public attention for keeping New Yorkers calm during the influenza outbreak of 1918." See Wikipedia.com.

179. Witmark and Goldberg, *The Story of the House of Witmark*, 348; "Woman Playwright's Secret of Success," n.p.

180. Elizabeth Lonergan, "Women Who Write Plays, *Strand* (June 1911): 596.

181. Burns, "Women Dramatists," 634.

182. Mary E. Mullett, *New York Sun*, reprinted in *Kansas City Star*, May 14, 1917, p. 7.

183. *Dramatic Mirror*, April 10, 1909, n.p., clipping, BR.

184. *Morning Telegraph*, January 28, 1910, p. 4.

185. "Rida Johnson Young Robbed," *New York Times*, March 4, 1913, p. 1.

186. "The Great American Playwright Belt."

187. Letters and notes to the Shuberts indicate her New York address was always changing. Various residences for Young included: Hotel Somerset, Madison Square Apartments, Central Park Apartments, Hotel Blackstone, Gainsboro Studios, The Oregon, and several different apartments.

188. Mullett, *New York Sun*, p. 7.

189. Ibid.

190. "Woman Playwright's Secret of Success."

191. Ibid.

192. Mullett, *New York Sun*, p. 7.

193. "Actresses to Grow War Relief Crops," *New York Times*, May 4, 1917, p. 18.

194. Mullett, New York Sun, p. 7.

195. Kenneth Andrews, "Broadway, Our Literary Signpost," *Bookman* (July 1921): 411.

196. *New York Tribune*, September 9, 1920, p. 3.

197. Both of the Shuberts sought properties, often operating independently from one another.
Sometimes one may surmise to which Shubert Young was writing (J. J. often directed and produced, while Lee served mostly as producer), but letters sel- dom identify whether it was Lee or J. J. Shubert Young addressed as "Dear Mr. Shubert," and responding letters from the Shuberts are generally unsigned copies.

198. Letter from R. J. Young to Shubert, September 19, 1917, SA.

199. Letter from R. J. Young to Shubert, November 2, 1917, SA.

200. Letter from R. J. Young to Shubert, March 13, 1918, SA.

201. Letters from Jack Morris, June 19, 1919; October 15, 1919; October 19, 1919, SA.

202. Letter from R. J. Young to Jack Morris, October 21, 1919, SA.

203. Letter from Jack Morris, October 22, 1919, SA.

204. Letter from R. J. Young to Lee Shubert, SA.

205. Letter from R. J. Young to Lee Shubert, November 19, 1919, SA.

206. Letter from R. J. Young to Lee Shubert, February 1920, SA.
207. Letter from Lee Shubert to R. J. Young, February 10, 1920, SA
208. Letter from Lee Shubert to R. J. Young, February 23, 1920, SA.
209. The Dramatists' Theatre was formed by a group of playwrights to stage new works. While Young was not a member, those who founded the company were Owen Davis, James Forbes, Cosmo Hamilton, William Anthony McGuire, Arthur Richman, and Edward Child's Carpenter, chairman. *Sentinel* (Stamford, CT), April 21, 1924. *Telegram* (NY), March 26, 1924, clipping MCNY.
210. *Sentinel* (Stamford), April 21, 1924, clipping MCNY.
211. *Advocate* (Stamford), April 21, 1924, clipping MCNY.
212. *Boston Globe*, April 27, 1924, clipping MCNY.
213. Stark Young, *New York Times*, October 14, 1924, p. 23.
214. *Telegram* (NY), October 14, 1924, clipping MCNY.
215. *Cock o' the Roost* had eighteen performances at the Garrick Theatre, London, July 1926.
216. "Rida Johnson Young Playwright, Dies," *New York Times*, May 9, 1926, p. E9; the record in Probate Court for the District of Stamford gives her age as fifty-four, but this differs from all other accounts.
217. *Bridgeport Telegram* (CT), August 16, 1927, n.p.
218. Last Will and Testament of Rida Johnson Young, September 10, 1924, Stamford Probate Records.
219. *New York Sun*, December 7, 1936, clipping, BR.
220. *New York Times*, April 9, 1907, p. 9.
221. Burns, "Women Dramatists," 634.
222. Frame, "Women Who Have Written Successful Plays," ix.
223. Lucy France Pierce, "Women Who Write Plays," *The World Today* 15 (July 1908): 729.
224. Anna Steese Richardson, "Lady Broadway," *McClure's*, December 1917, p. 67.
225. Broeck, "Rida Young," 250.

APPENDIX

New York Plays and Musicals by Women, April 1885- June 1925

Includes adaptations, dramatizations, translations, books, lyrics, music, and collaborators; cited are the theatres, date, and length of run or number of performances when known (in parentheses), and the nationality (where known) of the writer, if not American.

1885

Favette, the Story of a Waif, dramatized by Estelle Clayton
    Union Square Theatre, April 6, 1885

1887

In the Fashion, Selina Dolaro
    Wallack's Theatre, December 26, 1887

1888

Philip Herne, Mary Fiske
    Fifth Avenue Theatre, August 27, 1888
Her Husband, Alice Lewis Johnson
    Windsor Theatre, September 24, 1888 (1 wk)
The Quick or the Dead? Amélie Rives
    Fifth Avenue Theatre, October 1, 1888
A Sad Coquette, dramatized by Estelle Clayton
    Fifth Avenue Theatre, October 17, 1888
Little Lord Fauntleroy, Frances Hodgson Burnett
    Broadway Theatre, December 3, 1888

1889

Hélèn, Martha Morton
    Union Square Theatre, October 29, 1889 (2 wks)

1890

The Prince and the Pauper, Abby Sage Richardson
    Broadway Theatre, January 20, 1990

1891

The Pharisee, Mrs. Lancaster Wallis and Malcolm Watson (English)
    Madison Square Theatre, March 16, 1891
The Witch, Philip G. Hubert, Jr. and Marie Madison People's
    Theatre, May 4, 1891
The Merchant, Martha Morton
    Madison Square Theatre, May 4, 1891 (7 wks)

1892

Countess Roudine, Paul Kester and Minnie Maddern Fiske
    Union Square Theatre, January 13, 1892
Incog, Mrs. Romualdo Pacheco (Rosana)
    Bijou Theatre, February 22, 1892
Ten Thousand a Year, Emma Sheridan
    Garden Theatre, February 23, 1892
Geoffrey Middleton, Gentleman, Martha Morton
    Union Square Theatre, March 31, 1892 (1 1/2 wks)
White Roses, Lottie Blair Parker
    Lyceum Theatre, April 25, 1892
The Rose, Minnie Maddern Fiske (one-act)
    Daly's Theatre, May 2, 1892
Captain Lettarblair, Marguerite Merington
    Lyceum Theatre, August 16, 1892
Love's Young Dream, Frances Hodgson Burnett
    Standard Theatre, October 31, 1892
Drifting, Evelyn Greenleaf Sutherland and Emma Sheridan Fry (one-act)
    23rd Street Theatre, December 15, 1892

1893

The Belle Stratagem, Hannah Cowley (English)
  Daly'sTheatre, January 3, 1893
The Knave, Clothilde Graves
  Daly's Theatre, January 3, 1893
Captain Herne, U.S.A., Margaret Barrett Smith
  Union Square, January 9, 1893
The Basoche, Madeleine Lucette Ryley
  Casino Theatre, February 27–March 11, 1893
Brother John, Martha Morton
  Star Theatre, March 20, 1893 (1 month)
The Player, Blanche Marsden
  Star Theatre, August 14, 1893

1894

Christmas, Martha Morton (one-act)
  Empire School of Acting, January 9, 1894 (1)
Charley's Uncle, Ellie Norwood (English)
  Bijou Theatre, May 7, 1894
The Great Brooklyn Handicap, Alice E. Ives
  Grand Opera, September 17, 1894
To Nemesis; or Love and Hate, Mrs. Romualdo Pacheco (Rosana)
  Star Theatre, December 2, 1894

1895

His Wife's Father, Martha Morton
  Fifth Avenue Theatre, February 25, 1895 (104)
A Social Highwayman, dramatized by Mary T. Stone
  Garrick Theatre, September 24, 1895
Christopher, Jr., Madeleine Lucette Ryley
  Empire Theatre, October 7, 1895 (64)
Journeys End in Lovers' Meeting, John Oliver Hobbes (Mrs. Craigie)
  Abbey's Theatre, October 29, 1895 (one-act)
A Bowery Girl, Ada Lee Bascom
  Grand Opera Theatre, December 2, 1895

1896

The Awakening, Beatrice Sturges (one-act)
   Empire Theatre School, January 23, 1896 (1)

A Rainy Day, Frances E. Johnson (one-act)
   Empire Theatre School, January 23, 1896 (1)

The Time of Strife, Madeleine Lucette Ryley (one-act)
   Empire Theatre School, January 27, 1896 (1)

The Flying Wedge, Grace Livingston Furniss (one-act)
   Empire Theatre School, January 27, 1896 (1)

Marsa Van, Emma Sheridan Frye and Evelyn Greenleaf Sutherland
   Empire Theatre, February 17, 1896 (one-act)

A Light From St. Agnes, Minnie Maddern Fiske (one-act)
   Garden Theatre, March 19, 1896

The Facts in the Case, Julie M. Lipman (one-act)
   Empire Theatre School, March 26, 1896 (1)

The Wife of Willoughby, Helen Bogart and Theo B. Sayre (one-act)
   Empire Theatre School, March 26, 1896 (1)

The Village Postmaster, Jerome H. Eddie and Alice E. Ives 14th Street
   Theatre, April 13, 1896

An Innocent Sinner, Lawrence Marston and Lillian Lewis
   Star Theatre, November 16, 1896

A Fool of Fortune, Martha Morton
   Fifth Avenue Theatre, December 1, 1896 (40)

The Wife of Willoughby, Helen Bogart and Theo B. Sayre (one-act)
   Lyceum, December 14, 1896

Miss Eagleston's Brother, Mrs. E. Sagendorf (one-act)
   Empire Theatre School, December 14, 1896 (1)

On the King's Highway, Helen Bogart and Theo. Bart Sayer (one-act)
   Empire Theatre School, December 14, 1896 (1)

The White Flower, Minnie Maddern Fiske (one-act)
   Lyceum Theatre, December 31, 1896

1897

The First Gentleman of Europe, from novel by Frances Hodgson Burnett,
   adapted by George Fleming (Constance Fletcher)
   Lyceum Theatre, January 25, 1897

When George IV Was King, Frances Moore
  Knickerbocker, February 8, 1897
The Mysterious Mr. Bugle, Madeleine Lucette Ryley
  Lyceum Theatre, April 19, 1897 (56)
The Widow Goldstein, Lillian Lewis and Lawrence Marston
  14th Street Theatre, May 17, 1897
A Coat of Many Colors, Madeleine Lucette Ryley
  Wallack's Theatre, September 13, 1897 (48)
A Bachelor's Romance, Martha Morton
  Garden Theatre, September 20, 1897 (48)
An American Citizen, Madeleine Lucette Ryley
  Knickerbocker Theatre, October 11, 1897 (96)
For Liberty and Love, Lillian Lewis, Lawrence Marston, and Albert B. Paine
  Grand Opera, October 11, 1897
A Lady of Quality, adapted by Frances Hodgson Burnett and
  Stephen Townsend
      Wallack's Theatre, November 1, 1897
The Secret Enemy, Elmer Grandin and Eva Mountford
  Grand Opera Theatre, December 20, 1897

1898

Joan, Frances Aymar Matthews
  Fifth Avenue Theatre, January 29, 1898
Way Down East, Lottie Blair Parker
  Manhattan Theatre, February 7, 1898
Dangerfield '95, Mildred Dowling
  Hoyt's Theatre, February 28, 1898
A Bit of Old Chelsea (one-act), Mrs. Oscar Beringer
  Fifth Avenue Theatre, April 11, 1898
Love Finds the Way, Marguerite Merington
  Fifth Avenue Theatre, April 11, 1898
Po' White Trash, Evelyn Greenleaf Sutherland (one-act)
  Lyceum, NY, April 22, 1898
A Bit of Instruction, Evelyn Greenleaf Sutherland (one-act)
  Lyceum Theatre, April 22, 1898
Devil's Island, Vera De Noie and Arthur D. Hall

14th Street Theatre, August 29, 1898

The Young Wife, Hannah May Ingham
Murray Hill Theatre, October 3, 1898

On and Off, adapted by Madeleine Lucette Ryley
Madison Square Theatre, October 18, 1898 (80)

A Colonial Girl, Grace Livingston Furniss and Abby Sage Richardson
Lyceum Theatre, October 31, 1898

At the Sign of the Buff Bible, Beulah Marie Dix (one-act)
Empire Theatre, December 1, 1898 (1)

The End of the Way, Evelyn Greenleaf Sutherland (one-act)
Lyceum Theatre, 1898 (1)

1899

That Man, Anita Vivanti Chartres
Herald Square Theatre, January 16, 1899

Americans at Home, Grace Livingston Furniss and Abby Sage
Richardson
Lyceum Theatre, March 13, 1899

The Dairy Farm, Eleanor Merron
14th Street Theatre, September 16, 1899 (82)

1900

The Ambassador, John Oliver Hobbes (Pearl Mary Teresa Richards
Craigie)
Daly's Theatre, February 5, 1900 (51)

The Pride of Jennico, Abby Sage Richardson and Grace L. Furniss
Criterion Theatre, March 6, 1900 (111)

A Man and His Wife, George Fleming (Constance Fletcher) Empire
Theatre, April 2, 1900 (24)

Quo Vadis, dramatized by Jeannette L. Gilder Herald Square
Theatre, April 9, 1900 (32)

Borderside, Eva Foster Riggs and Virginia Calhoun Lyceum Theatre,
April 30, 1900 (16)

The Greatest Thing in the World, Harriet Ford and Beatrice de Mille
Wallack's Theatre, October 8, 1900 (41)

The Sprightly Romance of Marsac, Molly Elliot Seawell and William Young
 Republic Theatre, December 3, 1900 (32)
The Village Postmaster, Alice E. Ives and Jerome H. Eddy
 14th Street Theatre, December 24, 1900 (16)

1901

My Lady Dainty, Madeleine Lucette Ryley
 Madison Square Theatre, January 8, 1901 (39)
Nell Gwyn, Mrs. Charles Doremus (Elizabeth Ward)
 Murray Hill Theatre, January 21, 1901
Richard Savage, Madeleine Lucette Ryley
 Lyceum Theatre, February 4, 1901 (26)
The Mormon Wife, Howard Hall and Madeline Merli
 14th Street Theatre, August 19, 1901 (32)
Up York State, David Higgins and Georgia Waldron
 14th Street Theatre, September 16, 1901 (16)
Miranda of the Balcony, Anne Crawford Flexner
 Manhattan Theatre, September 24, 1901 (62)
Under Southern Skies, Lottie Blair Parker
 Republic Theatre, November 12, 1901 (71)
The Unwelcome Mrs. Hatch, Mrs. Burton Harrison Manhattan
 Theatre, November 25, 1901 (63)
Beaucaire, Evelyn Greenleaf Sutherland and Booth Tarkington
 Herald Square Theatre, December 2, 1901 (64)
The Helmet of Navarre, Bertha Runkle and Lawrence Marston
 Criterion Theatre, December 2, 1901 (24)
A Gentleman of France, Harriet Ford
 Wallack's Theatre, December 30, 1901 (120)

1902

Joan o' the Shoals, Evelyn Greenleaf Sutherland
 Republic Theatre, February 3, 1902 (8)
Her Lord and Master, Martha Morton
 Manhattan Theatre, February 24, 1902 (69)
The Diplomat, Martha Morton
 Madison Square Theatre, March 20, 1902 (76)

Hearts Aflame, Genevieve G. Haines
  Garrick Theatre, May 12, 1902 (8)
Mrs. Jack, Grace Livingston Furniss
  Wallack's Theatre, September 2, 1902 (72)
A Rose O' Plymouth Town, Beulah Marie Dix and Evelyn Greenleaf
  Sutherland
    Manhattan Theatre, September 29, 1902 (21)
An American Invasion, Madeleine Lucette Ryley
  Bijou Theatre, October 20, 1902 (24)
Audrey, Harriet Ford and E. F. Bodington
  Madison Square Theatre, November 24, 1901 (44)
The Altar of Friendship, Madeleine Lucette Ryley
  Knickerbocker Theatre, December 1, 1902 (50)
The Cross-ways, Mrs. Lillie Langtry and J. Hartley Manners
  Garrick Theatre, December 29, 1902 (24)

1903

Gretna Green, Grace Livingston Furniss
  Madison Square Theatre, January 5 (28)
The Little Princess, Frances Hodgson Burnett
  Criterion Theatre, January 14, 1903 (34)
Mice and Men, Madeleine Lucette Ryley
  Garrick Theatre, January 19, 1903 (120)
The Bishop's Move, John Oliver Hobbs (Pearl Mary Teresa Richards Craigie)
  Manhattan Theatre, March 2, 1903 (24)
Pretty Peggy, Frances Aymar Mathews
  Herald Square Theatre, March 23, 1903 (48)
Little Lord Fauntleroy, Frances Hodgson Burnett
  Casino Theatre, April 13, 1903 (12)
My Lady Peggy Goes to Town, Frances Aymar Mathews
  Daly'sTheatre, May 4, 1903 (24)
The Light That Failed, George Fleming (Constance Fletcher)
  Knickerbocker Theatre, November 9, 1903 (32)
The Pretty Sister of Jose, Frances Hodgson Burnett
  EmpireTheatre, November 10, 1903 (58)

Lady Rose's Daughter, George Fleming (Constance Fletcher)
  Garrick Theatre, November 16, 1903 (16)
Way Down East, Lottie Blair Parker
  Academy of Music, December 14, 1903 (48)

1904

Terence, Mrs. Edward Nash Morgan
  New York Theatre, January 5, 1904 (56)
That Man and I, Frances Hodgson Burnett
  Savoy Theatre, January 25, 1904 (23)
The Triumph of Love, Martha Morton
  Criterion Theatre, February 8, 1904 (1)
A Venetian Romance, Cornelia Osgood Tyler, libretto
  Knickerbocker Theatre, May 2, 1904 (31)
Ingomar, Maria Lovell
  Empire Theatre, May 16, 1904 (1)
Mrs. Wiggs of the Cabbage Patch, Anne Crawford Flexner
  Savoy Theatre, September 3, 1904 (150)
The Fortunes of the King, Mrs. Charles A. Doremus and Leonidas
  Westervelt
      Lyric Theatre, December 6, 1904 (38)
In Newport, lyrics and music by J. W. Johnson, Bob Cole and
  Rosamond Johnson
      Liberty Theatre, December 26, 1904 (24)

1905

Once Upon a Time, Genevieve Greville Haines
  Berkeley Lyceum, January 2, 1905 (8)
Richter's Wife, Julie Herne
  Manhattan Theatre, February 27, 1905 (5)
A Woman's Pity, E. Mora Davison (one-act)
  Berkeley Lyceum, February 27, 1905 (8)
The Trifler, Murray Carson and Nora Keith
  Princess Theatre, March 16, 1905 (4)
The Lady Shore, Mrs. Vance Thompson and Lena R. Smith
  Hudson Theatre, March 27, 1905 (16)

A Light from St. Agnes, The Eyes of the Heart, and *The Rose,* Minnie Maddern Fiske
  Manhattan Theatre, March 27, 1905 (one-act) (3)
Sergeant Brue, music Liza Lehman and Clare Kummer w/others
  Knickerbocker Theatre, April 21, 1905 (152)
Mary and John, Edith Ellis Baker
  Manhattan Theatre, September 11, 1905 (12)
The Man on the Box, Grace Livingston Furniss Madison
  Square Theatre, October 3, 1905 (111)
The Truth Tellers, Martha Morton
  Grand Opera Theatre, October 16, 1905 (1 wk.)
The Player Maid, Louise Mallory
  Liberty Theatre, October 13, 1905 (1)
Veronique, lyrics, Lilian Eldee and Percy Greenbank
  Broadway Theatre, October 30, 1905 (81)
The Marriage of William Ashe, Margaret Mayo
  Garrick Theatre, November 20, 1905 (40)
Madeline, Mrs. W. K. Clifford (one-act)
  Garrick Theatre, December 25, 1905 (16)

1906

Julie Bonbon, Clara Lipman
  Field's Theatre, January 1, 1906 (98)
The Redemption of David Corson, Lottie Blair Parker
  Majestic Theatre, January 8, 1906 (16)
Mexicana, book and lyrics, Clara Driscoll
  Lyric Theatre, January 29, 1906 (82)
Brown of Harvard, Rida Johnson Young
  Princess Theatre, February 26, 1906 (101)
The Greater Love, Ivy Ashton Root
  Madison Square Theatre, March 19, 1906 (32)
The Strength of the Weak, Alice M. Smith
  Liberty Theatre, April 17, 1906 (27)
The Eyes of the Heart and *The Light from St. Agnes,* Minnie Maddern Fiske
  Manhattan Theatre, April 24, 1906 (3)
The Girl Patsy, Jane Mauldin
  Savoy Theatre, May 26, 1906 (17)

La belle Marseillaise, adapted by Madeleine Lucette Ryley
　　Knickerbocker Theatre, July 22, 1906 (29)
The Kreutzer Sonata, adapted by Lena Smith and Mrs. Vance
　　Thompson
　　　　Manhattan Theatre, August 13, 1906 (29)
John Hudson's Wife, Alicia Ramsey and Rudolph de Cordova
　　Weber's Theatre, September 20, 1906 (27)
Mizpah, Ella Wheeler Wilcox and Luscombe Searelle
　　Academy of Music, September 24, 1906 (24)
The Three of Us, Rachel Crothers
　　Madison Square Theatre, October 17, 1906 (227)
The Measure of Man, Cora Maynard
　　Weber's Theatre, October 20, 1906 (15)
The House of Mirth, Edith Wharton and Clyde Fitch
　　Savoy Theatre, October 22, 1906 (14)
A Tenement Tragedy, Clothilde Graves (one-act)
　　Savoy Theatre, November 20, 1906 (14)
The Double Life, Rinehart Roberts (Mary Roberts Rinehart)
　　Bijou Theatre, December 24, 1906 (12)
The Road to Yesterday, Beulah Marie Dix and Evelyn Greenleaf
　　Sutherland
　　　　Herald Square Theatre, December 31, 1906 (216)

1907

The Good Hope, Christopher St. John (English)
　　Empire Theatre, January 28, 1907 (8)
Genesee of the Hills, Marah Ellis Ryan and McPherson Turnbull
　　Astor Theatre, February 11, 1907 (26)
The Lilac Room, Beulah Marie Dix and Evelyn Greenleaf Sutherland
　　Weber's Theatre, April 3, 1907 (4)
The Boys of Company B, Rida Johnson Young
　　Lyceum Theatre, April 8, 1907 (96)
Divorcons, adapted by Margaret Mayo
　　Wallack's Theatre, April 15, 1907 (54)
The Lemonade Boy, Gladys Unger
　　Lyceum Theatre, April 30, 1907 (4)

The Builders, Marion Fairfax
  Astor Theatre, May 20, 1907 (16)
The Shoo-Fly Regiment, music by J. Rosamond Johnson
  Bijou Theatre, August 6, 1907 (15)
When Knights Were Bold, Charles Marlowe (Harriet Jay) (English)
  Garrick Theatre, August 20, 1907 (100)
Classmates, William C. de Mille and Margaret Turnbull
  Hudson Theatre, August 29, 1907 (102)
The Movers, Martha Morton
  Hackett Theatre, September 3, 1907 (23)
The Man on the Case, Grace Livingston Furniss
  Madison Square Theatre, September 4, 1907 (21)
After the Opera, adapted by Gladys Unger (one-act)
  Daly's Theatre, October 15, 1907 (2 months)
A Grand Army Man, David Balasco, Pauline Phelps and Marion Short
  Stuyvesant Theatre, October 16, 1907 (149)
The Top o' th' World, music by Manuel Klein and Anne Caldwell
  Majestic Theatre, October 19, 1907 (156)
The Coming of Mrs. Patrick, Rachel Crothers
  Madison Square Theatre, November 6, 1907 (13)
The Rejuvenation of Aunt Mary, Anne Warner
  Garden Theatre, November 12, 1907 (56)
The Lancers, Rida Johnson Young and J. Hartley Manners
  Daly's Theatre, December 3, 1907 (12)
Polly of the Circus, Margaret Mayo
  Liberty Theatre, December 23, 1907 (160)

1908

The Rising of the Moon, Lady Gregory (Irish) (one-act)
  Savoy Theatre, February 24, 1908 (24)
Adrienne Lecouvreur, adapted by Olga Nethersole
  Daly's Theatre, February 8, 1908 (3 wks)
Papa Lebonnard, adapted by Kate Jordan
  Bijou Theatre, April 28, 1908 (31)
Love Watches, adapted by Gladys Unger
  Lyceum, August 27, 1908 (172)

Diana of Dobson's, Cicely Hamilton (English)
  Savoy Theatre, September 5, 1908 (17)
Glorious Betsy, Rida Johnson Young
  Lyric Theatre, September 7, 1908 (24)
Agnes, George Cameron (Gladys Rankin Drew)
  Majestic Theatre, October 5, 1908 (16)
Myself—Bettina, Rachel Crothers
  Daly's Theatre, October 5, 1908 (32)
Mary Jane's Pa, Edith Ellis
  Garden Theatre, December 3, 1908 (89)
The Chaperon, Marion Fairfax
  Maxine Elliott Theatre, December 30, 1908 (62)

1909

The Dawn of a Tomorrow, Frances Hodgson Burnett
  Lyceum Theatre, January 25, 1909 (152)
The Goddess of Reason, Mary Johnston
  Daly's Theatre, February 15, 1909 (48)
Votes for Women, Elizabeth Robins
  Wallack's Theatre, March 15, 1909 (16)
Sham, Geraldine Bonner
  Wallack's, March 27, 1909 (65)
Billy, George Cameron (Gladys Rankin Drew)
  Daly's Theatre, August 2, 1909 (64)
The Ringmaster, Olive Porter
  Maxine Elliott Theatre, August 9, 1909 (32)
The Awakening of Helena Richie, Charlotte Thompson
  Savoy Theatre, September 20, 1909 (120)
On the Eve, Martha Morton
  Hudson Theatre, October 4, 1909 (24)
The Fourth Estate, Joseph Medill Patterson and Harriet Ford
  Wallack Theatre, October 6, 1909 (93)
The Debtors, Margaret Mayo
  Bijou Theatre, October 12, 1909 (15)
The Belle of Brittany, music by Marie Horne
  Daly Theatre, November 8, 1909 (72)

Seven Days, Mary Roberts Rinehart and Avery Hopwood
  Astor Theatre, November 10, 1909 (397)
The Lottery Man, Rida Johnson Young
  Bijou Theatre, December 6, 1909 (200)
Mrs. Dakon, Kate Jordan
  Hackett Theatre, December 14, 1909 (2)
A Little Brother of the Rich, Joseph Medill Patterson and Harriet Ford
  Wallack Theatre, December 27, 1909 (24)

1910
Little Town of Bethlehem, Katrina Trask
  The Ben Greet Repertory, January 17, 1910
Three Wonder Tales, Rose Meller O'Neil
  The Ben Greet repertory, January 17, 1910
A Lucky Star, Anne Crawford Flexner
  Hudson Theatre, January 18, 1910 (95)
Ragged Robin, Rida Johnson Young w/ Rita Olcott
  Academy of Music, January 24, 1910 (16)
The Watcher, Cora Maynard
  Comedy Theatre, January 27, 1910 (12)
A Man's World, Rachel Crothers
  Comedy Theatre, February 8, 1910 (71)
Baby Mine, Margaret Mayo
  Daly Theatre, August 23, 1910 (287)
The Deserters, Robert Peyton Carter and Anna Alice Chapin
  Hudson Theatre, September 20, 1910 (63)
Rebecca of Sunnybrook Farm, Kate Douglas Wiggin and Charlotte
  Thompson
    Republic Theatre, October 3, 1910 (216)
The Scarlet Pimpernel, Baroness Orczy and Montague Barstow
  Knickerbocker Theatre, October 24, 1910 (40)
Naughty Marietta, book and lyrics, Rida Johnson Young
  New York Theatre, November 7, 1910 (136)

1911

Barry of Ballymore, book and lyrics, Rida Johnson Young,
  Academy of Music, January 30, 1911 (24)
The Piper, Josephine Preston Peabody
  New Theatre, January 30, 1911 (in repertory)
Seven Sisters, adapted by Edith Ellis
  Lyceum Theatre, February 20, 1911 (32)
The Arrow Maker, Mary Austin
  New Theatre, February 27, 1911 (in repertory)
Sauce for the Goose, Geraldine Bonner and Hutcheson Boyd
  Playhouse Theatre, April 15, 1911 (2)
The Real Thing, Catherine Chisholm Cushing
  Maxine Elliott Theatre, August 10, 1911 (60)
Next!, Rida Johnson Young
  Daly's Theatre, September 28, 1911 (18)
The Garden of Allah, Robert Hichens and Mary Anderson
  Century Theatre, October 21, 1911 (241)
Mrs. Avery, Gretchen Dale and Howard Estabrook
  Weber Theatre, October 23, 1911 (8)
Uncle Sam, Anne Caldwell and James O'Dea
  Liberty Theatre, October 30, 1911 (48)
The Three Lights, May Robson and Charles T. Dazey
  Bijou Theatre, October 31, 1911 (7)
The Strugglers, H. M. Horkheimer and Lucile Sawyer
  Bijou Theatre, November 6, 1911 (8)
The Workhouse Ward, Lady Gregory (Irish)
  Maxine Elliott Theatre, November 20, 1911 (in repertory)
The Rising of the Moon, Lady Gregory (Irish)
  Maxine Elliott Theatre, November 20, 1911 (in repertory)
The Gaol Gate, Lady Gregory (Irish)
  Maxine Elliott Theatre, November 20, 1911 (in repertory)
Hyacinth Halvey, Lady Gregory (Irish)
  Maxine Elliott Theatre, November 20, 1911 (in repertory)
The Jackdaw, Lady Gregory (Irish)
  Maxine Elliott Theatre, November 20, 1911 (in repertory)
Falsely True, Johanna Redmond (Irish)

Maxine Elliott Theatre, November 20, 1911 (in repertory)
The Image, Lady Gregory (Irish)
Maxine Elliott Theatre, November 20, 1911 (in repertory)
Spreading the News, Lady Gregory (Irish)
Maxine Elliott Theatre, November 20, 1911 (in repertory)
The Senator Keeps House, Martha Morton
Garrick Theatre, November 27, 1911(80)
The Marionettes, adaptation by Gladys Unger Lyceum Theatre,
December 5, 1911 (63)
The Wedding Trip, music by Regina de Koven Broadway Theatre,
December 25, 1911 (48)

1912

Just to Get Married, Cicely Hamilton (English) Maxine
Elliott's Theatre, January 1, 1912 (24)
A Fool of Fortune, Martha Morton
Garrick Theatre, January 12, 1912 (1)
Elevating a Husband, Clara Lipman and Roi Cooper Megrue
Liberty Theatre, January 22, 1912 (21)
Macushla, Rida Johnson Young
Grand Opera House, February 5, 1912 (21)
Monsieur Beaucaire, Booth Tarkington and Evelyn Greenleaf
Sutherland Daly's Theatre, March 11, 1912 (64)
The Wall Street Girl, Margaret Mayo and Edgar Selwyn
Comedy Theatre, April 15, 1912 (56)
The Merry Countess, Gladys Unger
Casino Theatre, August 22, 1912 (135)
The Governor's Lady, Alice Bradley
Republic Theatre, September 10, 1912 (135)
The Daughter of Heaven, Pierre Loti and Judi Gautier
Century Theatre, October 12, 1912 (98)
Little Women, dramatized by Marian de Forest
Playhouse Theatre, October 14, 1912 (184)
The Lady of the Slipper, Anne Caldwell and Lawrence McCarty
Globe Theatre, October 28, 1912 (232)
Our Wives, adapted by Frank Mendel and Helen Kraft
Wallack's Theatre, November 4, 1912 (40)

The Red Petticoat, book, Rida Johnson Young
  Daly's Theatre, November 13, 1912 (61)
Racketty-Packetty House, Frances Hodgson Burnett
  Children's Theatre, December 23, 1912 (81)
Rutherford and Son, K. G. (Githa) Sowerby (English)
  Little Theatre, December 24, 1912 (63)
The Argyle Case, Harriet Ford and Harvey O'Higgins
  Criterion Theatre, December 24, 1912 (191)
Years of Discretion, Frederic and Fanny Hatton
  Belasco Theatre, December 25, 1912 (190)
His Wife by His Side, Ethelyn Emery Keays
  Berkeley Theatre, December 30, 1912 (16)
Cheer Up, Mary Roberts Rinehart
  Harris Theatre, December 30, 1912 (24)

1913

A Good Little Devil, Rosemonde Gerard and Maurice Rostand
  Republic Theatre, January 8, 1913 (133)
The Poor Little Rich Girl, Eleanor Gates
  Hudson Theatre, January 21, 1913 (160)
The Man with Three Wives, version by Paul M. Potter and Agnes Morgan
  Weber and Fields' Theatre, January 23, 1913 (52)
The Isle o' Dreams, Rida Johnson Young
  Grand Opera House, January 27, 1913 (32)
The Jackdaw, Lady Gregory (Irish)
  Wallack's Theatre, February 4, 1913 (in repertory)
Spreading the News, Lady Gregory (Irish)
  Wallack's Theatre, February 4, 1913 (in repertory)
The Rising of the Moon, Lady Gregory (Irish)
  Wallack's Theatre, February 4, 1913 (in repertory)
The Gaol Gate, Lady Gregory (Irish)
  Wallack's Theatre, February 4, 1913 (in repertory)
Damer's Gold, Lady Gregory (Irish)
  Wallack's Theatre, February 4, 1913 (in repertory)
The Workhouse Ward, Lady Gregory (Irish)
  Wallack's Theatre, February 4, 1913 (in repertory)
Coats, Lady Gregory (Irish)

Wallack's Theatre, February 4, 1913 (in repertory)

Widow by Proxy, Catherine Chisholm Cushing
  Cohan Theatre, February 24, 1913 (88)

Mary's Manoeuvres, a suffrage sketch, Alice E. Ives
  Lyceum Theatre, February 25, 1913 (1)

Revenge or the Pride of Lillian Le Mar, Rachel Crothers
  Lyceum Theatre, February 25, 1913 (1)

Mary Dressler's All Star Gambol, Marie Dressler
  Weber and Fields' Theatre, March 10, 1913 (8)

Ann Boyd, dramatized by Lucille La Verne
  Wallack's Theatre, March 31, 1913 (8)

Divorcons, adapted by Margaret Mayo
  Playhouse Theatre, April 1, 1913 (55)

The Lady from Oklahoma, Elizabeth Jordon
  48th Street Theatre, April 2, 1913 (13)

The Purple Road, Fred de Gresac (Mme. Frederique Morel) and
  William Cary Duncan
    Liberty Theatre, April 7, 1913 (136)

The Necken, Elizabeth G. Crane
  Lyceum Theatre, April 15, 1913 (1)

The Passing of the Idle Rich, Margaret Townsend
  Garden Theatre, May 1, 1913 (4)

Are You a Cook? William J. Hurlbut and Frances Whitehouse
  Longacre Theatre, May 1, 1913 (12)

Sweethearts, Harry B. Smith and Fred de
  Gresac (Frederique Morel) (French)
    New Amsterdam Theatre, September 8, 1913 (136)

The Marriage Market, adapted by Gladys Unger
  Knickerbocker Theatre, September 22, 1913 (80)

Mice and Men, Madeleine Lucette Ryley
  Shubert Theatre, September 29– December 29, 1913,
    in repertory

The Love Leash, Anna Steese Richardson and Edmund Breese
  Harris Theatre, October 20, 1913 (16)

The Girl and the Pennant, Rida Johnson Young and Christy
  Mathewson Lyric Theatre, October 23, 1913 (20)

The Marriage Game, Anne Crawford Flexner
    Comedy Theatre, October 29, 1913 (78)
Ourselves, Rachel Crothers
    Lyric Theatre, November 12, 1913 (29)
Children of Today, Clara Lipman and Samuel Shipman
    Harris Theatre, December 1, 1913 (24)
Rachel, Carina Jordan
    Knickerbocker Theatre, December 1, 1913 (16)
We are Seven, Eleanor Gates
    Belasco Theatre, December 24, 1913 (21)

1914

Young Wisdom, Rachel Crothers
    Criterion Theatre, January 5, 1914 (56)
Kitty Mackay, Catherine Chisholm Cushing
    Comedy Theatre, January 7, 1914 (278)
The Deadlock, Margaret Turnbull
    Maxine Elliott Theatre, January 20, 1914 (23)
Shameen Dhu, Rida Johnson Young
    Grand Opera House, February 2, 1914 (32)
When Claudia Smiles, farce with songs devised by Anne Caldwell
    39th Street Theatre, February 2, 1914 (56)
Maids of Athens, English version by Carolyn Wells
    New Amsterdam Theatre, March 18, 1914 (22)
Jerry, Catherine Chisholm Cushing
    Lyceum Theatre, March 28, 1914 (41)
The Dummy, Harvey J. O'Higgins and Harriet Ford
    Hudson Theatre, April 13, 1914 (200)
The Worth of a Man, Mrs. Vere Campbell
    48th Street Theatre, April 27, 1914 (1)
Vik, Myra Wiren
    Wallack Theatre, April 29, 1914 (5)
Twin Beds, Salisbury Field and Margaret Mayo
    Fulton Theatre, August 14, 1914 (411)
Cordelia Blossom, George Randolph Chester and Lillian Chester
    Gaiety Theatre, August 31, 1914 (16)

A Modern Girl, Marion Fairfax and Ruth C. Mitchell
    Comedy Theatre, September 12, 1914 (17)
Daddy Long-Legs, Jean Webster
    Gaiety Theatre, September 28, 1914 (264)
Evidence, J. (Jean) and L. (La Margaret) du Rocher Macpherson
    Lyric Theatre, October 7, 1914 (21)
Across the Border, Beulah Marie Dix (one-act)
    Princess Theatre, October 17, 1914 (in repertory)
Chin-Chin, book and lyrics by Anne Caldwell and R. H. Burnside
    Globe Theatre, October 20, 1914 (295)
The Lilac Domino, book/lyrics by Emerich Von Gatti & Bela Jenbach
    44th Street Theatre, October 28, 1914 (109)
The Traffic, Rachael Marshall and Oliver D. Bailey
    New York Theatre, November 16, 1914 (8)
Polygamy, Harvey O'Higgins and Harriet Ford
    Playhouse Theatre, December 1, 1914 (159)
The Marriage of Kitty, Fred De Gresac (Mme. Frederique Morel)
    and Francois De Croisset
        Comedy Theatre, December 18, 1914 (27)
Just Herself, Ethel Watts Mumford
    Playhouse Theatre, December 23, 1914 (13)
Lady Luxury, book and lyrics, Rida Johnson Young
    Casino Theatre, December 25, 1914 (35)
Secret Strings, Kate Jordan
    Longacre Theatre, December 28, 1914 (24)

1915

Children of Earth, Alice Brown
    Booth Theatre, January 12, 1915 (39)
The Dickey Bird, Harvey O'Higgins and Harriet Ford
    Park Theatre, February 22, 1915 (64)
Three of Hearts, Martha Morton
    39th Street Theatre, June 3, 1915 (20)
Some Baby! Zellah Covington and Jules Simonson
    Fulton Theatre, August 12, 1915 (72)
Mr. Myd's Mystery, Lillian Trimble Bradley

Comedy Theatre, August 16, 1915 (16)

Just Boys, Katherine Browning and Allena Kanka
 Comedy Theatre, September 13, 1915 (16)

Moloch, Beulah Marie Dix
 New Amsterdam Theatre, September 20, 1915 (32)

Overtones, Alice Gerstenberg (one-act)
 Bandbox Theatre, October 4, 1915 (in repertory)

The Red Cloak, Josephine A. Meyer and Lawrence Langer
 Bandbox Theatre, October 4, 1915 (in repertory)

Our Mrs. McChesney, dramatized by George V. Hobart and Edna Ferber
 Lyceum Theatre, October 19, 1915 (151)

The Mark of the Beast, Georgia Earle and Fanny Cannon
 Princess Theatre, October 20, 1915 (13)

Mrs. Boltay's Daughters, Marion Fairfax
 Comedy Theatre, October 23, 1915 (17)

The Great Lover, Leo Ditrichstein and Frederick and Fanny Hatton
 Longacre Theatre, November 10, 1915 (245)

The Courtship of Then and *Now and To-morrow* (one-acts), Anna Wynne
 Bramhall Playhouse, November 17, 1915 (10)

The Unborn, Beulah Poynter
 Princess Theatre, November 29, 1915 (16)

The Devil's Garden, adaptation, Edith Ellis
 Harris Theatre, December 28, 1915 (23)

1916

Erstwhile Susan, adaptation, Marian de Forest
 Gaiety Theatre, January 18, 1916 (167)

The Fear Market, Amelie Rives (Princess Troubetzkoy)
 Booth Theatre, January 26, 1916 (118)

Captain Kidd, Jr., Rida Johnson Young (128 perf.)
 Cohan and Harris Theatre, November 13, 1916

Her Soldier Boy, Rida Johnson Young, book and lyrics
 Astor Theatre, December 6, 1916 (198)

Pay-day, Oliver D. Bailey and Lottie Meanie
 Cort Theatre, February 26, 1916 (49)

Pom-pom, book and lyrics by Anne Caldwell

Cohan Theatre, February 28, 1916 (128)

A King of Nowhere, J. (Jean) and L. (La Margaret) du Rocher Macpherson

Maxine Elliott Theatre, March 20, 1916 (58)

The Co-respondent, Alice Leal Pollack and Rita Weiman

Booth Theatre, April 10, 1916 (48)

His Bridal Night, revised by Margaret Mayo

Republic Theatre, August 16, 1916 (77)

The Guilty Man, Ruth Helen Davis and Charles Klein

Astor Theatre, August 17, 1916 (52)

The Happy Ending, J.& L (La Margaret) du Rocher Macpherson

Shubert Theatre, August 21, 1916 (16)

The Sugar House, Alice Brown (one-act) (repertory)

Comedy Theatre, August 30, 1916

Trifles, Susan Glaspell (one-act) (repertory)

Comedy Theatre, August 30, 1916

Mr. Lazarus, Harvey O'Higgins and Harriet Ford

Shubert Theatre, September 5, 1916 (39)

Pollyanna, adapted by Catherine Chisholm Cushing

Hudson Theatre, September 18, 1916 (112)

Upstairs and Down, Frederic and Fanny Hatton

Cort Theatre, September 25, 1916 (320)

Betty, Frederick Lonsdale and Gladys Unger

Globe Theatre, October 3, 1916 (63)

Hush!, Violet Pearn

Little Theatre, October 3, 1916 (39)

Go to It, John L. Golden, John E. Hazzard and Anne Caldwell

Princess Theatre, October 24, 1916 (23)

Old Lady 31, Rachel Crothers

39th Street Theatre, October 30, 1916 (160)

Good Gracious Annabelle, Clare Kummer

Republic Theatre, October 31, 1916 (111)

Captain Kidd, Jr., Rida Johnson Young

Cohan and Harris Theatre, November 13, 1916 (128)

Voices, Hortense Flexner (in repertory)

30th Street Theatre, November 27, 1916

Her Soldier Boy, adapted by Rida Johnson Young
   Astor Theatre, December 6, 1916 (198)
Little Women, dramatized by Marian De Forest
   Park Theatre, December 18, 1916 (24), revival
Editha's Burglar, Frances Hodgson Burnett's story dramatized by
   Jacob Heniger
      Cohan and Harris Theatre, December 26, 1916 (2)
The Travelling Man, Lady Gregory (Irish) (one-act)
   Cohan and Harris Theatre, December 26, 1916 (2)
Mary Christmas, Daddy, Mary Austin
   Cohan and Harris Theatre, December 26, 1916 (2)

1917

A Successful Calamity, Clare Kummer
   Booth Theatre, February 5, 1917 (144)
Lilac Time, Jane Cowl and Jane Murfin
   Republic Theatre, February 6, 1917 (176)
The Brat, Maude Fulton
   Harris Theatre, March 5, 1917 (136)
His Little Widows, Rida Johnson Young, book and lyrics
   Astor Theatre, April 30, 1917 (72)
Mary's Ankle, May Tully
   Bijou Theatre, August 6, 1917 (80)
Daybreak, Jane Cowl and Jane Murfin
   Harris Theatre, August 14, 1917 (71)
Maytime, book and lyrics, Rida Johnson Young
   Shubert Theatre 16 August 1917 (492)
The Pawn, Azelle M. Aldrich and Joseph Noll
   Fulton Theatre, September 8, 1917 (17)
Hamilton, Mary Hamlin and George Arliss
   Knickerbocker Theatre, September 17, 1917 (80)
Lombardi, Ltd., Frederic and Fanny Hatton
   Morosco Theatre, September 24, 1917 (296)
Mother Carey's Chicken, Kate Douglas Wiggin and Rachel Crothers
   Cort Theatre, September 25, 1917 (39)

The Land of the Free, Fannie Hurst and Harriet Ford
    48th Street Theatre, October 2, 1917 (32)
The Rescuing Angel, Clare Kummer
    Hudson Theatre, October 8, 1917 (32)
Eve's Daughter, Alicia Ramsey
    Playhouse Theatre, October 11, 1917 (36)
Jack O'Lantern, Anne Caldwell and R. H. Burnside
    Globe Theatre, October 16, 1917 (265)
The Land of Joy, adaptation and lyrics by Ruth Boyd Ober
    Park Theatre, October 31, 1917 (86)
Blind Alleys, Grace Latimer Wright (one-act)
    Comedy Theatre, October 31, 1917 (in repertory)
Neighbors, Zona Gale (one-act)
    Comedy Theatre, October 31, 1917 (in repertory)
Yum Chapab, Beatrice de Holthoir and J. Garcia Pimentel (one-act)
    Comedy Theatre, October 31, 1917 (in repertory)
Suppressed Desires, George Cram Cook and Susan Glaspell (one-act)
    Comedy Theatre, October 31, 1917 (in repertory)
Enter the Hero, Theresa Helburn (one-act)
    Comedy Theatre, October 31, 1917 (in repertory)
Barbara, Florence Lincoln
    Plymouth Theatre, November 5, 1917 (16)
Six Months' Option, Ancella Anslee
    Princess Theatre, November 29, 1917 (29)
Good Morning, Rosamond, Constance Lindsay Skinner
    48th Street Theatre, December 10, 1917 (8)
Flo-Flo, Fred De Gresac (Mme. Frederique Morel)
    Cort Theatre, December 20, 1917 (220)

1918
Success, Adeline Leitzbach and Theodore A. Liebler, Jr.
    Harris Theatre, January 28, 1918 (64)
The Indestructible Wife, Frederic and Fanny Hatton
    Hudson Theatre, January 30, 1918 (22)
Her Country, Rudolph Besier and Sybil Spottiswoode
    Punch and Judy Theatre, February 21, 1918 (76)

Sick-a-Bed, Ethel Watts Mumford
   Gaiety Theatre, February 25, 1918 (80)
The Garden of Allah, dramatized by Robert
   Hichens and Mary Anderson
     Manhattan Opera House, February 25, 1918 (24)
The Squab Farm, Frederic and Fanny Hatton
   Bijou Theatre, March 13, 1918 (45)
Love's Lightning, Ada Patterson and Robert Edeson
   Lexington Theatre, March 25, 1918
Fancy Free, book by Dorothy Donnelly and Edgar Smith
   Astor Theatre, April 11, 1918 (116)
Once Upon a Time, Rachel Crothers
   Fulton Theatre, April 15, 1918 (24)
A Woman's Honor, Susan Glaspell (one-act) Greenwich
   Village Theatre, May 20, 1918 (2 wks)
Rock-a-Bye Baby, book by Edgar Allan Woolf and Margaret Mayo
   Astor Theatre, May 11, 1918 (85)
Marriages Are Made, Bess Lipschultz (one-act)
   Fulton Theatre, June 10, 1918 (2 wks)
Allegiance, Prince and Princess Troubetzkoy
   Maxine Elliott Theatre, August 1, 1918 (44)
The Blue Pearl, Anne Crawford Flexner
   Longacre Theatre, August 8, 1918 (36)
The Woman on the Index, Lillian Trimble Bradley and George
   Broadhurst
     48th Street Theatre, August 29, 1918 (52)
Another Man's Shoes, Laura Hinkley and Mabel Ferris
   39th Street Theatre, September 12, 1918 (20)
Crops and Croppers, Theresa Helburn
   Belmont Theatre, September 12, 1918 (20)
The Walk-offs, Frederic and Fanny Hatton
   Morosco Theatre, September 17, 1918 (31)
The Awakening, Ruth Sawyer
   Criterion Theatre, October 1, 1918 (29)
Information Please, Jane Cowl and Jane Murfin
   Selwyn Theatre, October 2, 1918 (46)

Sometime, book and lyrics, Rida Johnson Young
    Shubert Theatre, October 4, 1918 (283)
A Stitch in Time, Oliver D. Bailey and Lottie M. Meaney
    Fulton Theatre, October 15, 1918 (71)
The Riddle: Woman, Charlotte E. Wells and Dorothy Donnelly
    Harris Theatre, October 23, 1918 (165)
Glorianna, book and lyrics, Catherine Chisholm Cushing
    Liberty Theatre, October 28, 1918 (96)
Peter's Mother, Mrs. Henry de la Pasture
    Playhouse Theatre, October 29, 1918 (15)
Be Calm, Camilla, Clare Kummer
    Booth Theatre, October 31, 1918 (84)
Little Simplicity, book and lyrics, Rida Johnson Young
    Astor Theatre, November 4, 1918 (112)
Daddy Long Legs, Jean Webster
    Henry Miller Theatre, November 16, 1918 (17)
Betty at Bay, Jessie Porter
    39th Street, December 2, 1918 (16)
The Gentile Wife, Rita Wellman
    Vanderbilt Theatre, December 24, 1918 (31)
A Little Journey, Rachel Crothers
    Little Theatre, December 26, 1918 (252)
The Melting of Molly, Maria Thompson Davies
    Broadhurst Theatre, December 30, 1918 (88)

1919

Tillie, Helen R. Martin and Frank Howe, Jr.
    Henry Miller Theatre, January 6, 1919 (32)
The Net, Maravene Kennedy Thompson
    48th Street Theatre, February 10, 1919 (8)
Penny Wise, Mary Stafford Smith and Leslie Vyner
    Belmont Theatre, March 10, 1919 (40)
39 East, Rachel Crothers
    Broadhurst Theatre, March 31, 1919 (160)
Papa, Zoe Akins
    Little Theatre, April 10, 1919 (12)

She's a Good Fellow, libretto and lyrics, Anne Caldwell
    Globe Theatre, May 5, 1919 (120)
The Lady in Red, book and lyrics, Anne Caldwell
    Lyric Theatre, May 12, 1919 (48)
Lusmore, Rita Olcott and Grace Heyer
    Henry Miller's Theatre, September 9, 1919 (23)
Nighty-Night, Martha M. Stanley and Adelaide Matthews
    Princess Theatre, September 9, 1919 (154)
Thunder, Peg Franklin
    Criterion Theatre, September 22, 1919 (33)
Where's Your Wife? Thomas Springer, Fleta Springer & Joseph Noel
    Punch and Judy Theatre, October 4, 1919 (65)
Declassee, Zoe Akins
    Empire Theatre, October 6, 1919 (257)
Hello, Alexander, book, Edgar Smith and Emily Young
    44th Street Theatre, October 7, 1919 (56)
On the Hiring Line, Harvey O'Higgins and Harriet Ford
    Criterion Theatre, October 20, 1919 (48)
Fifty-fifty, Ltd., book, Margaret Michael and William Lennox
    Comedy Theatre, October 27, 1919 (40)
The Unknown Woman, Marjorie Blaine and Willard Mark
    Maxine Elliott's Theatre, November 10, 1919 (64)
The Rise of Silas Lapham, Lillian Sabine
    Garrick Theatre, November 25, 1919 (47)
Elsie Janis and Her Gang, book, Elsie Janis
    George M. Cohan Theatre, December 1, 1919 (55)
Forbidden, Dorothy Donnelly
    Manhattan Opera House, December 20, 1919 (18)

1920

The Acquittal, Rita Weiman
    Cohan and Harris Theatre, January 5, 1920 (138)
The "Ruined" Lady, Frances Nordstrom
    The Playhouse, January 19, 1920 (33)
Pietro, Maud Skinner and Jules Eckert Goodman
    Criterion Theatre, January 19, 1920 (41)

Mama's Affair, Rachel Barton Butler
    Little Theatre, January 19, 1920 (98)
The Night Boat, lyrics by Anne Caldwell
    Liberty Theatre, February 2, 1920 (148)
He and She, Rachel Crothers
    Little Theatre, February 12, 1920 (28)
Shavings, Pauline Phelps and Marion Short
    Knickerbocker Theatre, February 16, 1920 (122)
The Wonderful Thing, Mrs. Lillian Trimble Bradley
    The Playhouse, February 17, 1920 (120)
The Piper, Josephine Preston Peabody
    Fulton Theatre, March 19, 1920 (8)
What's in a Name? book and lyrics, John Murray Anderson, Anna
    Wynne O'Ryan and Jack Yellen
        Maxine Elliott's Theatre, March 19, 1920 (87)
Mrs. Jimmie Thompson, Norman S. Rose and Edith Ellis
    Princess Theatre, 29 March 1920 (64)
Lassie, book and lyrics, Catherine Chisholm Cushing
    Nora Bayes Theatre, April 16, 1920 (63)
Footloose, adapted by Zoe Akins
    Greenwich Village Theatre, May 10, 1920 (162)
All Soul's Eve, Anne Crawford Flexner
    Maxine Elliott's Theatre, May 12, 1920 (21)
His Chinese Wife, Forrest Halsey and Clara Beranger
    Belmont Theatre, May 17, 1920 (16)
Seeing Things, Margaret Mayo and Aubrey Kennedy
    The Playhouse, June 17, 1920 (103)
The Charm School, Alice Duer Miller and Robert Milton
    Bijou Theatre, August 2, 1920 (88)
Scrambled Wives, Adelaide Matthews and Martha M. Stanley
    Fulton Theatre, August 4, 1920 (60)
Enter Madame, Gilda Varesi and Dolly Bayrne
    Garrick Theatre, August 16, 1920 (350)
Spanish Love, Avery Hopwood and Mary Roberts Rinehart
    Maxine Elliott Theatre, August 17, 1920 (308)

The Checkerboard, Frederick and Fanny Hatton
 39th Street Theatre, August 19, 1920 (29)
The Bat, Mary Roberts Rinehart and Avery Hopwood
 Morosco Theatre, August 23, 1920 (332)
The Sweetheart Shop, book and lyrics, Anne Caldwell
 Knickerbocker Theatre, August 31, 1920 (55)
Little Old New York, Rida Johnson Young
 Plymouth Theatre, September 8, 1920 (308)
The Tavern, Cora Dick Gantt
 Cohan Theatre, September 27, 1920 (252)
Tip Top, book and lyrics, Anne Caldwell and R. H. Burnside
 Globe Theatre, October 5, 1920 (27)
Hitchy-Koo, book and lyrics, Glen MacDonough and Anne Caldwell
 New Amsterdam Theatre, October 19, 1920 (71)
The Prince and the Pauper, adapted by Amelie Rives
 Booth Theatre, November 1, 1920 (155)
When We Are Young, Kate L. McLaurin
 Broadhurst Theatre, November 22, 1920 (40)
Rollo's Wild Oat, Clare Kummer
 Punch and Judy Theatre, November 23, 1920 (228)
The Young Visitors, dramatized by Mrs. George Norman and
 Margaret MacKenzie
   39th Street Theatre, November 29, 1920 (16)
Lady Billy, book and lyrics, Zelda Sears
 Liberty Theatre, December 14, 1920 (188)
Miss Lulu Bett, Zona Gale
 Belmont Theatre, December 27, 1920 (198)

1921
The White Villa, adapted by Edith Ellis
 Eltinge Theatre, February 14, 1921 (18)
Bridges, Clare Kummer (one-act)
 Punch and Judy Theatre, February 28, 1921 (5)
The Choir Rehearsal, Clare Kummer (one-act)
 Punch and Judy Theatre, February 28, 1921 (5)
The Robbery, Clare Kummer (one-act)

Punch and Judy Theatre, February 28, 1921 (5)
Chinese Love, Clare Kummer (one-act)
Punch and Judy Theatre, February 28, 1921 (5)
Nice People, Rachel Crothers
Klaw Theater, March 2, 1921 (120)
Clair de Lune, Michael Strange (Blanche Oelrichs Barrymore)
Empire Theatre, April 18, 1921 (64)
Just Married, Adelaide Matthews and Ann Nichols
Comedy Theatre, April 26, 1921 (307)
The Teaser, Martha M. Stanley and Adelaide Matthews
Playhouse, July 27, 1921 (29)
Back Pay, Fannie Hurst
Eltinge Theatre, August 30, 1921 (79)
Daddy's Gone A-Hunting, Zoe Akins
Plymouth Theatre, August 31, 1921 (129)
Blossom Time, adapted by Dorothy Donnelly
Ambassador Theatre, September 29, 1921 (295)
Main Street, adapted by Harvey O'Higgins and Harriet Ford
National Theatre, October 5, 1921 (86)
Love Dreams, Ann Nichols
Times Square Theatre, October 10, 1921 (40)
The Six-Fifty, Kate McLaurin
Hudson Theatre, October 24, 1921 (24)
Good Morning Dearie, book and lyrics, Anne Calwell
Globe Theatre, November 1, 1921 (265)
Golden Days, Sidney Toler and Marion Short
Gaiety Theatre, November 1, 1921 (40)
The Great Way, Horace Fish and Helen Freeman
Park Theatre, November 7, 1921 (8)
We Girls, Frederic and Fannie Hatton
48th Street Theatre, November 9, 1921 (30)
Nature's Nobleman, Samuel Shipman and Clara Lipman
Apollo Theatre, November 14, 1921 (74)
The Verge, Susan Glaspell
Provincetown Theatre, November 14, 1921 (38)
The Man's Name, Marjorie Chase and Eugene Walter

Republic Theatre, November 14, 1921 (24)
Everyday, Rachel Crothers
Bijou Theatre, November 16, 1921 (30)
The Varying Shore, Zoe Akins
Hudson Theatre, December 5, 1921 (66)
The Fair Circassian, Gladys Unger
Republic Theatre, December 6, 1921 (7)
The Mountain Man, Clare Kummer
Maxine Elliott Theatre, December 12, 1921 (163)
The White Peacock, Mme. Olga Petrova
Comedy Theatre, December 26, 1921 (102)
Face Value, adapted by Solita Solano
49th Street Theatre, December 26, 1921 (41)

1922

Elsie Janis and Her Gang, Elsie Janis
Gaiety Theatre, January 16, 1922 (56)
Marjolaine, book by Catherine Chisholm Cushing
Broadhurst Theatre, January 24, 1922 (136)
The Nest, adapted by Grace George
48th Street Theatre, January 28, 1922 (161)
Voltaire, Leila Taylor and Gertrude Purcell
Plymouth Theatre, March 21, 1922 (16)
Just Because, book and lyrics, Anne Wynne O'Ryan and
Helen S. Woodruff, Music, Madelyn Sheppard
Earl Carroll Theatre, March 22, 1922 (46)
Taboo, Mary Hoyt Wiborg
Sam H. Harris Theatre, April 4, 1922 (3)
The Green Ring, Zinaida Hippius Neighborhood
Playhouse, April 4, 1922 (30)
The Goldfish, adapted by Gladys Unger
Maxine Elliot Theatre, April 17, 1922 (70)
Lady Bug, Frances Nordstrom
Appollo Theatre, April 17, 1922 (5)
The Night Call, Adeline Hendricks
Frazee Theatre, April 26, 1922 (29)

Chains of Dew, Susan Glaspell
    Provincetown Theatre, April 27, 1922 (16)
The Advertising of Kate, Annie Nathan Meyer
    Ritz Theatre, May 8, 1922 (24)
The Red Geranium, Ruth M. Woodward
    Princess Theatre, May 8, 1922 (16)
Abie's Irish Rose, Anne Nichols
    Fulton Theatre, May 23, 1922 (2,327)
Red Pepper, book, Edgar Smith and Emily Young
    Shubert Theatre, May 29, 1922 (24)
Whispering Wires, Kate McLaurin
    49th Street Theatre, August 7, 1922 (352)
Orange Blossoms, Fred de Gresac (Mme. Frederique Morel)
    Fulton Theatre, September 19, 1922 (95)
Banco, adapted by Clare Kummer
    Ritz Theatre, September 20, 1922 (69)
Malvaloca, Serafin and Joaquin Alvarez Quintero
    48th Street Theatre, October 2, 1922 (48)
The Ever Green Lady, Abby Merchant
    Punch and Judy Theatre, October 11, 1922 (13)
To Love, trans. by Grace George
    Bijou Theatre, October 17, 1922 (55)
The Texas Nightingale, Zoe Akins
    Empire Theatre, November 20, 1922 (32)
The Bunch and Judy, Anne Caldwell and Hugh Ford
    Globe Theatre, November 28, 1922 (63)
Gringo, Sophie Treadwell
    Comedy Theatre, December 12, 1922 (35)
The Masked Woman, trans. by Kate Jordan
    Eltinge Theatre, December 22, 1922 (115)
The Clinging Vine, Zelda Sears
    Knickerbocker Theatre, December 25, 1922 (184)
Secrets, Rudolf Besier and May Edginton
    Fulton Theatre, December 25, 1922 (168)

1923

The Humming Bird, Maude Fulton
    Ritz Theatre, January 15, 1923 (40)
Mary the 3D, Rachel Crothers
    39th Street Theatre, February 5, 1923 (152)
Humoresque, Fannie Hurst
    Vanderbilt Theatre, February 27, 1923 (32)
The Love Habit, adapted, Gladys Unger
    Bijou Theatre, March 14, 1923 (69)
Sandro Botticelli, Mercedes de Acosta
    Provincetown Theatre, March 26, 1923 (24)
The Dice of the Gods, Lillian Barrett
    National Theatre, April 5, 1923 (20)
For Value Received, Ethel Clifton
    Longacre Theatre, May 7, 1923 (48)
The Apache, Josephine Turck Baker
    Punch and Judy Theatre, May 7, 1923 (16)
The Rut, Sarah Sherman Pryor
    Bayes Theatre, May 7, 1923 (1)
A Thousand Generations and One, Ethelyn E. Keays
    Bayes Theatre, May 8, 1923 (1)
The Will O' the Wisp, Doris F. Halman
    Bayes Theatre, May 10, 1923 (1)
The Pot Boiler, Alice Gerstenberg
    Bayes Theatre, May 10, 1923 (1)
Three Pills in a Bottle, Rachel Lyman Field
    Bayes Theatre, May 11, 1923 (1)
The Mistletoe Bough, Dorothy Stockbridge
    Bayes Theatre, May 11, 1923 (1)
Sun Up, Lula Vollmer
    Provincetown Theatre, May 25, 1923 (28)
Adrienne, Frances Bryant and William Stone
    Cohan Theatre, May 28, 1923 (24)
The Breaking Point, Mary Roberts Rinehart
    Klaw Theatre, August 16, 1923 (68)

The Whole Town's Talking, John Emerson and Anita Loos
   Bijou Theatre, August 29, 1923 (178)
Poppy, book and lyrics, Dorothy Donnelly
   Apollo Theatre, September 2, 1923 (328)
A Lesson in Love, Rudolph Besier and May Eddington
   39th Street Theatre, September 24, 1923 (72)
Floriani's Wife, adapted by Ann Sprague MacDonald
   Greenwich Village Theatre, October 13, 1923 (16)
The Magic Ring, Zelda Sears
   Liberty Theatre, October 1, 1923 (96)
Launzi, adapted by Edna St. Vincent Millay
   Plymouth Theatre, October 10, 1923 (16)
The Shame Woman, Lula Vollmer
   Greenwich Village Theatre, October 16, 1923 (278)
Stepping Stones, Anne Caldwell and R. H. Burnside
   Globe Theatre, November 6, 1923 (274)
A Royal Fandango, Zoe Akins
   Plymouth Theatre, November 12, 1923 (24)
Go West, Young Man, Fay Pulsifer and Cara Carelli
   Punch and Judy Theatre, November 12, 1923 (48)
Meet the Wife, Lynn Starling
   Klaw Theatre, November 26, 1923 (232)
One Kiss, adapted by Clare Kummer
   Fulton Theatre, November 27, 1923 (95)
In the Next Room, Eleanor Robson and Harriet Ford
   Vanderbilt Theatre, November 27, 1923 (154)
The Business Widow, Gladys Unger
   Ritz Theatre, December 10, 1923 (32)
Hurricane, Olga Petrova
   Frolic Theatre, December 25, 1923 (125)
The Wild Westcotts, Anne Morrison
   Frazee Theatre, December 24, 1923 (24)
Roseanne, Nan Bagby Stephens
   Greenwich Village Theatre, December 29, 1923 (41)

1924

Lollipop, Zelda Sears
  Knickbocker Theatre, January 21, 1924 (152)
Mr. Pitt, Zona Gale
  39th Street Theatre, January 22, 1924 (87)
The Gift, Julia Chandler and Alethea Luce
  Greenwich Village Theatre, January 22, 1924 (7)
Fashion, Anna Cora Mowatt
  Provincetown Playhouse, February 3, 1924 (152)
The New Englander, Abby Merchant
  48th Street Theatre, February 7, 1924 (36)
The Moon-Flower, adapted by Zoe Akins
  Astor Theatre, February 25, 1924 (48)
The Strong, Karen Bramson
  49th Street Theatre, February 26, 1924 (2)
The Outsider, Dorothy Brandon
  49th Street Theatre, March 3, 1924 (104)
The Lady Killer, Alice and Franke Mandel
  Morosco Theatre, March 12, 1924 (13)
Sweet Seventeen, L. Westervelt, John Clements, Harvey O'Higgins
and Harriet Ford -- Lyceum Theatre, March 17, 1924 (72)
The Main Line, Grace Griswold and Thomas McKean
  Klaw Theatre, March 25, 1924 (18)
Nancy Ann, Dorothy Heyward
  49th Street Theatre, March 31, 1924 (40)
Helena's Boys, dramatized by Ida Lublenski
  Henry Miller Theatre, April 7, 1924 (40)
Expressing Willie, Rachel Crothers
  48th Street Theatre, April 16, 1924 (69)
Peg-O'-My-Dreams, lyrics by Anne Caldwell
  Jolson Theatre, May 5, 1924 (32)
On Vengeance Height, Allan Davis and Cornelia C. Vencill
  Belasco Theatre, May 5, 1924 (1)
Lamplight, Claire Carvalho
  Belasco Theatre, May 9, 1924 (1)

Tired, Juliet Wilbor Tompkins
  Belasco Theatre, May 9, 1924 (1)
Blossom Time, Dorothy Donnelly
  Jolson Theatre, May 19, 1924 (24)
Grand Street Follies, music, Lily Hyland, book and lyrics, Agnes Morgan
  Neighborhood Playhouse, May 20, 1924 (30)
The Dream Girl, book and lyrics, Rida Johnson Young
  Ambassador Theatre, August 20, 1924 (118)
The Werewolf, adapt. by Gladys Unger
  49th Street Theatre, August 25, 1924 (112)
Top-Hole, revised by Gladys Unger
  Fulton Theatre, September 1, 1924 (104)
Pigs, Anne Morrison and Patterson McNutt
  Little Theatre, September 1, 1924 (312)
Stepping Stones, lyrics by Anne Caldwell; book, Anne Caldwell and R. H.
  Burnside
    Globe Theatre, September 1, 1924 (40)
Izzy, Mrs. Trimble Bradley and George Broadhurst
  Broadhurst Theatre, September 16, 1924 (71)
My Son, Martha Stanley
  Princess Theatre, September 17, 1924 (278)
Minick, George S. Kaufman and Edna Ferber
  Booth Theatre, September 24, 1924 (141)
The Red Falcon, Mrs. Trimble Bradley and George Broadhurst
  Broadhurst Theatre, October 7, 1924 (15)
In His Arms, Lynn Starling
  Fulton Theatre, October 13, 1924 (40)
Cock o' the Roost, Rida Johnson Young
  Liberty Theatre, October 13, 1924 (24)
Tiger Cats, adapted by Mme. Karen Bramson
  Belasco, October 21, 1924 (48)
Annie Dear, book, music, and lyrics, Clare Kummer
  Times Square Theatre, November 4, 1924 (103)
Mme. Pompadour, adapted by Clare Kummer
  Martin Beck Theatre, November 11, 1924 (80)

Blind Alleys, Alice Fleming Sidman and Victoria Montgomery
 Punch and Judy Theatre, November 17, 1924 (8)
The Magnolia Lady, book and lyrics, Ann Caldwell
 Shubert Theatre, November 25, 1924 (47)
Close Harmony, Dorothy Parker and Elmer Rice
 Gaiety Theatre, December 1, 1924 (24)
The Student Prince in Heidelberg, Dorothy Donnelly
 Jolson Theatre, December 2, 1924 (183)
Topysy and Eva, Catherine Chisolm Cushing
 Sam H. Harris Theatre, December 23, 1924 (159)
The Habitual Husband, Dana Burnet
 48th Street Theatre, December 24, 1924 (12)
The Bully, Julie Helene Percival and Calvin Clark
 Hudson Theatre, December 25, 1924 (37)

1925

Mrs. Partridge Presents, Mary Kennedy and Ruth Hawthorne
 Belmont Theatre, January 5, 1925 (144)
Lass O'Laughter, Edith Carter and Nan Marriott Watson
 Comedy Theatre, January 8, 1925 (28)
The Valley of Content, Blanche Upright
 Apollo Theatre, January 13, 1925 (39)
Beyond, translated by Rita Matthias
 Provincetown Theatre, January 25, 1925 (16)
She Had to Know, adapted by Grace George
 Times Square Theatre, February 2, 1925 (80)
Puzzles of 1925, conceived by Elsie Janis
 Fulton Theatre, February 2, 1925 (104)
Tangletoes, Gertrude Purcell
 39th Street Theatre, February 17, 1925 (23)
White Collars, adapted by Edith Ellis
 Cort Theatre, February 23, 1925 (104)
The Virgin of Bethulia, adapted by Gladys Unger
 Ambassador Theatre, February 23, 1925 (16)
Two by Two, John Turner and Eugenie Woodward
 Selwyn Theatre, February 23, 1925 (16)

Puppets, Frances Lightner
   Selwyn Theatre, March 9, 1925 (54)
The Legend of the Dance, Agnes Morgan
   Neighborhood Theatre, March 31, 1925 (37)
The Dunce Boy, Lulu Vollmer
   Daly's Theatre, April 1, 1925 (43)
The Sapphire Ring, adapted by Isabel Leighton
   Selwyn Theatre, April 15, 1925 (13)
O, Nightingale, Sophie Treadwell
   49th Street Theatre, April 15, 1925 (29)
For Distinguished Service, Florence Clay Knox
   Wallack's Theatre, 4 May 1925 (1)
Aria Da Capo, Edna St. Vincent Millay
   Wallack's Theatre, May 4, 1925 (1)
Marsyas, the Faun, Jane Kerley
   Wallack's Theatre, May 5, 1925 (1)
As I Remember You, Sada Cowan
   Wallack's Theatre, May 7, 1925 (1)
Gloria Mundi, Patricia Brown
   Wallack's Theatre, May 4, 1925 (1)
The Family Failing, Elfrida and Clarence Derwent
   Princess Theatre, June 9, 1925 (1)

SOURCES

Bordman, Gerald. *American Theatre: A Chronicle of Comedy and Drama, 1869–1914*. New York: Oxford University Press, 1994.

Bzowski, Frances Diodato. *American Women Playwrights, 1900–1930, A Checklist*. Westport, CT: Greenwood, 1992.

Kritzer, Amelia Howe. *Plays by Early American Women, 1775–1850*. Ann Arbor: University of Michigan Press, 1998.

Mantle, Burns, ed. *The Best Plays of 1919–1920*. New York: Dodd, Mead and Company, 1947.

———. *The Best Plays of 1920–1921*. New York: Dodd, Mead and Company, 1921, 1960.

———. *The Best Plays of 1921–1922*. Boston: Small, Maynard and Company, 1922.

———. *The Best Plays of 1922–1923*. Boston: Small, Maynard and Company, 1923.

———. *The Best Plays of 1923–1924*. Boston: Small, Maynard and Company, 1924.

———. *The Best Plays of 1924–1925*. Boston: Small, Maynard and Company, 1925.

Mantle, Burns and Garrison P. Sherwood, ed. *The Best Plays of 1909–1919*. New York: Dodd, Mead and Company, 1933.

———. *The Best Plays of 1899–1909*. Philadelphia: Blakiston, 1944. New York Times, various articles

Rigdon, Walter, ed. "New York Productions." *The Biographical Encyclopedia and Who's Who in the American Theatre*. New York: James H. Heineman, 1966.

www.ingramcontent.com/pod-product-compliance
Lightning Source LLC
Chambersburg PA
CBHW020433130626
46549CB00001B/122